The Scarecrow Author Bibliographies Series

BENJAMIN DISRAELI:

A list of writings by him, and writings about him, with notes

by

R.W. STEWART

The Scarecrow Author Bibliographies, No. 7

The Scarecrow Press, Inc.
Metuchen, N.J.   1972

Library of Congress Cataloging in Publication Data

Stewart, R   W
    Benjamin Disraeli.

    (The Scarecrow author bibliographies, no. 7)
    1. Beaconsfield, Benjamin Disraeli, 1st Earl of,
1804-1881--Bibliography.
~~Z8082.S8~~   942.081'0924   72-3906
ISBN 0-8108-0489-1

DA 564. B3S7

CONTENTS

ACKNOWLEDGMENTS

The British Museum
The National Trust, and particularly the members of the
    staff at Hughenden Manor
The National Library of Scotland
The Bodleian Library
The University Library, Birmingham
The University Library, Cambridge
The University Library, Leeds
The University Library, London
The University Library, Manchester
The Library, University College, London
The Librarian, Pusey House, Oxford
Sion College Library
St. Deiniol's Library, Hawarden, Flintshire
Birmingham City Libraries
Leeds City Libraries
Manchester City Libraries
Sheffield City Libraries
The City of London Guildhall Library
The Wiener Library, London
Deutsche Staatsbibliothek
Bibliothèque Nationale, Paris
Buckinghamshire County Record Office
Shropshire (Salop) County Record Office
Somerset County Record Office
The Times, London
The late Sir John Murray, K. C. V. O., D. S. O., F. S. A.
Lord Blake, Provost of The Queen's College, Oxford
Professor Curtis Dahl
C. C. Nickerson, Esq., Trinity College, Oxford
Mrs. L. Collins
Mrs. A. Kaucky
Mrs. S. Lamb

None of these individuals or institutions is in any way re-
sponsible for the errors or inadequacies of this work. The
typescript for this book was prepared with unfailing care,
ingenuity, and patience by Mrs. J. R. Butler.

Benjamin Disraeli, from a photograph by Mayall, in the possession of the National Trust. (By permission of the National Trust, Hughenden Manor.)

INTRODUCTION

The object of this work has been to bring together systematically the published writings of Benjamin Disraeli, and writings relating to him. The scope and arrangement of the lists are described below.

No such full list of writings on Disraeli has previously been published. I regard its justification as lying in the interest of Disraeli's unique career both as writer and politician, and in the perennial fascination, which is illustrated in the lists, of his personality. His centrality in Parliamentary politics, at the period of their greatest importance, particularly in the 27 years of his leadership of his party in the Commons, demands attention. It has been said (item 1030), "From Trollope's runically-titled shelf, the greatest Victorian political novel of all is missing: How Did He Do It?" Disraeli's progress from a lawyer's office to the premiership shows that there was a career open to the talents, or, as his enemies would say, to unscrupulous opportunism, in nineteenth-century Britain. If not quite the first "outsider" to hold the highest office, he was the first to hold it for so long. He was certainly the only Jewish person, and probably the only person whose ancestry has been so recently non-British, to hold it, but, though without the advantages of rank or conventional education, his rise was no Victorian text-book success story. Disraeli's enemies denounced the way he had risen (e. g., 1132) though, as he said in old age, after fifty years they could think of nothing more original to say than that he was an "adventurer."

It is not necessary to claim that Disraeli's writings are in the first rank in order to adduce their interest, variety and merit as additional reasons for recording them and their criticisms. The political and literary aspects of Disraeli's career cannot be isolated from each other. His political career in the political context was, indeed, more important than his literary career in the literary context, but the interconnection was unusual. It is, to say the least, less easy to overlook Disraeli's political and public career than that of, say, Scott, and on the other side, Disraeli's writings are of greater significance to his political career than those of, say, Gladstone. Other prime ministers published essays, translations, or historical works, but these excursions, in general, were neither so significant in the writer's political career, nor so important in themselves, as Disraeli's writings. The political significance of Disraeli's novels may have been exaggerated, but few other novels by active politicians have had the impact of Coningsby and Sybil. Contemporary criticism of Disraeli's novels tended to be political rather than literary, and this tendency has persisted. His novels have had, in my opinion, less serious attention than they deserve. It has been said that by going into politics, Disraeli destroyed the potentiality of becoming a significant literary figure (e. g. , 1250); it has been answered that his significant novels, from Coningsby onwards, were possible only because he was a politician, and that he invented a new genre, the political novel (e. g. , 262, 1320).

I am in general agreement with the latter view. Disraeli was first and longest a politician, whose writings, where they were not mere pot-boilers, were essentially political. The exclusively "literary" character of Disraeli's family background has been exaggerated, not least by Disraeli himself in his Memoir of his father (704). Isaac D'Israeli, though never involved in party politics, was, as the historian of Charles I, whose life and times appear with such frequency in his son's works, not lacking in interest in political questions. Although it is true that most of Disraeli's writings appeared before he went into Parliament, it is misleading to say that he was diverted from literature to politics; the most important of his works date from 1837. Among his writings were numerous polemical works, of which the best known are 151 and 493, and his writings in the press in the 1830s were chiefly, though not entirely, political.

Disraeli's first connection with public affairs was in the launching of John Murray's newspaper, The Representative, in 1825 (see 735). The details are still unclear in several crucial aspects, but there is no doubt that after Disraeli had been associated with Murray's publishing ventures for several months there was a breach between them and that immediately afterwards Disraeli wrote his first published novel, Vivian Grey (14). This work, at least in

the first two volumes, is a disguised account of the newspaper venture. The plot concerns the formation of a new
political party, nominally led by a character who stands for
Murray, with J. G. Lockhart, who had been offered the
editorship of The Representative, as its spokesman, and the
eponymous hero, Disraeli, as the manipulator behind the
scenes. It has been too readily assumed that Vivian Grey
was a picture of a "literary" scene transposed to the "political." The transposition was less marked than might at
first appear. The Representative was a highly political
venture, and the Quarterly Review, which Murray also
owned, and of which Lockhart secured the editorship, was
the leading Tory journal of opinion. J. D. Powles, the
third partner with Murray and Disraeli in launching the
paper, was a financier whose foreign interests inevitably
led him into politics and for whom Disraeli had written,
and Murray published in 1825, the three "Mining pamphlets"
(7, 11, 12), which, where they are not advertising, are
political diatribes. In the air of hectic optimism preceding
the financial crisis at the end of 1825, and in the prevailing
fluidity of parties, it is not impossible that a new political
grouping was sought, of which Disraeli saw himself as the
Tadpole or Taper. These plans collapsed utterly.

After the publication of the first part of Vivian Grey,
Disraeli travelled on the continent, and published a further
three volumes (15) in 1827. Thereafter, he suffered a pro-
longed nervous breakdown, from which he recovered during
an extended tour in the eastern Mediterranean (June 1830 to
October 1831), which exercised a disastrous influence, certainly on his novels, and perhaps on the history of Europe.
Disraeli made relatively few visits abroad after 1831, but
the effect of his visit to Jerusalem can be seen throughout
his works, particularly in Tancred and Lothair. He had
possibly made some attempt to enter politics before leaving
for the East, and on his return he began the political
career which was to end only with his life. From the out-
set, he wrote as well as spoke on political matters. It
cannot be denied that there was probably some very dubious
work behind his first political book, England and France
(85), or that the means by which he sought advancement
were not over-scrupulous. During the mid-1830s he was an
occasional anonymous contributor to the press (465 ff.),
both as a "literary" writer and as a political commentator.
After his election to Parliament in 1837, and particularly
after his failure to secure a place in the government of
Peel in 1841, this miscellaneous writing almost ceased.

After Peel's refusal to give him office, he became involved with the group known as "Young England" and produced the central works of his genius, the novels Coningsby, Sybil, and Tancred, which are discussed below. Thereafter, as leader of the Conservative Party in the House of Commons, he abandoned novel-writing until, after his defeat in 1868, he published Lothair in 1870. His last published novel, Endymion, appeared only a few months before his death, and in it he surveyed the scene in which he had lived, and sketched some of the personalities he had known.

Disraeli's novels have tended to be dismissed as if they consisted entirely of absurd pageantry revolving around heroes of ancient lineage, unbounded wealth, and impossible virtue. Although these elements are by no means lacking, it is well to note that Disraeli often looks on them with a very sardonic eye. There is, however, much more than this. Although it is true that Disraeli does not explore the profundities of the human spirit, for good or ill, and that he does not express a coherent world view throughout his work, there is much that he does well. Possibly there is too much that he does well enough, and nothing that he does supremely well, unless it be his satirical portraits of politicians. The portrait of Peel in Sybil book 6, chapter 1, is a miniature masterpiece. There are certain recurring themes: the influence of women, the strength of youth, the power of will, and, it is to be feared, the significance of race. Disraeli desired his life to be "perpetual romance," and incorporated the wish into his novels, in which the women are generally more interesting and more effective than the nominal heroes.

Disraeli did seek, particularly in the trilogy and in Lothair, to deal with matters of serious import. He did not altogether succeed, as is suggested in the discussion of individual novels, but the attempt has often been insufficiently recognised. Disraeli was too much of a dilettante to produce a great novel or, indeed, to become a great statesman. He lacked the capacity for unremitting hard work which made a Peel, a Palmerston, or a Gladstone but, had he had it, he would have lost the lightness of touch, the airy persiflage, the soufflé quality, which mark much of his writing and his table-talk; he would not have been, as Maurois a trifle fancifully puts it, "some old Spirit of Spring, ever vanquished and ever alive, as a symbol of what can be accomplished in a cold and hostile universe, by a long youthfulness of heart." That youthfulness can be seen in the letters (564) which he wrote in his seventies to his beloved

friends, Lady Bradford and Lady Chesterfield, and in
Endymion, published when he was 76.

The great ideas expressed in the novels, the Crown,
the Church, the Aristocracy, Faith, Imagination, Race, and
Time, tend to abstraction.   Here he was at home, half-
dreaming of an ideal world strangely compounded of English
chivalry and eternal Jewish wisdom.   As to details, these
could be left to others.   He was no Peel, to oversee the
work of every department of the state.   It is true that he
was old, tired and widowed before he attained real power,
but it is not likely that he would have acted differently had
he reached "the top of the greasy pole" earlier.   His interest was essentially in the relation of states, "real politics," and one may suppose that the supremest moment of
his political career was when he smoked with Bismarck,
under the impression that the pair of them ruled Europe.
It was the summit of all his political advice--the personal
dealing of the men who run states.

How, as Trollope should have asked, did he do it?
With all that has been published, there remains this question.
He made himself indispensable, though not until he had been
prime minister.   Perhaps he did so because he was the
observant outsider in the most English party, devoted to the
party's interest, but not personally committed to its beliefs,
prejudices and passions.   Carlyle called him "a superlative
Hebrew conjurer" and so he was.

His name proclaimed his people.   As a Jew, he
defended his people, flaunted in the face of Celt and Saxon
that his ancestors had been priests in the Temple of Solomon while theirs were savages in an unknown forest, and
propounded in his novels, and in his political writings and
speeches, the view that Christendom owed an incalculable
debt to the Jews.   As to this, there can be no doubt of
his sincerity, or his courage, even if one must deplore the
racial views which he frequently expressed.

Abused and adored, vilified and revered, the creator
of the modern Conservative Party, the journalist, the novelist, the Jew: Disraeli has been seen from many angles;
the writings containing these views form the content of this
work.

SCOPE AND ARRANGEMENT

The lists have been based primarily on the collections of
the British Museum and the Bodleian Library, and the
printed material preserved at Hughenden.   To these have
been added information from other libraries listed in the
Acknowledgments and from reference works of which those
most used are listed below.

Works in languages other than English have normally been
included only where they have been found to be available
in British libraries.   Publications up to the end of 1970
have been included, though some recent publications may
have been inadvertently omitted.

Sources

Besides the bibliographies listed as 1-6, lists of writings
by and about Disraeli, including the more significant later
editions of his works, appear in the Cambridge Bibliography
of English Literature, vol. 3, 1940, and the New Cambridge
Bibliography of English Literature, vol. 3, 1969.   Lists of
varying scope and quality appear in several of the studies
listed and these are not necessarily confined, as this list
is, to works directly relating to Disraeli.   Among the more
notable lists is that in 1047, which is recent and extensive,
but with few comments.   There is a useful summary list in
1045; and there are useful lists in some of the German dissertations, e. g. , 989.   There are also bibliographical notes
in the volumes of 661.   Monypenny and Buckle provided no
bibliography.

Among general works on which particular reliance has been
placed are:
Annual Bibliography of English Language and Literature,
1920-1968;
Bibliographies of Studies in Victorian Literature, 1932-1944,
edited by W. D. Templeman, and 1945-54, edited by A.
Wright, and the subsequent annual Victorian Bibliographies;

Readers' Guide to Periodical Literature;
International Index, and Social Science and Humanities Index,
to 1969;
Subject Index to Periodicals, 1926-61, and British Humani-
ties Index, 1962-70;
Essay and General Literature Index, 1900/33-1970;
The Wellesley Index to Victorian Periodicals, vol. I.

Arrangement

Bibliographies
Disraeli's writings
Separately published works;
Writings not originally published separately;
Writings, published and unpublished, collected and published
after Disraeli's death;
Speeches;
Collected editions;
Selections;
Miscellaneous letters and speeches;
Anonymous works ascribed to Disraeli.

The arrangement in each section is chronological. The
Disraeli canon, with the exception of items 723, 725, 727,
and 730 is well agreed, and is recorded, with varying de-
grees of completeness, in items 1-6. I have been able to
make two additions, both of signed verses, which have previously been overlooked. (519, 528). I have presented the
available evidence in the case of works of doubtful authorship but without reaching any new conclusions.

The list is intended to be a comprehensive list of Disraeli's
published writings, but some exceptions should be noted.
Letters in newspapers have been included only where they
appear to be of particular importance. Speeches have been
included only where they were separately published, or have
appeared in collections: no reference has been made to
the reports in Hansard. Election addresses have been
placed at the end (1693-1720), where Disraeli's own addresses and related election material have been listed together.

Later editions and reprints of Disraeli's works have been
included where they contain significant editorial matter or
are otherwise important. Continental reprints, contemporary
and later, by Tauchnitz and other publishers are omitted.

Except in a few special cases, I have included only notes of

the existence of such translations of Disraeli's works as
have been readily traceable. There are, no doubt, other
translations, possibly some in non-European languages,
which have not been noticed.

There may be, in newspapers and magazines, particularly
of the period 1832-1837, other anonymous, pseudonymous,
or even signed, articles by Disraeli which have so far
escaped attention.

Writings on Disraeli

The arrangement in each section is chronological.

Separately published works

I have normally included only those works of which Disraeli
is the only, or principal, subject, with some important
accounts of events in which Disraeli was closely involved
(e.g., 792, 993, 1068). Translations of works published
in English, and of works published in languages other than
English into third languages, have been included where they
have been noticed.

Pamphlets and ephemera published up to 1901

In general, only items more or less directly connected
with Disraeli have been included. General political pamphlets on events with which Disraeli was concerned have
not been included, apart from those "addressed" to him.
In this section, there is at least a representative collection
of contemporary polemic, though there will be a considerable
number of items which have not come to my attention.

Articles in books

These have generally been confined to articles which are
distinctly separate works, many of which first appeared in
periodicals. It has not been possible to locate the original
publication of all of these articles. Essays in collectaneous
works have normally been included. Chapters in general
accounts of the period and in encyclopedias and reference
works are omitted.

Articles in periodicals

The collection of these, and the choice of those which ought
to be listed, have been perhaps the most laborious parts of

the work, despite the assistance afforded by the reference
works cited. Brief and cursory articles have been omitted.

Dissertations

The list in Altick, R. D. and Matthews, W. R: Guide to
doctoral dissertations in Victorian literature, 1960, has
been invaluable, and has been supplemented by holdings
in the British Museum and the Bodleian. The list is, however, representative only.

Novels and plays about Disraeli, or in which Disraeli is
supposed to appear, have been noted.

The Disraeli family. The principal sources of information
have been listed.

Election addresses and ephemera include both Disraeli's
own addresses and speeches, as well as other works relating to his election contests. See the note before 1693.

Reviews

Reviews in periodicals have throughout been listed with the
works reviewed, and do not appear again in the list of
periodical articles. The year of publication of reviews is
omitted where it is the same as that of the book reviewed.

It has not seemed practicable to adopt wholly consistent
criteria for the inclusion of reviews. Disraeli's writings
range from anonymous advertising brochures (7, 11, 12) to
Endymion (429), published 55 years later by the ex-prime
minister, and said to have been then the most highly-
priced work of fiction ever bought by a publisher. The
notice accorded to Disraeli's various writings naturally dif-
fered markedly, and the whole range of periodical literature
had immensely expanded during his lifetime. I have, in
noting reviews, as in other parts of the list, paid particular
attention to the earlier and relatively lesser-known works
and for the books before Coningsby, I have included most
of the references found, though some are cursory in the
extreme. Mere series of extracts have generally been
omitted, particularly where other reviews of the same work
are noted.

In the "General Preface" to his novels, published with
Lothair in 1870 (419), Disraeli began,

An American gentleman, with more than courtesy, has forwarded to me a vast number of notices of LOTHAIR which have appeared in the leading journals of his country. He tells me that, irrespective of literary "organs," there are in the Union five thousand newspapers, and it is not impossible that some notice of "Lothair" might appear in each of these. However various may be the opinions of those which I thus possess, they appear to me generally to be sincere, and in point of literary ability; taste, style, and critical acumen; I think they need not fear competition with the similar productions of our own land.

My English publishers also have made a collection of the notices of this work in our own country, and though we have not yet five thousand newspapers, the aggregate of articles is in amount perhaps unprecedented. I have nothing to complain of in their remarks. One could hardly expect at home the judicial impartiality of a foreign land.

Among the papers at Hughenden are preserved some 150 notices of Lothair and a somewhat larger number relating to Endymion, though only a small proportion in each case is from United States or Canadian sources. The great majority are from British daily or weekly newspapers; only about 30 and 20 reviews respectively, are listed here. Reviews in daily newspapers have been excluded, except for the substantial notices in The Times. Reviews in weekly newspapers which were not avowedly literary organs have normally been excluded. Reviews in monthly and quarterly periodicals, regardless of their particular interests, have normally been included, unless they are very cursory. Consideration has, of course, been given to the standing of the paper, and of the reviewer, where known, in deciding on inclusion or exclusion. The search for reviews has been hampered by the frequent absence of indexes, even where these were published, from bound volumes, particularly of weekly newspapers, preserved in libraries. The principal British journals of literary and political opinion have been checked for reviews of Disraeli's books published during their currency. Most of the significant journals in which at least one review was found, either in the reference works, or in the very miscellaneous collection of cuttings at Hughenden, have been checked for reviews of other works. Reviews which notice Disraeli's works with other works have not usually been included. However, I have no doubt

that other reviews, for example, of new editions and reprints, and other articles, can be found by further search-
ing, particularly of nineteenth-century periodicals.

Less emphasis has been given to reviews of works on Disraeli, though representative reviews of the more significant
studies have been noted. Reviews, like other material, in
languages other than English, have been noted where traced,
but no systematic searches have been made.

Index

The index lists the authors of all items included, other than
Disraeli himself; the titles of all Disraeli's writings included;
the names of all persons referred to in connection with Disraeli, including the editors, illustrators and translators of
Disraeli's works, where noted, and publishers of first editions; the titles of all periodicals referred to; the editors
of collectaneous works listed; the titles of anonymous works;
pseudonyms used by Disraeli and others.

In the index under Disraeli are listed references to particular subjects, e.g., Disraeli as a novelist, his Judaism, and
the names of places at which he made speeches, that are
otherwise of particular significance. In addition there is a chronological list of published speeches listed here and a list of
references by language, to works and translations in languages other than English.

Enumeration

All items included are numbered consecutively throughout.
Cross references have been made, between different forms
of the same article; between items related to one another,
e.g., from particular books to reviews or comments which
do not appear in periodicals; and between continuations and
replies and their main articles.

Cross references have not been made between items by the
same author, which will be found listed in the index.

Annotations   Notes have been given on each of Disraeli's
books, according to their significance.

Although not all books and pamphlets have been annotated,
I have included descriptions of, or extracts from, some of
the more remarkable polemical works, and have drawn
attention to special features where this has appeared neces-

sary.   The lists of periodical articles have not been annotated.

Descriptions

I have used the following arrangement for each of Disraeli's
books

a. transcript of title-page
b. collation
c. references to other bibliographies
d. date of publication
e. note of dedication
f. note of circumstances of writing and publication
g. Reviews
    Name of periodical, reference, title of review, if sig-
    nificant, author, if known.   These reviews are not
    again listed in the list of periodical articles (1373-1589)
    but reviews and articles in individual periodicals are
    brought together in the index.
h. contemporary pamphlets, satires etc.
i. later editions of significance; date, publisher, editor,
    note on text used etc.
j. translations.   Language and date only, unless of par-
    ticular significance.
k. later comments: non-contemporary periodical articles,
    and references to items in the lists of writings on Dis-
    raeli
l. Manuscript: location, notes

This arrangement is followed, so far as is appropriate, for
other separately published works throughout the lists.   The
transcripts of Disraeli's title-pages preserve the capitalisa-
tion and punctuation, but do not indicate different types used.
The collations have been given in summary form: for details,
consult the works by Michael Sadleir (3 & 4).

Note

It is not to be supposed that the writings listed here exhaust
the available material on Disraeli.   No reference has been
made to material in works not primarily concerned with
him.

The primary source of information is the "Hughenden Papers"
in the possession of the National Trust; while these have
provided material for some specialised studies, two works
are in a special category, having been based on the

systematic use of the papers, namely, the "official," and
long-delayed, life by Monypenny and Buckle (853), which
contains copious extracts from the papers, and the more
recent biography by Lord Blake (1053), which has amplified,
supplemented and re-interpreted in the light of recent research the account presented by the "official" authors. This
is, and will remain for many years, the authoritative work
on Disraeli.

Of the other books on Disraeli, all those before "Monypenny
and Buckle" were based on "public" sources, and are chiefly
of interest for their interpretations. After the completion
of "Monypenny and Buckle" in 1920, several lives based on
its materials appeared. Of more recent works on particular
aspects, Roth on Disraeli's Jewishness (1018) and Jerman
on his early years (1028) merit particular attention. Of
avowedly literary studies, two are outstanding, Brandes
(771) and Maitre (1047); with these may be mentioned
Levine (1072) and though not entirely devoted to Disraeli,
Speare (1320).

To specify particular studies in books and periodicals would
extend this note too far, but the index is intended to point
to various topics dealt with. It may be noted that writers
so various as Thackeray (1362), Bagehot (1369), Sir Leslie
Stephen (1250), Louis Cazamian (1282), J. R. Lowell (1292),
Henry James (1364), Lytton Strachey (1339), and A. J. P.
Taylor (1363) have, with others, contributed to the interpretation of Disraeli's life and writings. An indication of the
interest in Disraeli in non-English-speaking countries is given
in the list of works in languages other than English at the
end of the index.

I am conscious of the inevitable errors and omissions in a
work of this nature. I shall be grateful for corrections and
additions. In particular, I shall welcome the assistance of
specialists, particularly in tracing translations of Disraeli's
works and other works published in languages other than
English, in extending the lists of "ephemera," and in identifying the authors of anonymous publications.

SYNOPSIS

Disraeli's speeches

611-612   The Crisis examined. 1834
613   At the dinner of the Printers' Pension Society.
           1845
614   In the House of Commons. 15th May 1846
615-617   England and Denmark. 1848
618   The New Parliamentary reform. 1848
619-620   The Parliament and the Government. 1848
621   Brompton Hospital. 1849
622   Financial policy. 1851
623   Parliamentary reform. 1852
624-625   The New Budget. 1852
626   Parliamentary reform. 1859
627   Public expenditure. 1862
628   Oxford Diocesan Society meeting. 1862
629-630   Church policy. 1864
631   On the Re-distribution of Seats Bill. 1866
632   At Edinburgh. 1867
633   On Church and state. 1868
634-636   At Manchester. 1872
637-638   At the Crystal Palace. 1872
639   Mr. Osborne Morgan's Burials Bill. 1873
640-641   Inaugural address ... at Glasgow. 1873
642   To the Conservative Association of Glasgow. 1873
643-644   At Aylesbury. 1876
645   At Berlin. 1878
646   The Agricultural situation. 1879

Collected editions of Disraeli's writings

647   1839 Philadelphia
648   1850 Philadelphia
649   1853 Bryce
650   1858 Routledge
651   1862-63 Shilling edition, Routledge
652   1868 New edition, Warne
653   1870-71 Longmans
654   1881 "Hughenden" edition, Longmans
655   1881 Seaside library, New York
656   1888 "Primrose" edition, Routledge
657   1888 Sixpenny edition, Ward Lock
658   1892 "Primrose" edition, Ward Lock
659   1904 "Empire" edition
660   1904 "Centenary" edition, edited by L. Wolf
661   1904 "Young England", edited by B. N. Langdon-
           Davies
662   1905-06 Bodley Head, edited by the Earl of
           Iddesleigh
                              xxiii

Selections from Disraeli's writings and speeches

Miscellaneous

Books on Disraeli (including all separately published works after 1902)

743-744	Francis, G. H.	:	The Right Honourable Benjamin Disraeli. 1852
745-752	(MacKnight, T.)	:	The Right Honourable Benjamin Disraeli. 1854
753-755	Mill, J.	:	Disraeli, the author, orator, and statesman. 1863
756	M'Gilchrist, J.	:	The Life of Benjamin Disraeli. 1868
757-770	O'Connor, T. P.	:	Benjamin Disraeli, Earl of Beaconsfield. 1877 etc.
771-783	Brandes, G.	:	Lord Beaconsfield. 1878 etc.
784	Valmont, V.	:	La jeunesse de Lord Beaconsfield. 1878
785	Finkelhaus, J. J.	:	Bohater wieku. Lord Beaconsfield. 1879
786-790	Hitchman, F.	:	The Public life of ... the Earl of Beaconsfield. 1879
791	Towle, G. M.	:	Beaconsfield. 1879
792-793	Clayden, P. W.	:	England under Lord Beaconsfield. 1880
794	Cucheval-Clarigny, A	:	Lord Beaconsfield et son temps. 1880
795	Benjamin Disraeli, Earl of Beaconsfield. (Anon.) 1881		
796-798	Apjohn, L.	:	The Earl of Beaconsfield. 1881
799	Bonghi, R.	:	Disraeli e Gladstone. 1881
800-801	Brown, C.	:	An Appreciative life of ... the Earl of Beaconsfield. 1881
802	Ewald, A. C.	:	The Right Hon. Benjamin Disraeli, Earl of Beaconsfield, K. G., and his times. 1881
803	"Oedipus, David"	:	Benjameni de Israeli. 1881
804-805	Walford, E.	:	The Life and political career of the Earl of Beaconsfield. 1881
806	Thompson, G. C.	:	Public opinion and Lord Beaconsfield. 1886

807	Garnett, R.	:	Shelley and Lord Beaconsfield. 1887
808-810	Kebbel, T. E.	:	Life of Lord Beaconsfield. 1888
811-812	Brewster, F. C.	:	Disraeli in outline. 1890
813-821	Froude, J. A.	:	Lord Beaconsfield. 1890
822-824	Fraser, W.	:	Disraeli and his day. 1891
825	Lake, H.	:	Personal reminiscences of the ... Earl of Beaconsfield. 1891
826			
	Aronstein, P.	:	Benjamin Disraeli's Dichtungen. 1892
827			
	Gorst, H. E.	:	The Earl of Beaconsfield. 1900
828			
829-840	Courcelle, M.	:	Disraëli. 1902
	Meynell, W.	:	Benjamin Disraeli, an unconventional biography. 1903
841-847	Sichel, W.	:	Disraeli. 1904
848-850	Sichel, W.	:	Beaconsfield. 1904
851	Mendes, H. P. and Arnot, R. : The Earl of Beaconsfield, K. G. Keys to the famous characters ... 1904		
852	Howes, R. W.	:	Disraeli, a key to the characters ... 1907
853-930	Monypenny, W. F. and Buckle, G. E. : The Life of Benjamin Disraeli. 1910-1920		
931-932	Cromer	:	Disraeli. 1912
933-935	Schmitz, O. A. H.	:	Lord Beaconsfield. 1911
936	Birrell, A.	:	On a dictum of Mr. Disraeli's. 1912
937	Külischer, A.	:	(Lord Beaconsfield, 1804-1832) 1923
938-947	Somervell, D. C.	:	Disraeli and Gladstone. 1925
948-953	Raymond, E. T.	:	Disraeli, the alien patriot. 1925
954-959	Clarke, E.	:	Benjamin Disraeli. 1926
960-979	Maurois, A.	:	La Vie de Disraëli. 1927
980-985	Murray, D. L.	:	Disraeli. 1927
986-987	Segalowitsch, B.	:	Benjamin Disraelis Orientalismus. 1930
988	Seikat, H.	:	Die Romankunst Disraelis. 1933
989-992	Rühl, H.	:	Disraelis Imperialismus ... 1935

993	Seton-Watson, R. W. :	Disraeli, Gladstone, and the Eastern Question. 1935
994-996	Beeley, H. :	Disraeli. 1936
997-1000	Craemer, R. :	Benjamin Disraeli. 1941
1001-1005	Stapledon, R. G. :	Disraeli and the new age. 1943
1006-1007	Gelber, N. M. :	(Lord Beaconsfield's plan for a Jewish state) 1946
1008-1017	Pearson, H. :	Dizzy. 1951
1018-1021	Roth, C. :	Benjamin Disraeli, Earl of Beaconsfield. 1952
1022-1025	Masefield, M. :	Peacocks and primroses. 1953
1026	Jaffe, B. :	Benjamin Disraeli. 1956
1027	Frietzsche, A. H. :	"The Monstrous clever young man. " 1959
1028-1039	Jerman, B. R. :	The Young Disraeli. 1960
1040-1043	Faber, R. :	Beaconsfield and Bolingbroke. 1961
1044	Frietzsche, A. H. :	Disraeli's religion. 1961
1045	Bloomfield, P. :	Disraeli. 1961
1046	Komroff, M. :	Disraeli. 1963
1047	Maitre, R. :	Disraeli, homme de lettres. 1963
1048-1052	Smith, S. M. :	Mr. Disraeli's readers. 1966
1053-1067	Blake, R. :	Disraeli. 1966
1068	Cowling, M. :	1867, Disraeli, Gladstone and revolution. 1967
1069	Pilát, J. :	Benjamin Disraeli. 1967
1070	Smith, P. :	Disraelian Conservatism and social reform. 1967
1071	Feuchtwanger, E. J. :	Disraeli, democracy and the Tory Party. 1968
1072	Levine, R. A. :	Benjamin Disraeli. 1968
1073	Phillips, O. S. :	The Boy Disraeli. 1968
1074-1075	Blake, R. :	Disraeli. 1969
1076	Blake, R. :	Disraeli and Gladstone. 1969
1077	Grant, N. :	Benjamin Disraeli, Prime Minister extraordinary. 1969

Pamphlets on Disraeli

1078	Stammers, J. :	The Case of the Queen v. D'Israeli. 1838

1145	Bendizzy's vision. 1878?	
1146	Ben's dream about the "Schemers of Philistia." 1878	
1147	Constantinople, and who is to have it? 1878	
1148	Earl Beaconsfield, a political sketch. 1878	
1149	Impeachment of Lord Beaconsfield. 1878	
1150	A Letter to Lord Beaconsfield. 1878	
1151	The Life of the Earl of Beaconsfield. 1878	
1152	Two imperial policies. 1878	
1153	Dizzi-ben-Dizzi or the orphan of Bagdad. 1878	
1154	Carter, L. M.	: Lord Beaconsfield and the Irish Catholic University Scheme. 1879
1155	Du Vivier, J. H.	: Mr. Gladstone & Lord Beaconsfield. 1879
1156	Rumer, A.	: Lord Beaconsfield and his foreign policy. 1879
1157-1158	Shaw, A. C.	: The Book of Benjamin. 1879?
1159	Shaw, A. C.	: The Second book of Benjamin
1160	Smith, G. and Smith,	G. A.: Whom to follow ... 1879
1161	Snape, J.	: Lord Beaconsfield. 1879
1162	Taylor, J.	: Grocers' licences. 1879
1163	Turnerelli, T.	: The Truth about the wreath. 1879
1164	Turnerelli, T.	: Tracy's death and burial. 1879
1165	The Apparition of the late Lord Derby to Lord Beaconsfield. 1879?	
1166-1167	Lord Beaconsfield, a sketch. 1879	
1168	The Premier's defence of his administration. 1879	
1169	Squire Bull, and his bailiff, Benjamin. 1879	
1170	Drew, F. B.	: How Ben behaved himself. 1880
1171-1172	Stafford, J. P.	: Beaconsfield the immaculate, a reply. 1880
1173	Bits of Beaconsfield. 1880?	
1174	Lord Beaconsfield's imperialism. 1880	
1175	Lord Beaky's lies, and England's allies. 1880	
1176	Atkinson, J. A.	: Lessons from the life of the Earl of Beaconsfield. 1881
1177	Bentley, H.	: A Sermon ... on occasion of the death of Lord Beaconsfield. 1881

1178	Hancock, A.	:	The Life and career of the Earl of Beaconsfield. 1881
1179	Hyndman, F. A.	:	A Sketch of the public career of the late ... Earl of Beaconsfield. 1881
1180	Jellinek, A.	:	Im Vaterhause Lord Beaconsfield's. 1881
1181-1183	Manners, J.	:	Some personal recollections of the later years of the Earl of Beaconsfield. 1881

1184   The Late Earl of Beaconsfield's first constituency. 1881

1185   The Life and work of the Earl of Beaconsfield (The Times) 1881

1186   A Memoir of the Earl of Beaconsfield (The Times) 1881

1187   Memorials of Lord Beaconsfield (The Standard) 1881

1188   Life and death of the Earl of Beaconsfield. 1881

1189   Yorkshire Conservative Newspaper Co. : The Late Lord Beaconsfield. 1881

1190	Burton, R. F.	:	Lord Beaconsfield. 1882

1191   The Life of the Earl of Beaconsfield. 1882

1192   This is the tree that Ben raised. 1883

1193	Nelson, T. J.	:	An Incredible story. 1884
1194	Hennessy, J. P.	:	Lord Beaconsfield's Irish policy. 1885

1195-96   Lord Beaconsfield's ghost. 1886

1197	De Haye, A.	:	Lamartine et Lord Beaconsfield. 1895
1198	Pitman, J. A.	:	Lord Beaconsfield as a writer, from a political view. 1899
1199	Lovat-Fraser, J. A. :		Disraeli. 1901

Verse

1200	Collins, M.	:	A Letter to ... Disraeli. 1869

1201-1202   Ginx's blot removed. 1876

1203-1204   Beaconsfield, a mock-heroic poem. 1878

1205   The Premier's dream. 1878?

1206   The Pretty little coronet and great big B! 1878

ABBREVIATIONS

AHR	American Historical Review
DGK	Deutscher Gesamtkatalog
EHR	English Historical Review
frontis.	frontispiece, not included in the pagination
H. & L.	Halkett, S. and Laing, J. : Dictionary of anonymous and pseudonymous English literature, new edition by J. Kennedy etc. , 1926 etc.
H. P.	The Hughenden Papers, in the possession of the National Trust, at Hughenden Manor. See 742
JMH	Journal of Modern History
L. B. L.	Lord Beaconsfield's Letters (551)
MB	Monypenny, W. F. and Buckle, G. E. : Life of Disraeli, new edition, 1929 (926)
MLR	Modern Language Review
n. d.	no date of publication in the book
n. d. (1879)	no date of publication in the book, the date being supplied from internal or external evidence
(1879)	the date of publication, appearing in the book elsewhere than on the title-page

N. & Q.	Notes and Queries. The series number is given up to and including the 15th series. For the weekly issues, the month is given in Roman numerals.
NCBEL	The New Cambridge Bibliography of English Literature, volume 3, edited by George Watson. Cambridge, 1969
NCF	Nineteenth Century Fiction
NYRB	New York Review of Books
pl.	plate or plates, not included in the pagination
pseud	in the Index, indicates a pseudonym
publ. advts.	publisher's advertisements, forming part of the book as issued
Sadleir, Excursions	See item 3. The page number is given
Sadleir, XIX C. F.	See item 4. The item number is given
Smiles	Smiles, Samuel: A publisher and his friends, memoir and correspondence of the late John Murray. London, 1891
T. L. S.	Times Literary Supplement
VNL	Victorian Newsletter
VS	Victorian Studies
W. I.	The Wellesley Index to Victorian Periodicals, Vol. I, 1966
*	A work by Disraeli reprinted in Tales and Sketches, edited by J. Logie Robertson (554)
+	A work by Disraeli reprinted in Whigs and Whiggism, edited by W. Hutcheon (558)

In references to periodicals, volume numbers are given without prefix; issue numbers are prefixed by "no." Arabic numerals are used throughout.

Throughout the lists, the place of publication of books is London, except where otherwise stated. The place of publication of periodicals has been given only in cases of identity or similarity of title.

SIGNIFICANT DATES IN DISRAELI'S LIFE

1804	Dec. 21	Born, probably in London
1817	July 31	Baptized at S. Andrew's, Holborn, London
1825		In partnership with John Murray (See 735)
1826	April	Vivian Grey published
1830-1831		Tour of the Eastern Mediterranean
1832		Contested Wycombe twice unsuccessfully
1834		Contested Wycombe unsuccessfully
1837	July	Elected M. P. for Maidstone
1839	Aug. 28	Married Mary Anne, widow of Wyndham Lewis
1841		Elected M. P. for Shrewsbury
1844		Coningsby published
1844-1846		Increasing attacks on Peel's government
1847		Purchased Hughenden Manor
		Elected M. P. for Buckinghamshire (until 1876)
1852		Chancellor of the Exchequer
1858-1859		Chancellor of the Exchequer

1866-1868		Chancellor of the Exchequer
1868	Feb. -Dec.	Prime Minister
1870		Lothair published
1872	Dec. 16	Death of Mary Anne, since 1868 Viscountess Beaconsfield
1874	Feb.	Prime Minister
1876	Aug. 12	Created Earl of Beaconsfield
1880	April	Defeated at General Election, and resigned
	Nov.	Endymion published
1881	April 19	Died at 19 Curzon Street, London

BENJAMIN DISRAELI

A list of writings by him, and writings about him

Bibliographies

1. "Contributions to a bibliography of Benjamin Disraeli, Earl of Beaconsfield," by George Angus in N. & Q., 8th ser., 3, 321-23, 361-63, 401-03, 443-45, 482-83 and 4, 22-24. (1893)
   Many of the ephemeral pieces were first listed here.

2. "A complete bibliography chronologically arranged of the writings of the Earl of Beaconsfield, K. G. Critically surveyed by the late ... Lord Rowton ...", in 659, v. 20. 13 pp. (1904)
   No further information is given about the sources of this list. Compared to 1, it follows the same order, which is distinctive at some points, and though numerous items in 1 are omitted, there are no additional items; the descriptions are similar, and there are frequent parallels in wording. It seems that 2 is an abridged version of 1, with some inexplicable omissions, and several mistakes. It cannot be regarded as an independent authority.

3. Sadleir, Michael: Benjamin Disraeli: essay and bibliography in Excursions in Victorian bibliography, 1922, 107-125. Editiones principes.

4. Sadleir, Michael: XIX Century Fiction, a bibliographical record ..., 1951, I, 110-114. (Items no. 709-738)

5. Dahl, Curtis: Benjamin Disraeli in Victorian fiction, a guide to research, edited by Lionel Stevenson. Harvard U. P., 1964, 22-35.
   The principal critical discussion of writings on Disraeli.

6. Stewart, R.W.: Writings of Benjamin Disraeli, in 1053, pp. 772-778. (1966)

DISRAELI'S WRITINGS

Works originally published separately

Inquiry into ... the American Mining Companies

The first published work known to be by Disraeli. Like the two following titles, published at the request of J.D. Powles, to boost his companies' shares, and to divert the attention of Parliament from the affairs of the companies speculating in the minerals of Central and South America. All three were anonymous.

7. An inquiry into the plans, progress, and policy of the American mining companies. London: John Murray, Albemarle Street. MDCCCXXV.
Pp. 88, title on p. (1)
Sadleir, Excursions, 113; XIX C.F., 715
Published March 1825

8. Gentleman's Magazine, 95, (1), 440

9. 1825 Second edition. Pp. 88. new footnotes on pp. 20, 36 and 49-50, resulting in re-setting of pages.

10. 1825 "Third edition, with considerable additions," containing a new "Advertisement" (pp.(v)-vi) and "Supplement" (pp. 132-35); the text enlarged. Pp. vi, (7)-135+(1) Half-title.

Lawyers and Legislators

11. Lawyers and Legislators: or notes on the American mining companies. (Quotation) London: John Murray, Albemarle Street. MDCCCXXV.
Pp. (viii)+99+(1 advt.) No half-title.
Sadleir, Excursions, 113; XIX C.F., 716
Published April/May 1825
Dedicated to Canning, "Who is not more eminent for his brilliant wit, and classic eloquence, than for that sedate sublimity of conception, which distinguishes the practical statesman, from the political theorist, these pages are, without permission, dedicated by his sincere admirer."

Present state of Mexico

12. The present state of Mexico: as detailed in a report
presented to the General Congress, by the Secretary of
State for the Home Department and Foreign Affairs, at
the opening of the session in 1825. With notes, and a
memoir of Don Lucas Alaman. London: John Murray,
Albemarle Street. MDCCCXXV.
Pp. 130
The "Memoir" (pp. (9)-55) and the notes appear to
have been added by Disraeli.
Sadleir, Excursions, 113
Published May/June 1825
Dedicated to Canning.

13. (A second edition?) containing, in addition, pp. (131)-
152, with subsidiary half-title, p. (131) "Gold and sil-
ver." On verso of half-title, announcements of Inquiry,
Ed. 3. and Lawyers and legislators.
Sadleir, XIX C. F., 722

Vivian Grey

14. Vivian Grey. "Why then the world's mine oyster,
Which I with sword will open." London: Henry Colburn, New Burlington Street. 1826.
Two volumes. Pp.(iv)+266+(2 pp. advts.) No half-
title; (iv)+236+(4 pp. advts.) Half-title.
Sadleir, Excursions, 114; XIX C. F., 734
Published 22 April 1826. This, Disraeli's first published novel, appeared anonymously, though the secret
of the authorship was discovered in a few weeks. The
plot is based on Disraeli's partnership with Murray in
the latter part of 1825 in launching the newspaper, The
Representative (735).
For the circumstances, see Jerman (1028), and
Stewart (56). It was, and continued, very popular,
though Disraeli came to regard it as a mistake, and in
the General Preface to his novels, 1870, called it
"essentially a puerile work." It featured largely in
later polemics (e.g. 1137, 1408). To appreciate the
feeling it aroused, it should be read in the original:
Disraeli made extensive revisions for the 1853 edition
(42) and the revised text was used for Longmans'
standard editions. Colburn paid Ł200 for it.

15. (Part II) Three volumes. Pp. (ii)+333+(3), (335)
& (336) advts. No half-title; (ii)+362+ (2 advts.) No
half-title; (iv)+324. Half-title.

41

Published 23 February 1827. Though the authorship was known, it was not then acknowledged, and Colburn tried to pretend there was some mystery about it. He paid Ł500 for it. These volumes describe Vivian Grey's tedious adventures on the Continent: Gladstone (in 1874) called it "trash," though he allowed that the earlier volumes were "extremely clever."

Reviews of Part I

16.   The Atlas,   1, 170-71 (30 July) Review of Ed. 2.
17.   Blackwood's,   20, 98 (July) in "Noctes Ambrosianae," no. 27
18.   Literary Chronicle, no. 367, 323-27 (27 May)
19.   Literary Gazette,   no. 483, 241-44 (22 April) Possibly by William Jerdan.
20.   Literary Magnet, new ser., 2, 1-6 "Nuisances of the press. No. 1. The New Unknown."
21.   London Magazine, new ser., 5, 207-17 (June)
22.   Monthly Review, new ser., 2, 329-30 (July)
23.   New Monthly Magazine, 18, 173 (April)
24.   Revue française, no. 1, 46-99 (1828) "Moeurs politiques anglaises" (Vivian Grey and "De Vere." Said to be by François Guizot)
25.   Star Chamber, pp. 16, 33-38 and
26.   Star Chamber, 114-16 (Key). For Disraeli's connection with this see 723. See 36, 58
27.   United States Review and Literary Gazette, 1, 231-32 (W. C. Bryant)

Reviews of Part II

28.   The Atlas,   2, 138 (4 March)
29.   Literary Chronicle, no. 407, 131-34 (3 March)
30.   Literary Gazette, no. 528, 134-35 (3 March)
31.   London Magazine, new ser., 7, 472-83 (April)
32.   Monthly Review, new ser., 5, 420-26 (July)
33.   New Monthly Magazine, 19, 297-304. This is probably based on a review by Isaac D'Israeli, corrected by Disraeli himself. See 55 and 587
34.   North American Review, 25, 199-203
35.   United States Review and Literary Gazette, 2, 224-25 (W. C. Bryant)

36. (on front wrapper) <u>Drawing of a key</u> / TO VIVIAN
GREY!!! / Being a complete Exposition of the / Royal
Noble & Fashionable / CHARACTERS / who figure in
that most extraordinary work / <u>drawing</u> (with litho-
grapher's name) / London / Printed for WILLIAM
MARSH, / Public Subscription Reading Rooms. / 137 &
145 Oxford Street
(on title-page) Key / to / Vivian Grey. / <u>rule</u> /
Pandarus. Here, here, here's an excellent place; here
we may / see most bravely. I'll tell you them all by
their names as they / pass by. / Cressida. Speak not
so loud. * * * Who's that? / Shakspeare. / <u>rule</u> /
London: / Printed for / William Marsh, 137, Oxford
Street. / 1827.
Pp. (iv)+25+(3 publ. advts.) Yellow wrappers, all
but (i) blank. There are variant states, e. g. the copies
in the Bodleian and at Hughenden differ in text and advts.
The lay-out of the wrapper of the Bodleian copy differs
slightly from that above. The "Key" to the first two
volumes taken from <u>Star Chamber</u> (26 & 723) which was
also published by <u>William Marsh</u>. The pamphlet contains also a "review" of, extracts from, and a key to
the "Continuation." See 58

37. A "tenth edition" (1827) See 1, where the Keys are
reprinted (N. & Q., 8th ser., <u>3</u>, 321-22)

For Key to Vivian Grey, by H. P. Mendes see 851

For Key to Vivian Grey, by R. W. Howes see 852

<u>Later editions</u>

38. 1826 "New edition" (of Part I) (so title-page; described as "Second edition" on labels). 2 volumes,
pagination as Ed. 1
39. 1827 "Third edition." 4 volumes. Vol. 1 (= Vols. 1
and 2) Pp. (iv)+ 380
40. 1827 2 volumes. Philadelphia, Carey, Lea and Carey
41. 1833 5 volumes in 4. Bentley. (Colburn's modern
novelists) The first edition in which Disraeli's
authorship was acknowledged.
42. 1853 1 volume, in uniform edition of novels, Bryce.
With an Advertisement, dated Nov. 1853. The
text was heavily revised, according to Wolf (45)
by Sarah Disraeli.

43. 1870 In Longmans' standard edition, with revised
        text. Frequently reprinted.
        Also reprinted in London by Warne, and Rout-
        ledge, and in New York by Munro, between 1858
        and 1888 at least.
44. 1904 Edited by Bernard N. Langdon-Davies, illustrated
        by Byam Shaw. The first volume of "Young Eng-
        land" (661). The original text is printed, with
        notes on the omissions, and on the "Keys." The
        revised text may be readily distinguished by the
        fact that Book I contains only 9 chapters, whereas
        the original contained 10.
45. 1904 2 volumes, edited by Lucien Wolf, part of a
        projected "Centenary edition" (see also 81) De
        La More Press. Original text. The introduction
        is particularly useful for the Jewish background.
        (See 1683)
46.   N. & Q., 10th ser., 4, 539 (30.xii.1905)
47. 1906 In uniform edition, edited by Lord Iddesleigh.
        John Lane, the Bodley Head. (662)
48. 1968 1 volume, edited by Herbert Van Thal, with an
        introduction by Stephanie Nettell, Cassell. (The
        First novel library)

Translations

49. German (1827)
50. Danish (1840-41)

Later comments

51. Samuel, H. B.   : Two dandy novels, Vivian
                         Grey and Pelham in Acad-
                         emy, 67, 316-17 (1904)
52. Samuel, H. B.   : (Review of Wolf's edition)
                         ibid., 657-58
53. Horrabin, J. F.   : Vivian Grey, ibid., 68, 157-
                         58 (1905)
54. Caspar, Maria   : Disraeli's Vivian Grey II
                         als politischer Schlüssel-
                         roman, in Archiv, 153, 37-
                         60 (1928) (See 1604)
55. Maitre, R.   : Un point de critique Dis-
                         raelienne: le lancement
                         de la deuxième partie de
                         "Vivian Grey" in Etudes
                         anglaises, 5, 227-31 (1952)
56. Stewart, R. W.   : The publication and reception

			of Disraeli's Vivian Grey in Quarterly Review, 298, 409-17 (1960)
57.	Maxwell, J. C.	:	Words from "Vivian Grey" in N. & Q., 206, 225-6 (June 1961); 207, 190 (May 1962); 210, 195 (May 1965)
58.	Fido, Martin	:	The "Key to Vivian Grey" of 1827 in N. & Q., 210, 418-19 (Nov. 1965)
59.	Nickerson, Charles C.	:	Vivian Grey and Dorian Gray in T. L. S., 14 Aug. 1969, 909, and subsequent correspondence.
60.	N. & Q., 9th ser., 6, 209 (15. ix. 1900); 11th ser., 5, 445 (8. vi. 1912)		

See 587, 665, 1296, 1304, 1595, 1602, 1604

Manuscript   Hughenden Papers E/I/7

Popanilla

61. The voyage of Captain Popanilla. By the author of "Vivian Grey." "Travellers ne'er did lie, tho' fools at home condemn 'em." London: Henry Colburn, New Burlington Street 1828.
     Pp. viii+243+(1)
     Sadleir, Excursions, 114; XIX C. F., 735
     Published 3 June 1828. Dedicated to Plumer Ward.
     A political satire against the Utilitarians; "Popanilla" visits England ("Vraibleusia") from a remote island where a collection of the tracts of the Society for the Diffusion of Useful Knowledge has been washed up. It was apparently a re-writing of "Aylmer Papillon" (740). Plumer Ward compared it to Swift and Voltaire, but no-one else seems to have taken much notice of it.

Reviews

62.	Athenaeum,	no. 34, 531-32 (18 June)
63.	Literary Gazette,	no. 594, 360 (7 June)
64.	New Monthly Magazine,	24, 286 (July)

Later editions

65.	1828	Philadelphia, Carey, Lea and Carey
66.	1829	The voyage of Captain Popanilla, to the glorious island of Vraibleusia, the wonderful city of

Hubbabub, and the peaceable isle of Blunderland.
By the author of "Vivian Grey." (quotation as
above) A new edition. With illustrations from
drawings by Daniel Maclise. (Colburn), 1829.
　　Pp. xiv+ 243+(1); after p. vi, a 4-page advt.
containing a review of Vivian Grey (24). Sadleir,
XIX C. F. , 735a
　　Not again published separately. Published with
"Ixion" and other works in Bryce's uniform edition
of 1853, for which the text was heavily revised
(471); with "Alroy" and other works in Longmans'
standard editions, (125); with "Alroy, " edited by
Iddesleigh (127), and with other works in 663.

67.　Translated into French, 1866

Later comment

68.　Maxwell, J. C.　　　　　: Words from "Popanilla, " N.
　　　　　　　　　　　　　　　& Q. , 206, 330 (Sept. 1961)

The Young Duke

69.　The young Duke. "A moral Tale, though gay. " By
the author of "Vivian Grey." London: Henry Colburn
and Richard Bentley, New Burlington Street. 1831.
　　Three volumes. Pp. iv+ 300; (iv)+ 269+ (3); (iv)+ 265+
(3).
　　Sadleir, Excursions, 114; XIX C. F. , 738
　　This contains some "Notes" omitted from later editions.
　　Written at top speed, avowedly for money to pay for
his tour to the East; offered to Murray in 1830; Murray
would not overlook the ill-treatment he believed himself
to have suffered from Disraeli in the Representative af-
fair, and declined to see him, while offering to consider
the manuscript "in the ordinary way of business. " Disraeli declined, and offered it to Colburn, who paid £500
for it, and published it in April 1831, when Disraeli was
abroad.
　　There has been some discussion about the autobio-
graphical content of the novel (81), but his father's comment "What does Ben know of dukes?" is perhaps the
best criticism. It was generally favourably received,
except by the Benthamite Westminster Review. The text
was heavily revised for the 1853 edition, according to
Wolf (81) by Sarah Disraeli. The only one of his full-

length novels which Disraeli does not mention in his "General Preface" of 1870.

Reviews

70.	Athenaeum,	no.	183, 276-77 (30 April)
71.	Court Journal,	no.	104, 291-92 (23 April) &
		no.	106, 324-25 (7 May)
72.	Examiner,	no.	1232, p. 579 (11 Sept.)
73.	Literary Gazette,	no.	743, 242-43 (16 April)
74.	New Monthly Magazine,	32,	360-61 (Oct.) and 33,
			205 (May)
75.	Spectator,	4,	425-27 (30 April)
76.	Westminster Review,	15,	399-406 (an attack)

Later editions

77. 1831 New York, Harper, 2 volumes.
78. 1832 ?Second edition (announced in Literary Gazette, 7 Jan. 1832)
79. 1853 in Bryce's edition
80. 1871 in Longmans' standard edition, with "Court Alarcos"
    other editions by Ward Lock, Warne and Routledge, and in New York by Harper and Munro
81. 1905 edited by Lucien Wolf, uniform with his edition of "Vivian Grey " (45). The usefulness of the introduction is reduced by his insistence that the scenes of the novel were drawn from Disraeli's own experience.
82. N. & Q., 10th ser., 4, 498 (16.xii.1905)
83. 1906 edited by Lord Iddesleigh, with "The Rise of Iskander" and "The Infernal Marriage" (662)

Later comments

Hudson (1545) suggests that this was one of Disraeli's works burlesqued by Poe.
84. Maxwell, J. C.   : Words from "The Young Duke" in N. & Q., 209, 29 (Jan. 1964)
    See 665, 1595
    Manuscript sold to the Duke of Albany at Christie's, 1881.

England and France

85. England and France; or, A cure for the Ministerial

Gallomania. (Quotation from Wellington) London: John
Murray, Albemarle Street. 1832.
    Pp. (?iv)+ viii+ 268. Sadleir, Excursions, 115;
    XIX C. F., 713. There are possibly variant states.
    The dedication, to Lord Grey, is dated 14 April 1832,
Saturday morning. 8 a. m.
    The circumstances of the writing of this work remain
obscure. It is an attack on the policy of friendship with
France, and contains a "Secret History" of the French
Revolution of 1830.
    Disraeli was involved, it appears, with supporters of
the exiled Charles X, one of whom, De Haber, perhaps
wrote the French sections. The more general parts,
dealing with British affairs, seem to be by Disraeli, and
there is a manuscript of them in his hand. He denied
to Murray that he was the sole author, but acknowledged
it at the time of the Taunton election of 1835. (1702)
His connection with the work was noticed by at least
one contemporary writer. (1373) There seems to have
been an intention to influence the fate of the Reform Bill,
which had just passed its Second Reading in the House
of Lords, though Disraeli denied any hostility to "the
general measure of Reform." It does not appear to have
figured in later controversies, presumably because it
made little impression at the time, and was forgotten.

Reviews

86.	Athenaeum,	no. 234, 254 (21 April)
87.	Examiner,	no. 1264, 260 (22 April)
88.	John Bull,	12, 134 (22 April)
89.	Literary Gazette,	no. 800, 311 (19 May)
90.	Monthly Review,	1832, part 2, 100-16
91.	Morning Chronicle,	(19 April)
92.	Spectator,	5, 376 (21 April)
93.	Times,	(20 April)

It has never been re-published.

Manuscript, lacking the chapters of "Secret History,"
Hughenden Papers E /I /9

Contarini Fleming

94. Contarini Fleming a psychological auto-biography. London: John Murray, Albemarle-Street. MDCCCXXXII.
    Four volumes. Pp. (iv)+ 288; iv+ 247+ (1);
    (iv)+ 194+ (2); (iv)+ 230+ (2).
    Sadleir, Excursions, 115; XIX C. F., 711

Much of this was apparently written abroad. The original title, "A psychological romance," was changed by Murray, on the suggestion of Milman, who read it for him. (See Smiles, II, 332-41.) Published anonymously, May 1832, though the authorship was known. Praised by Beckford, Fanny Burney, and Heine.

Reviews

95.	Athenaeum,	no. 237, 298-300 (12 May)
96.	Atlas,	7, 347-48 (27 May)
97.	Court Journal,	no. 161, 349-50 (26 May) Disraeli told his sister this was by P. G. Patmore (L. B. L., May 26, 1832)
98.	Gentleman's Magazine,	102, (2), 240-41 (Sept.)
99.	Literary Gazette,	nos. 798, 799, pp. 277-78, 289-91 (5 and 12 May) (See Smiles, II, 340; Disraeli told Sarah it was by Letitia Landon)
100.	Literary Guardian,	2, 115-16 (26 May)
101.	New Monthly Magazine,	35, 26-28
102.	Spectator,	5, 471 (19 May)

Later editions

103.   1834   Contarini Fleming or The psychological romance.
By D'Israeli the younger, author of "Vivian Grey,"
"Alroy," and "Ixion in Heaven." Second edition.
London: Edward Moxon, Dover Street.
MDCCCXXXIV.
    Four volumes. Pp. viii+ 288. Other volumes
as first edition.
    Sadleir, Excursions, 115; XIX C. F., 711a
    The sheets of the Murray edition re-issued,
with a preface, dated 11 December 1833, explaining the change in the sub-title.

104.   Literary Gazette, no. 892, 135-36 (22 February)

105.   The young Venetian; or, The victim of imagination.
By Granville Jones, Esq. Glasgow: Richard Griffin and Company. 1834.
    Four volumes
    This is undoubtedly the sheets of "Contarini
Fleming" (with the same imprint "William Clowes,
Stamford Street"), with new title-pages. See 1028,

224ff., where it is suggested that Disraeli may not
have been innocent of the deception.

106. 1846 Published with "Alroy" by Colburn, with a new
preface, dated July 1845.
Three volumes
Sadleir, XIX C. F., 711

107. 1853 in Bryce's uniform edition

108. 1871 and later, with "The Rise of Iskander" in Longmans' standard edition

109. 1905 edited by Lord Iddesleigh, with the 1845 preface. See 662, 655

Translations

110. German (1846)

111. French (1863)
See 669

Later comments

112. Gilbert, F.   : The Germany of Contarini
Fleming in Contemporary
Review, 149, 74-80 (1936)

113. Cline, C. L.   : The failure of Contarini
Fleming in N. & Q., 15th
ser., 183, 69 (1 August
1942)
For "Contarini Fleming," a psychological satire, see
1208, 1595
Manuscript sold to Sir Theodore Martin for the Queen
at Christie's, 1881. A few sheets are in Hughenden
Papers, E /I /16
For Wycombe election address, 27 June 1832, see 1693

Alroy

114. The Wondrous tale of Alroy. The rise of Iskander.
By the author of "Vivian Grey," "Contarini Fleming,"
&c. London: Saunders and Otley, Conduit Street.
1833.
Three volumes. Pp. xxv+ (iii)+ 303+ (1); (iv)+ 305+ (3);
(iv)+ 324+ (4)

The half-title to Vol. III reads, erroneously, "The
rise of Iskander.   Vol. III."
  Sadleir, Excursions, 116; XIX C. F. , 737
  Published March 5, 1833. Dedicated to ** ********.
  Dedication begins "Sweet sister, " i. e. Sarah. In the
"General Preface, " Disraeli said that he had started
this after publishing "Vivian Grey, " and resumed it after
his visit to Jerusalem in 1831. "Alroy" is described
by Roth (1018) as "one of the earliest, and perhaps indeed the earliest, of Jewish historical novels. "; it is
based on an historical incident of the twelfth century,
and tells of the resurgence of the Jewish nation. "The
rise of Iskander, " probably written at Bath in the winter
of 1832-33, is about a Christian hero who rose against
the Moslems in Albania, which Disraeli had also visited
on his Eastern tour.
  Murray refused it.   Saunders and Otley gave an advance of £ 300.

Reviews

115.   American Monthly Magazine, I, 261 (June)
116.   American Monthly Review, 4, 279-82
117.   Athenaeum,   no. 280, 150-51 (9 March)
118.   Atlas,   8, 178-79 (24 March)
119.   Court Journal,   no. 204, 202-03 (23 March)
120.   Examiner,   no. 1319, 293 (12 May)
121.   Literary Gazette,   no. 842, 146-48 (9 March)
122.   Monthly Review,   1833, part 1, 588-89
123.   New Monthly Magazine, 37, 342-46 (March)

Later editions

124.   1834 "A new edition" (Proof of title-pages of Vols.
           2 and 3 in Hughenden Papers, R /V /B /27)
(106.) 1846 Alroy, published by Colburn with "Contarini
           Fleming" with a preface dated July 1845
125.   1871 and later, in Longmans' standard edition, with
           "Ixion in Heaven, " "The infernal marriage" and
           "Popanilla"
126.   1881 "Miriam Alroy, a romance of the twelfth cen-
           tury. " New York, G. Munro. (Seaside Library)
           See 655
127.   1906 edited by Lord Iddesleigh, with "Popanilla, "
           "Count Alarcos" and "Ixion in Heaven" (662)
128.   Dramatised by Paul P. Grunfeld, 1896 and 1906
129.   (two versions)

Translations

130. German, 1833 and several subsequent versions
131. Hebrew, Warsaw, 1883
"The rise of Iskander" was published with "Contarini Fleming" in Longmans' standard edition (108), with "The young Duke" (83) in Iddesleigh's edition, and with "Popanilla" and other works in Guedalla's Bradenham edition, 1926 (663)

132. "The rise of Iskander," Greek, Nicosia, 1890

Later comments

133. Abrahams, Israel   :   Disraeli's "Alroy" in The Jewish World, no. 3005, 9-10, Tamuz 11, 5673 (16 July 1913) also in Beaconsfield Quarterly, no. 3, 41-43

134. Brandl, A.   :   Zur Quelle von Disraelis Alroy in Archiv für das Studium der neueren Sprachen und Literaturen, 148, 97-98 (1925)

135. Jean-Aubry, G.   :   Disraeli et le solitaire de Bath (i.e. Beckford), in Le Figaro, 5 Dec. 1931, 5-6

Manuscripts
Alroy Hughenden Papers, E/I/8 (incomplete). A Ms., or part, was sold at Christie's in 1881.
The Rise of Iskander B.M. Add. MSS., 36, 677. Offered at Christie's in 1881; bought by B.M. in 1902.

What is he?

136. "What is he?" By the author of "Vivian Grey." I hear that ******** is again in the field; I hardly know whether we ought to wish him success. "What is he?" --Extract from a Letter of an eminent Personage. London: James Ridgway, Piccadilly ... MDCCCXXXIII.
Pp. 16, the half-title as front wrapper. On the verso of half-title, advts. for "Alroy" and "The Turkish

Empire--Sketches in Greece and Turkey, 1832."
Sadleir, Excursions, 116; XIX C. F., 736
Issued in April 1833, at the time of an expected vacancy at Marylebone, for which Disraeli intended to stand. The "eminent personage" was supposed to be Lord Grey, the point of the question apparently being Disraeli's anti-Whig Radical position. See 1695

Later editions

137.   "A new revised edition," 1833. So described on title-page, on which there are also minor differences in punctuation; the advts. also differ, and there are some verbal changes in the text.
1884 Published with "Vindication of the English Constitution" (155)
1913 Published in "Whigs and Whiggism" (558)

Manuscript Hughenden Papers E/II/2 (incomplete)

Velvet Lawn

138.   Velvet Lawn. A sketch, written for the benefit of the Buckinghamshire Infirmary. By the author of "Vivian Grey." Wycombe: E. King. 1833.
Pp. 13+(1). Green wrappers. Sadleir, XIX C. F., 731
Copy in Hughenden Papers, E/III/15; no other copy traced.

The Revolutionary Epick

139.   The revolutionary epick. The work of Disraeli the younger, author of "The psychological romance." London: Edward Moxon, Dover Street. MDCCCXXXIV.
Part I, published March 1834. Pp. (vi)+viii+1-89+(3)
Part II, containing Books II and III, published June 16. Pp. xi+(i)+(91)-206
50 copies printed. Sadleir, Excursions, 117; XIX C. F., 723
An epic poem on the French Revolution, the idea for which Disraeli said came to him on the plains of Troy. Written at Bradenham and Southend in the winter of 1833-34. On 16th January 1834, Disraeli recited the first canto at the Austens' house, after which Samuel Warren improvised a burlesque, causing the audience to ridicule the "epick." The public reception was no more

favourable, and the poet, as he had threatened, or
promised, "hurled his lyre, without a pang, into Limbo."

Reviews

140.	American Monthly	Magazine, 3, 267-73 (June) condemnatory
141.	Athenaeum,	no. 335, p. 236 (29 March) no. 347, 468-69 (21 June)
142.	Atlas,	9, no. 424, 410-11 (29 June)
143.	Court Journal,	no. 257, 216-17 (29 March); no. 270, p. 457 (28 June); no. 272, 488-89 (12 July)
144.	Fraser's Magazine,	10, 361-64 (Sept.)
145.	Literary Gazette,	nos. 897, 909, 910, pp. 217-18, 427-28, 448-49 (29 March, 21 and 28 June)
146.	Monthly Review,	1834, part 2, 54-60
147.	Spectator,	7, 299-300, 592

Later editions

The "Epick" was occasionally used to provide texts
to attack Disraeli, but it was rescued from obscurity by
Bright quoting it in the Commons in 1864. Disraeli issued
a new edition, heavily revised, with an explanatory preface
dedicated to Lord Stanley, in which he claimed that the revision had been completed in 1837.

148.   1864   The revolutionary epick. By the Right Honor-
able Benjamin Disraeli. London: Longman, Green,
Longman, Roberts, & Green. 1864.
Pp. (ii)+ x+ (ii)+ 176+ (2).
Sadleir, Excursions, 121; XIX C.F., 723a

149.   1904   The Revolutionary Epick and other poems by
Benjamin Disraeli (Earl of Beaconsfield) Reprinted
from the Original Edition, and Edited by W. Davenport Adams   London   Hurst and Blackett ... 1904
Pp. (xvi)+ 240
This contains "Count Alarcos," poems from
several novels, and "The Dunciad of Today" (723):
there is no editorial matter, and no explanation
for the inclusion of the latter work.

Later comment

150.   Meynell, Wilfrid   : Lord Beaconsfield's lyre in

54

English Illustrated Magazine,
13, no. 1, 28-32 (1895)
Manuscript of Books 2 and 3: Hughenden Papers E/I/10
For The Crisis Examined see 611
For Disraeli's addresses and letters at the Taunton election, 1835, see 1695-1703

Vindication of the English Constitution

151. Vindication of the English constitution in a letter to a noble and learned Lord. By Disraeli the younger. London Saunders and Otley, Conduit Street. 1835.
    Pp. ix+ (i)+ (3)-210+ (2). Errata slip
    Sadleir, Excursions, 117; XIX C. F., 733
    Published December 1835; (not, as Ralph Disraeli and Sadleir, in January 1835). It is addressed to Lord Lyndhurst, at whose request Disraeli had written leading articles in the Morning Post (488), and who was perhaps aiming to replace Peel as Tory leader. Peel himself thanked Disraeli for a copy of the book.
    The most serious and sustained of Disraeli's purely political writings, this is a "vindication" of Disraeli's own unusual views of the development of English politics, to the effect that the "anti-national" faction, from the Roundheads to Lord Melbourne, have always sought to overthrow the true English polity with the help of the Scots or Irish, and to establish, despite their pretences, a theocratic or oligarchic despotism. Tories, from Strafford to Lyndhurst, have struggled to frustrate these knavish tricks. Disraeli's views, particularly on the Civil War and the Revolution of 1688, are further developed in "Coningsby" and "Sybil." Though Monypenny too optimistically stated that it had an important influence on political thought, it did, and does, provide, allowing for its polemical nature, an interesting counter to "the Whig interpretation of history."

Reviews

152.   London Review,   2, (also referred to as Westminster Review, 31), 533-52 (1836) signed S. A.
153.   Spectator,   9, 14-16 (2 Jan. 1836)
154.   Times,   22 December. (Third leader)

Later editions

155. 1884 Lord Beaconsfield on the constitution "What is

he?" and "A Vindication of the English Constitution" by "Disraeli the Younger," ... edited with
an anecdotical preface by Francis Hitchman author
of "The Public Life of the Earl of Beaconsfield,"
&c. London: Field & Tuer, Ye Leadenhalle Presse,
E. C. (&c.)
    n. d. (1884)
    Pp. 1x+ 210+ (8 advts.)

156. 1895 Rare reprint of the late Earl of Beaconsfield's
K. G. Vindication of the English Constitution etc.
With an introduction by Frederick A. Hyndman ...
London Ideal Publishing Union Ltd. 16, Farringdon
Street, E. C.
    n. d. (1895)
    Pp. iv+ 307+ (1)
    1913 Published in "Whigs and Whiggism" (558)

157. 1969 Reprinted by Gregg International Publishers (a
reduced facsimile reprint)

Manuscript Hughenden Papers E /I /11 (incomplete)
For The Letters of Runnymede see 496

Henrietta Temple

158. Henrietta Temple, A Love Story. By the author of
"Vivian Grey." (Quotation) London: Henry Colburn,
13, Great Marlborough Street. MDCCCXXXVII.
    Three volumes.
    Pp. (vi)+ 299+ (1); (iv)+ 309+ (3); (iv)+ 331+ (1)
    Sadleir, Excursions, 118; XIX C. F., 714
This was begun in 1833 or 1834, but put aside, and
completed in 1836, when Disraeli's need for money became very pressing.
    Published 1 December 1836.
    Dedicated to Count D'Orsay, who appears as "Count
Mirabel."
    The least political of all the novels.

Reviews

159.   American Monthly Magazine, new ser., 3, 509-10
160.   Athenaeum,   no. 476, 867-69 (10 Dec.)
161.   Atlas,   11, 790-91 (11 Dec.)
162.   Court Journal,   no. 397, 778-80
                          no. 398, 795-96 (3, 10 Dec.)
163.   Edinburgh Review, 66, 59-72 (with Venetia)
164.   Examiner,   no. 1507, 804-07 (18 Dec.)

165. Literary Gazette,   no. 1037, 771-72 (3 Dec.)
166. New Monthly Magazine, 49, 136-40
167. Southern Literary Messenger, 3, 325-31
168. Spectator,   9, 1186 (10 Dec.)
169. The Times,   21 Dec.

Later editions

170. 1853 in Bryce's uniform edition
171. 1871 and later, in Longmans' standard edition
172. 1906 edited by Lord Iddesleigh (662)
173. 1947 published with works by other authors in "Novels of high society from the Victorian age, edited by Anthony Powell."
174.   T. L. S., 11 Oct. 1947, 520

Translations

175. German (1837)
176. French (1850)
177. Swedish (1859)
178. Russian (1859 &c.)
179. Hungarian (1861)
180. Greek (1862)
181. Polish (1882)

Later comments

182. Walkley, A. B. in The Times, 5 July 1922, p. 12 (see 1316) "a delicious book. So are nearly all the earlier novels of Disraeli, written before he ruined his literary style by going into politics."
183. N. & Q., 11th ser., 2, 425 (26.xi.1910) See 1315, 1316

Manuscript Hughenden Papers E/I/12 (incomplete)

Venetia

184. Venetia. By the author of "Vivian Grey" and "Henrietta Temple." (Quotation) London: Henry Colburn, Publisher, 13, Great Marlborough Street. MDCCXXXVII.
     Three volumes.   Pp. (iv)+ 346; (ii)+ 377+ (1); (iv)+ 324.
     No half-titles.
     Sadleir, Excursions, 119; XIX C. F., 732
     Published May 1837.   Dedicated to Lord Lyndhurst.
     Based on two characters, who share the characteris-

tics of Byron and Shelley, and set at the time of the
American War of Independence. The confusion of the
real and the fictional was much criticised.

Reviews

185.   American Monthly Magazine, new ser. , 4, 393-94
186.   Athenaeum,   no. 499, 356-57 (20 May)
187.   Atlas,   12, 344-45 (28 May)
188.   Court Journal,   no. 421, 314-16 (20 May)
       Edinburgh Review see 163, 343
189.   Fraser's Magazine, 15, 773-89 (June)
190.   Literary Gazette,   no. 1061, 313-15 (20 May)
191.   Spectator,   10, 472-73 (20 May)

Later editions

192.   1837 Philadelphia, Carey & Hart
193.   1853 in Bryce's uniform edition
194.   1870 and later, in Longmans' standard edition
195.   1906 cditcd by Lord Iddcslcigh (662)
196.   1915 a German school edition

Translation

197.   Greek (1889)

Later comments

198.   N. & Q. , 5th ser. , 2, 37 (11. vii. 1874); 177 (29. viii.
       1874)   15th ser., 181, 8 (5. vii. 1941)
       See 1457, 1590, 1592

       Manuscript of Vol. I and part of Vol. II sold at Christie's
       in 1881. The remainder, or most of it, in Hughenden
       Papers, E /I /13.

       For Maidstone election addresses and speeches, July,
       1837 see 1704-1707

                    Tragedy of Count Alarcos

199.   The tragedy of Count Alarcos. By the author of "Viv-
       ian Grey." London: Henry Colburn, Publisher, Great
       Marlborough Street. 1839.
          Pp. vi+ (ii)+ 108+ (4 publ. advts.) No half-title. Erratum
       Sadleir, Excursions, 119; XIX C. F. , 729

Published May 1839.   Dedicated to Lord Francis
Egerton.

"An attempt to contribute to the revival of English
tragedy," with a verse version of a Spanish story which
he had heard in Spain, and which had been rendered into English by J. G. Lockhart and others.   The theme
was generally regarded as too horrific, and the poetry
was not thought successful.

Productions were staged in 1868 and 1879 (See 205)

Reviews

200.	Argus,	no. 20, p. 307 (16 June)
201.	Court Journal,	no. 530, p. 411 (26 June)
202.	Literary Gazette,	no. 1179, p. 541 (24 August)
203.	New Monthly Magazine,	56, 576-77 (August)

Later editions

204.   1847   25 copies "published by the Marchioness of Lon-
        donderry at her stall in the Grand Bazaar ... in
        the Regent's Park Barracks ...." With an "Ad-
        vertisement" dated May 17 1847.
        Pp. (iv)+(ii)+ 108; the sheets of the 1839 edition,
        with new preliminary pages.   Green wrappers.   A
        copy in Hughenden Manor.

(471.) 1853   with "Ixion in Heaven" and other works in Bryce's
        uniform edition
(80.)   1870   and later, with "The young Duke" in Longmans'
        standard edition
(149.) 1904   with "The Revolutionary Epick"
(127.) 1906   with "Alroy," edited by the Earl of Iddesleigh

Later comment

205.   Cline, C. L.   : Disraeli's only venture in
                                    dramatic composition in Uni-
                                    versity of Texas Studies in
                                    English, 16, 93-105 (1936),
                                    deals with the production of
                                    the play.
Manuscript Hughenden Papers E/I/14.   Up to the middle
of Act II, Scene IV, i.e., about half the total.

For Addresses at the Shrewsbury election, June 1841,
see 1708-1716

The Trilogy

Disraeli in 1870 wrote, "Coningsby, Sybil, and Tancred form a real trilogy; that is to say, they treat of the same subject, and endeavour to complete that treatment. The origin and character of our political parties, their influence on the condition of the people of this country, some picture of the moral and physical condition of that people, and some intimation of the means by which it might be elevated and improved, were themes which had long engaged my meditation." (General Preface)

In general terms, Coningsby deals with politics, Sybil with society, and Tancred with religion, though not exclusively, since Disraeli did not recognise any such artificial division. Although there are some references from the later to the earlier novels, each is based on a different central character, Coningsby, the aristocrat of the "new generation," Sybil, who links the "two nations," and Tancred, who sets out on a "new crusade." The first two novels have generally attracted greater attention than Tancred which, perhaps from the ambitious nature of the theme, is the least successful of the three. Taken together they express Disraeli's belief in Faith and Imagination, and his views both of English history and of the Jewish people. Disraeli explained his unusual views by writing that he had been "trained from early childhood by learned men who did not share the passions and the prejudices of our political and social life (and) had imbibed on some subjects conclusions different from those which generally prevail, and especially with reference to the history of our own country." (General Preface)

Much of Disraeli's history is open to question: he dealt largely in cloudy abstractions, and produced entertaining paradoxes; at least on some points the reader's attention is caught, and he may view a familiar matter in a new light. On another plane, Disraeli could paint merciless satirical portraits of politicians, aristocrats and churchmen, whose shortcomings are exposed by the lofty ideals which they profess but do not follow. His purpose, however, was avowedly to propose remedies for the evils he denounced. The remedies necessarily depended on the analysis of the causes: as Disraeli denied the economic interpretation of history, it is not surprising that he should have shown no sympathy with any scheme for the economic reconstruction of society. In producing a practical programme his invention flagged, and whether in these novels, or in more serious

60

contexts like his policy speeches of 1872, his practical sug-
gestions tended to be inadequate, sometimes embarrassingly
so.

Nevertheless, in Coningsby, Sybil, and at least the
first volume of Tancred, there is much of interest and
amusement. The interest is in the ideas and the circumstances, and only rarely in the characters: although some
minor characters are masterly in their way, the central fig-
ures are not sufficiently sustained and developed to be convincing.

Coningsby

206. Coningsby; or, The new generation. By B. Disraeli,
      Esq. M. P. Author of "Contarini Fleming." London:
      Henry Colburn, Publisher; Great Marlborough Street.
      1844.
         Three volumes. Pp. iv+ 319+ (1); (ii)+ 314; (ii)+ 350+
      (4 publ. advts.) No half-titles.
         Sadleir, Excursions, 119; XIX C. F., 709
         Published May 1844. Dedicated to Henry Hope, of
      Deepdene, where much of it was written. Jerman (1579)
      states that Disraeli received about £350 for each of the
      two first editions.

Disraeli stated, in the 1849 preface, that he had not
intended to treat his theme in fictional form. If this is true,
it is not difficult to see the advantages of a novel over a
pamphlet of the type of the Vindication. When Coningsby
was begun in the autumn of 1843, the rift between Disraeli
and Peel's government had already appeared, but it did not
become an open breach until early in 1845. Coningsby, in
effect, gave notice that Disraeli would not indefinitely support the Minister whose policies and principles are denounced
in its pages. The novel was regarded by the critics as the
manifesto of "Young England," a small group of young aristocrats with whom Disraeli was associated from the end of
1841. The leading characters in Coningsby are usually regarded as being portraits of the members of this group, and
some elements of their outlook are reflected in the novel.
It is possible to be too solemn about "Young England,"
which seems to have been hardly more than an undergradu-
ate coterie under the spell of romantic medievalism. Disraeli's genuine acceptance of the group's views were doubted
by its members, and his detachment from their background
allowed him to treat the "New Feudalism" with a certain

61

scepticism. It was impossible for him to take aristocratic regeneration as seriously as Manners or Smythe, and, in the end, "Young England" had little, if anything, to do with Disraeli's overthrow of Peel and rise to the Conservative leadership.

In Coningsby Disraeli traces political history from 1832 to 1841, introducing substantial passages of political polemic openly attacking the Conservative Party and Peel. The main points are (1) that the Whigs, ever since 1640, have tried to subvert the English constitution, and replace it by the Venetian, or, more recently, by abstract French theories, (2) that the modern Conservative Party is the heir, not of the Tory Party of Bolingbroke and the younger Pitt, but of the incompetent Pittites who abandoned principle for expediency, and (3) that Conservative government means "Tory men and Whig measures"; that it has no principles, and that its adherence to Church, Lords, and Crown is hypocrisy.

The remedies are characteristically vague, but include (1) restoring the power of the Sovereign, and (2) freeing the Church from Parliamentary control.

In general, Youth, Heroism, Faith, and Imagination are desirable. Throughout his career, one of the greatest of Parliamentarians denounced Parliamentary government. The dangers of these remedies, if they were meant to be taken seriously, are obvious.

There is, however, another line of argument, with no very obvious connection with the main one. This is the expression, through the character "Sidonia," of Disraeli's views on the Jewish people, views also frequently reiterated, most notably in Tancred and the 24th chapter of Lord George Bentinck, and directed to claiming for it a superiority based on purity of blood. Sidonia is a Jew from Spain, descended from a line of "New Christians," and there is a disquisition (Book IV, chapter 10) on Spanish history, with particular reference to the Expulsion of 1492, in which Disraeli believed, or affected to believe, that his own ancestors had left Spain rather than conform to Christianity. The details may be dubious as history, but there is no doubt of the satisfaction in the conclusion,

> The Spanish Goth, then so cruel and so haughty,
> where is he? A despised suppliant to the very

race which he banished .... Where is that tribunal? (the Inquisition) ... Where is Spain?

Here is also introduced the theory of racial purity, which in a civilised age and country, may have seemed merely the expression of an obvious fact, "You cannot destroy a pure race of the Caucasian organization," but which, inverted, has unleashed such horror. Disraeli undoubtedly regarded Jewry as a superior race, and superior as a race: there is no suggestion that it is under the special protection of Divine Providence. Indeed, the religious aspect of Judaism is, at least in Coningsby, wholly ignored. Jews and crypto-Jews dominated the art and the diplomacy of Europe, not least in Germany, and the Church itself. There is, of course, no suggestion that Jews need to assert their superiority by force: that was quite unnecessary. Whatever else Disraeli believed, he did believe in the uniqueness of his people, and in its special, if not very clearly defined, mission.

Coningsby did not make its author rich, but it did attract the attention of the politically-minded public. Whether or not there is a category, "the political novel" of which this may or may not be the first or the best, it clearly is a political novel; it is not merely set in politics; its whole purpose is political, the author's comments, and much of the dialogue are political, and all to a more exclusive degree than in any other of his novels. The plot, abstracted from the political content, is feeble: however, Disraeli's plots always were.

Reviews

207.	Ainsworth's Magazine, 5, 497-503. "Benjamin D'Israeli and the new generation."
208.	Athenaeum, no. 864, 446-47 (18 May)
209.	Atlas, 19, 339, 356-57 (18, 25 May)
210.	Christian Remembrancer, 7, 667-89
211.	Court Journal, no. 787, 351-52 (25 May)
212.	Critic (1st. ser.), 1, 186-88 (15 May)
213.	Eclectic Review, 4th ser., 16, 50-71
214.	Edinburgh Review, 80, 517-25 "Young England" (Abraham Hayward)
215.	Examiner, no. 1894, p. 307 (18 May)
216.	Fraser's Magazine, 30, 71-84
217.	Gentleman's Magazine, new ser., 22, 62 (July)

218.   Hood's Magazine,   1, 601-06.   "A few remarks
                            on Coningsby, by Real England."
                            (Possibly by R. Monckton
                            Milnes)
219.   John Bull,   24, 341-42, 357-58, 373-74,
                            390-91 (1-22 June)
220.   Literary Gazette,   no. 1426, pp. 315-19 (18 May)
221.   Mirror,   new ser., 5, 354-56
222.   Morning Chronicle, 13 May. (W. M. Thackeray)
                            See 1362
223.   New Monthly Magazine, 71, 206-15
224.   North British Review, 1, 561-79 (J. Moncrieff)
225.   Pictorial Times,   no. 63, p. 331 (25 May) (W.
                            M. Thackeray)
226.   Revue des deux mondes, n. s. 7, 385-417 (1 Aug.)
                            "De la jeune Angleterre, " by
                            E. Forcade
227.   Southern Literary Messenger, 10, 737-49
228.   Spectator,   17, 519-20 (1 June)
229.   Tait's Edinburgh Magazine, new ser., 11, 447-61
230.   The Times,   11, 15, 16, 20, 28 May
231.   Westminster Review, 42, 80-105

        For "Codlingsby" see 318

        Contemporary pamphlets

232.   1844 Key to the characters in Coningsby comprising
              about sixty of the principal personages of the story.
              London: Shelwood Gilbert and Piper, Paternoster
              Row. 1844. Pp. 7+ (1)
233.   1845 A new key to the characters in Coningsby. W.
              Strange, 21, Paternoster Row, London. (n. d.)
              Pp. 7+ (1)
              A single list of real names.
              A conflation of 232 and 233 is in 1 at p. 363.
234.   1844 Strictures on "Coningsby ..." With remarks
              on the present state of parties and the character
              of the age ...   London: James Ridgway, Picca-
              dilly. 1844. Pp. 36
235.   Anti-Coningsby; or, The new generation grown
              old. By an embryo M. P. ... London: T. C.
              Newby, 72, Mortimer Street, Cavendish Sq. 1844.
              Two volumes. By William North.
236.   Fraser's Magazine, 31, 211-22 (1845)
        See 280

Later editions

237. 1844   Second edition
238.   Third edition
239.   New York, Colyer
240.   Philadelphia, Carey and Hart
241. 1847   Fourth edition
242. 1849   Fifth edition. One volume. Pp. viii+ 469+ (3).
             With a new preface, dated May 1849
243. 1853   in Bryce's uniform edition
244. 1859   Routledge, Warnes & Routledge. One volume.
             Both prefaces
245. 1870   and later, in Longmans' standard edition
246. 1889   edited by Francis Hitchman, published by W. H.
             Allen
247. 1900   with an introduction by William Keith Leask,
             illustrated by Claude A. Shepperson. Gresham
             Publishing Co.
248. 1904   edited by Bernard N. Langdon-Davies, with il-
             lustrations by Byam Shaw. R. Brimley Johnson.
             "Young England, II. " See 661
249. 1905   edited by Lord Iddesleigh. See 662
250. 1911   Everyman's Library edition, with the introduc-
             tion and notes by B. N. Langdon-Davies
251. 1931   World's Classics edition, with a preface by
             André Maurois. Oxford U. P.
252. 1948   with an introduction by Walter Allen. John
             Lehmann ("The Chiltern Library. ")

Translations

253. German (1844-45)
254. French, with an introduction by P. Chasles, 1846
255. French, with a preface by André Maurois, Club
     Bibliophile de France, 1957
256. Hungarian (1862 and 1891)

Later comments

257. Lewes, G. H.   : Review of Ed. 5 in British
                               Quarterly Review, 10, 118-
                               38. (1849)
258. Purcell, Sir Gilbert K. T.: Disraeli, Eton and the
                               goose in T. L. S. , 30 Sept.
                               1920, 636
259. Bjerre, B.   : Den tredje markisen av
                               Hertford i verkligheten, i

			Coningsby samt i Vanity Fair (och Pendennis) in Edda, 25, 104-25. (1926)
260.	Cline, C. L.	:	Coningsby and three Victorian novelists in N. & Q., 15th ser., 186, 41. (15 January 1944)
261.	Griffiths, A.	:	The literary original of Disraeli's "Mr. Rigby" in N. & Q., 199, 396 (Sept. 1954)
262.	Edelman, M.	:	A political novel: Disraeli sets a lively pace in T. L. S., 7 August 1959. British books around the world, x-xi. Letter from Sir Henry D'Avigdor-Goldsmid, T. L. S., 14 August 1959, p. 471; reply by Edelman, T. L. S., 28 August 1959, p. 495
263.	Frietzsche, A. H.	:	Action is not for me: Disraeli's Sidonia and the dream of power in Utah Academy of Sciences, Arts and Letters, Proceedings, 37, (1959/60), 45-49
264.	Greene, D. J.	:	Becky Sharp and Lord Steyne--Thackeray or Disraeli? in NCF 16, 157-64. (1961)

265. N. & Q., 5th ser., 3, 186 (6. iii. 1875) & 316
     (17. iv. 1875);
           7th ser., 10, 505 (27. xii. 1890), 11, 93
     (31. i. 1891) & 277 (4. iv. 1891);
           12th ser., 4, 9 (Jan. 1918), 7, 290
     (9. x. 1920);
           15th ser., 183, 345 (5. xii. 1942), 184, 55
     (16. i. 1943), 186, 189 (8. iv. 1944)
     See 671, 699, 1267, 1362, 1600

Manuscript Hughenden Papers E/I/6

Sybil

266. Sybil; or, The two nations. By B. Disraeli, M. P.
     Author of "Coningsby." (Quotation) London: Henry
     Colburn, Publisher; Great Marlborough Street. 1845.

Three volumes.   Pp. viii+ 315+ (1);   (iv)+ 324;   (ii)+ 326+
(2 publ. advts.)
Sadleir, Excursions, 120; XIX C. F. , 726
Published May 1845.   Dedicated to Mrs. Disraeli.

Although it is the second book of the trilogy, Sybil is
not a sequel to Coningsby.   Disraeli described their relationship in the closing paragraphs of Sybil, "From the state of
parties (sc. in Coningsby) it now would draw public thought
to the state of the People whom those parties for two cen-
turies have governed. "   Coningsby covers the period from
1832 to 1841, Sybil that from 1837 to 1842, but they deal
almost entirely with different aspects of their common period, or, as with the "Bedchamber Plot, " with the same
event from quite different viewpoints.

Sybil illustrates Disraeli's inadequacies even more
strikingly than does Coningsby.   The sub-title, "The Two
Nations, " might warn of a certain over-simplification of a
complex problem.   The significant part of the book is his
description of the industrial towns, closely based on his own
observation and on the evidence of the Blue Books.   He
wrote in the "Advertisement" of 1845 that he had understated
the descriptions.   Miss Smith (300) suggests that this is
generally true, and that the exaggerations of which he might
be guilty lie in concentrating aspects of different real locali-
ties in one fictional place and in presenting relatively un-
common features of cruelty and degradation as normal.   Such
license is not unreasonable, and the effect of the contrast
between "Hellhouse Yard" and "Marney Abbey" is profound.
The observation and description are acute, if somewhat de-
tached, but no solution is offered, or, worse, the suggested
remedies are irrelevant.   On the one hand, we find Disraeli
using a tone almost reminiscent of the class war: "the
people, have not they shed their blood in battle, though they
may have commanded fleets less often than your lordship's
relatives?   And these mines and canals that you have exca-
vated and constructed, these woods you have planted, these
waters you have drained, had the people no hand in these
creations? ... "   (Bk. IV, Ch. 5.)

Nevertheless, though in both Coningsby and Sybil the
nobility is excoriated as being a travesty of an aristocracy
and having forgotten its duties, it is to the nobility that Disraeli at least pretends to look for a remedy.   The awful
conditions of the people do not make him an advocate of uni-
versal suffrage, nor of the overthrow of the capitalist econo-

my: they are used to point the danger to the governing classes of ignoring the lot of the people. It is not, as might appear, a mistake to reveal Gerard, the Chartist leader, as the rightful heir to a great estate, for it is implicit in the argument that leadership must come from the upper classes. "The people are not strong: the people never can be strong ... It is civilisation that has effected, that is effecting this change. It is that increased knowledge of themselves that teaches the educated their social duties ... The new generation of the aristocracy of England are not tyrants, not oppressors ... they are the natural leaders of the people ... they are the only ones." (Egremont, BK. IV, Ch. 15.)

The picture of the Chartist movement is powerful and sympathetic, as had been Disraeli's earlier speech on Chartism in the Commons. Through Sybil, the convent-sheltered daughter of the Chartist leader, we see the disillusionment caused by the realisation that the pure ideals of Chartism are being corrupted, and that the leaders of the people are no less prone to faction and self-seeking than members of Parliament. As well as displaying the condition of the people, Sybil seeks to show that the nobility is not altogether unworthy to provide leadership.

The practical remedies are vague, though they appear to include a revival of the power of the Throne, and a return to its proper work by the Church, including the revival of monastic charity. Disraeli was no democrat, in theory or in practice. The message of Sybil, as of Coningsby, is that beneficent change can come only through "energy and devotion," presumably among the aristocracy, but, most certainly, among the young, "The youth of a Nation are the trustees of posterity."

Sybil contains one of the most sustained, and coherent, accounts of Disraeli's view of English history (Book I, ch. 3), and one of his bitterest attacks on Peel (Book VI, ch. 1.) Like Coningsby, it is overlaid with a nostalgic and sentimental attachment to an imagined medieval Catholicism. Unlike Coningsby, however, the construction of the plot is relatively complex, and there is a real excitement, perhaps bordering on melodrama, in some scenes, particularly that in which Sybil hastens with difficulty through the London slums in search of her father. Sybil reaches Gerard just before the police, and is arrested, in circumstances reminiscent of the Cato Street conspirators. In that happy day, however, a

68

dangerous revolutionary, seized in the very act of plotting to overthrow the government, could confidently expect to be released on bail, and Sybil herself is released by the influence of her aristocratic admirer, Egremont.

It is far from clear whether any coherence can be found in Disraeli's views on the nobility, as expressed in Coningsby and Sybil. The origins of many noble families are attributed to the plunder of the Church, the philandering of kings, or the need of Pitt for support, all of which are no doubt true; others are attributed to concocted genealogies, like that of "Lord de Mowbray," whose father was a club waiter. In Coningsby, it appears that the mill-owners could form the nucleus of a new, genuine, aristocracy, enjoying privileges in return for the performance of real functions-- Disraeli's view that the basis of feudalism was that "the essence of all tenure is the performance of duty." In Sybil, the master locksmith, "Bishop" Hatton, a degraded and ignorant tyrant, is said to exemplify a real aristocracy, on the same grounds. Yet the idea of a "new" aristocracy, based presumably on wealth, was not worked out, and it is to the old, dubiously-descended families, that Disraeli seems to look for his new leaders--to the House of Manners, descended from a beneficiary of the Dissolution.

The impact of these outrageous ideas must have been considerable, and it can, to some extent, be gauged by the reaction of the reviewers, and in the letters to Disraeli which have been preserved, and of which some have been printed. (1048)

Reviews

267.   Ainsworth's Magazine, 7, 541-45
268.   Athenaeum,   no. 916, 477-79 (17 May)
269.   Atlas,   20, no. 992, 313-14 (17 May)
270.   British Quarterly Review, 2, 159-73
271.   Court Journal,   no. 838, 323 (17 May)
272.   Critic,   2, 55-57 (17 May)
273.   Douglas Jerrold's Shilling Magazine, 1, 557-65
                             (June)
274.   Examiner,   no. 1946, 308-09 (17 May)
275.   Fraser's Magazine, 31, 727-37
276.   Literary Gazette,   no. 1478, 305-08 (17 May)
277.   Morning Chronicle, 13 May (W. M. Thackeray)
                             See 1362
278.   New Monthly Magazine, 74, 281-86 (June)

279.   Oxford and Cambridge Review, 1, 1-11 (Possibly by
                Lord John Manners)
280.   Revue des deux mondes, n. s. , 10, 1011-21 (1 June)
                (P. Chasles) (with 235)
281.   Spectator,   18, 471-73 (17 May)
282.   The Times,   13, 19 May
283.   Westminster Review, 44, 141-52 (W. R. Greg)

Parodies

284.   Nihilism in Russia: in imitation of Sybil, in The
                World, 11, no. 272, 16 (17
                Sept. 1879). See 1266
285.   The Age of Lawn-Tennis, I (After Lord Beacons-
                field's "Sybil"), in Tennis cuts
                and quips, edited by Julian
                Marshall, 1884, 34-37. See
                1266

Later editions

286.   1853 in Bryce's uniform edition
287.   1871 &c. in Longmans' standard edition
288.   1895 illustrated by F. Pegram, with an introduction
           by H. D. Traill, published by Macmillan
289.   1904 edited by Bernard N. Langdon-Davies. "Young
           England, III. " See 661
290.   1905 edited by Lord Iddesleigh. See 662
291.   1925 World's Classics edition, with an introduction
           by W. Sichel. Oxford U. P.
292.   1934 illustrated by F. Pegram, edited by Victor
           Cohen. Macmillan. A school edition
293.   1954 Penguin edition, with an introduction by J. G.
           Watson
294.   1957 Nelson edition (first published 1913) re-issued,
           with an introduction by A. N. Jeffares

Translations

295.   German (1846 &c.)
296.   French (1847 &c.)
297.   Dutch (1889)

Later comments

298.   Hamilton, R.   : Disraeli and the two nations
                                in Quarterly Review, 288,

			102-15. (1950)
299.	Hackett, F.	:	Disraeli as a novelist in New Republic, 135 (no. 25), 27-28. (17 Dec. 1956)
300.	Smith, S. M.	:	Willenhall and Wodgate: Disraeli's use of Blue Book evidence in Review of English Studies, 13, 368-84. (1962)
301.	Andzhaparidze, G. A.	:	("Sybil" as a work of critical realism) In Russian in Moscow. University. Vestnik. Filologiya, I, 51-62. (1967)

302. N. & Q., 12th ser., 6, 88 (April 1920); 7, 209, 256, 276 (11. ix, 25. ix, 2. x. 1920);
14th ser., 160, 387 (30. v. 1931);
15th ser., 169, 130 (24. viii. 1935) "The Derby in literature"
See 686, 1048, 1266, 1362, 1587

Manuscript Hughenden Papers E/I/1

Tancred

303. Tancred: or, The new crusade. By B. Disraeli, M. P. Author of "Coningsby, " "Sybil, " etc. London: Henry Colburn, Publisher, Great Marlborough Street. 1847.
Three volumes. Pp. (ii)+ 338; (ii)+ 340; (ii)+ 298+ (12 publ. advts.)
Sadleir, Excursions, 120; XIX C. F., 728
Published March 1847. No preface or dedication.

According to the plan of the trilogy, Tancred should deal with the Church, and Disraeli presented it thus in his General Preface. There is little about the Church of England in the novel, and that little is not complimentary. The nobleman, Tancred, does not know what to do, or what to believe: this emerges in the first volume, which is set in England, and contains some of Disraeli's best social satire. Tancred goes to Palestine, where he fails to find answers at the Holy Sepulchre, and sets out for Sinai. He is kidnapped in the desert, in a complicated plot of the Emir Fakredeen, who is intriguing to set himself up as ruler of an independent Syria. Tancred is allowed to visit Mount Sinai, where the "Angel of Arabia" appears to him, with the

message which is presumably meant to be the message of
the novel, "the sublime and solacing doctrine of theocratic
equality." After this revelation, which inevitably suffers
from the undisguised comparison with the Biblical account
of Moses on the same spot, the novel becomes incoherent:
Disraeli seems to have been unable to think of what to do
next, and the book drags on to its unsatisfactory conclusion.

The main theme is essentially an impassioned asser-
tion of the superiority of the Jewish race, and the conclusions to be drawn therefrom. Together with the 24th chapter of Lord George Bentinck, Tancred gives Disraeli's views
of his people. How far he believed what he wrote, or how
far he wrote to startle, may be open to question. The
theme was too large for Disraeli: he did not have the necessary knowledge to support his reinterpretation of European
history as the consequences of accepting the Jewish faith,
then trying, in the French Revolution, to reject it. He was
seeking to re-interpret the Judaeo-Christian tradition, but
his interpretation virtually omitted everything that was specifically Christian. His attempted synthesis was acceptable to
neither Jew nor Christian; to Jews, inter alia, by the implications of his well-meant references to Jesus of Nazareth as
Son of God, and to the Jewish Maiden as Queen of Heaven;
to Christians, by omitting all mention of the Resurrection,
and by his more usual characterisation of Christ as a Jewish
Prince, and, apparently, nothing more; to both, by his racial theories.

In Tancred, the identification of the Divine purpose
is not merely with the race, but with the land: "God never
spoke except to an Arab" and "the Creator of the world
speaks with man only in this land." Disraeli's racism was
sufficiently elastic to embrace the Arabs "who are only Jews
on horseback," and his religion sufficiently accommodating
to admit that Mahomet was one of the prophets.

Throughout the Arabian episodes, Tancred is constantly emphasising the recent emergence of Europe, and
particularly the northern races, from barbarism, and ac-
quiesces in the remark that "God has never spoken to a
European." The implications are painfully obvious: Palestine had "never been blessed by that fatal drollery called a
representative government, tho' Omnipotence once deigned
to trace out the polity which should rule it," and not Palestine alone, but "regulate the human destiny." Christendom
ought to be governed by the Jewish Law, and presumably by

Jews, who were best fitted for the task, having been in touch with the Deity for so long. These implications are not clearly stated but it is difficult to see what else is meant by Disraeli's insistence that the Jewish race, having supplied for the Sacrifice of Calvary both the victim and the immolators, are the saviours of mankind.

What did it mean? Was it all merely day-dreaming, like Alroy? Was it a deliberate defiance of the prejudices of his countrymen and his party? or was it an elaborate joke which carried its author away? Yet he deliberately reiterated the main themes in Lord George Bentinck. It is all so apparently irrelevant to the alleged task of completing the trilogy: perhaps he was serious. Yet when he had actually visited Jerusalem, for one week in 1831, he wrote home "visited the Holy Sepulchre of course, though avoided the other coglionerie (foolishnesses); the House of Loretto is probability to them, but the Easterns will believe anything" (my italics).

Reviews

304.	Athenaeum,	nos. 1012, 1013, pp. 302-04, 329-30 (20, 27 March)
305.	Atlas,	22, no. 1,088, p. 218 (20 March)
306.	Bentley's Miscellany,	21, 385-89. "The Hebrew, the Saracen and the Christian"
307.	Christian Remembrancer,	13, 514-37
308.	Court Journal,	no. 934, 201-03 (20 March)
309.	Critic,	5, 239-41, 260-63 (27 March, 3 April)
310.	Douglas Jerrold's Shilling Magazine,	5, 377-82 (April)
311.	Dublin University Magazine,	30, 253-66
312.	Eclectic Review,	4th ser., 21, 717-32
313.	Edinburgh Review,	86, 138-55 (R. Monckton Milnes)
314.	Examiner,	no. 2042, 179-80 (20 March)
315.	Literary Gazette,	no. 1574, 225-26; no. 1575, 245-47 (20, 27 March)
316.	New Monthly Magazine,	79, 523-26
317.	North American Review,	65, 201-24 (J. R. Lowell) See 1292
318.	Punch,	12, 166, 198-99, 213-14, 223 (1847) "Codlingsby, by B. de Shrewsbury, Esq." (W. M.

Thackeray.) Reprinted 1236.
Listed here as being a parody
of "Tancred" rather than "Coningsby." See 463, 1266, 1580

319. Tait's Edinburgh Magazine, 14, 350-56 (May)
320. The Times,   2 April
321. Voice of Jacob: Judaism and the reviewer of
                         "Tancred" in the "Times, " new
                         ser., I, no. 16, 125-27, Iyar
                         7, 5607 (23 April 1847)
322. Westminster Review, 48, 241-43

Parodies

323.   De Tankard. By Benjamin Dizzyreally, Esq., M.
                       P. in The Puppet-Showman's
                       Album, 1849, pp. 16-18. See
                       1266
324.   "Bede, Cuthbert" (Bradley, Edward): Tancredi;
                       or, The new party. By the
                       Right Hon. B. Bendizzy, M.P.
                       in The Shilling Book of Beauty,
                       1856, 71-76. See 1266

Later editions

325. 1871 &c. in Longmans' standard edition
326. 1904 edited by Bernard N. Langdon-Davies. "Young
            England, IV." See 661
327. 1905 edited by Lord Iddesleigh. See 662

Translations

328. German (1847 &c.)
329. French (1851)
330. Russian (1878)
331. Polish (1879)
332. Hebrew (1883)

Later comments

333. Dahl, C.   : Baroni in Disraeli's "Tan-
                          cred" in N. & Q., 203, 152
                          (April 1958)
334. Levine, R. A.   : Disraeli's "Tancred" and
                          "The Great Asian mystery"
                          in NCF 22, 71-85 (June 1967)

74

335.   N. & Q., 5th ser., 2, 268 (3. x. 1874)
       See 675, 699, 1235, 1266, 1267, 1292, 1298

A dramatisation of Tancred by Edith Millbank was produced at the Kingsway Theatre, London, in 1923. (London Mercury, 8, 649-50, Oct. 1923)

Manuscript Hughenden Papers E /I /2
For To the electors of the County of Buckingham, May 1847, see 1717

Lord George Bentinck

336.   Lord George Bentinck: a political biography. By B. Disraeli, Member of Parliament for the County of Buckingham. "He left us the legacy of heroes; the memory of his great name and the inspiration of his great example." London: Colburn and Co., Publishers, Great Marlborough Street. 1852.
       Pp. viii+ 588
       Sadleir, Excursions, 120; XIX C. F., 719
       Published December 1851. Dedicated to Lord Henry Bentinck.

Reviews

337.   Athenaeum,   no. 1261, pp. 1367-69 (27
                                December 1851)
338.   Atlas,   30, 9-10 (3 Jan. 1852)
339.   Blackwood's Magazine, 71, 121-34 (W. E. Aytoun)
340.   Critic, London Literary Journal, 11, 5-7 (Jan.
                                1852)
341.   Dublin University Magazine, 39, 114-28 (Jan. 1852)
342.   Eclectic Review,   5th ser., 3, 190-204
343.   Edinburgh Review,   97, 420-61 (A. Hayward) with
                                "Venetia," and Francis' biog-
                                raphy. (April 1853)
344.   Examiner,   no. 2292, p. 5 (3 January 1852)
345.   John Bull,   32, 11-12 (3 Jan. 1852)
346.   New Monthly Magazine, 94, 104-10
347.   Revue des deux mondes, n. s. 13, 793-824 (E.
                                Forcade) (1 March 1852)
348.   Spectator,   25, 106-07 (31 January 1852)
349.   The Times,   26, 27 Dec.
350.   Westminster Review, new ser., 2, 205-46. "Sir
                                Robert Peel and his policy"
                                (by W. R. Greg), with works

75

on Peel. Reprinted, W. R. Greg: Essays on political and social science, II, 303-63. (1853)

Contemporary pamphlets

351.   Mr. D'Israeli's opinions, political and religious, recommended at the present moment to the serious consideration of the electors of Buckinghamshire. London: James Ridgway, Piccadilly. 1852.
      Pp. 12. Signed "An elector of Bucks." An attack.

352.   An answer to some of the opinions and statements respecting the Jews made by B. Disraeli, Esq., M. P., in the 24th chapter of his biographical memoir of Lord George Bentinck. (London, Longman, and Nottingham, T. Forman, "Guardian" Office), 1852.
      Pp. 19+ (1). The preface signed "Alfred Padley, " dated 11th February 1852

353.   The Bank Charter Act in the crisis of 1847; with an examination of certain passages in Mr. Disraeli's life of Lord George Bentinck. London: Richardson Brothers, 23, Cornhill. 1854.
      Pp. 56

Later editions

354. - 1852 Second, third, fourth (revised), fifth (revised)
357.   editions
358.   1858 Sixth edition. Routledge. Pp. viii+ 422. See 650
359.   1872 Eighth edition, revised. Longman. Pp. (ii)+ xiv+ 422+ (2) Preface dated Nov. 1871.
360.   1874 Ninth edition (As Ed. 8, with 1871 Preface)
361.   1881 Tenth edition
362.   1905 With an introduction by Charles Whibley. London, Constable. Pp. lvi+ 382+ (2) See 1301
363.   1969 Gregg International Publishers. A reduced photographic reprint of the Second Edition.

Translations

364.   German (1853)

365. Of Chapter 24, "Die Juden. Eine Vertheidigungs-
schrift" Leipzig, 1853

Later comments

366. Fraser's Magazine, 78, 363-74. (1868) "The religious creed and opinions of the Caucasian champion
of the Church. "
367. T. L. S., 20 Oct. 1905, 348 (review of 362)
368. N. & Q., 4th ser., 3, 529, 609 (5, 26. vi. 1869);
12th ser., 1, 167, 336 (26. ii, 22. iv. 1916)
"Was Mozart a Jew?"

Manuscript Hughenden Papers E /I /3
For Election addresses, 1852 and 1857, see 1718, 1719

Lothair

369. Lothair. By the Right Honorable B. Disraeli. 'Nôsse
omnia haec salus est adolescentulis.' Terentius. London: Longmans, Green, and Co. 1870.
Three volumes. Pp. (viii)+ 328+ (32 publ. advts.);
(iv)+ 321+ (3); (iv)+ 333+ (3)+ (4 publ. advts.); half-titles in
each volume.
Sadleir, Excursions, 122; XIX C. F., 720
Published May 1870. Dedicated to the Duc d'Aumale,
a Roman Catholic.

Lothair continues, though after a long interval, Disraeli's comments on current affairs, but the tone of didacti-
cism sometimes apparent in earlier novels is muted. The
theme is the Roman Catholic Church; the situation, the attempt to convert a rich young nobleman, inevitably recalled
the conversion of Lord Bute shortly before. Whereas, in
Tancred, Disraeli had indulged in grandiose socio-religious
abstractions, here he is concerned with contemporary events
--the failure of the Garibaldini at Mentana, and the approach
of the First Vatican Council. "Lothair" is the recurrent
Disraelian aristocrat, young, earnest, fabulously wealthy,
and seeking to discover what to do and what to believe. His
soul is contended for by the Roman Catholic Church, the
revolutionary secret societies, and Anglicanism, each repre-
sented by a woman, with each of whom Lothair falls in love.
It cannot be denied that Lothair is not a particularly interesting hero: his qualities are moderation and common sense,
but they are described rather than illustrated. He accepts
the propaganda of his various mentors somewhat passively,

and without very convincing counter-arguments, though in the end he makes up his own mind, of course in favour of Anglicanism.

The early parts of the novel are set in the houses of the high aristocracy in London and the country: the effulgence of the aristocratic characters prompted the suggestion that Disraeli was writing a parody of his own style. Lothair's erstwhile guardian, the Cardinal no less (perhaps a portrait of Manning), with the help of a Catholic family of the highest ton, and a swarm of insinuating monsignori, opens his campaign by dwelling on the common ground between Rome and Canterbury, and introduces the second central theme, that the Roman Catholic Church is not merely the strongest, but the only, bastion against the forces of the revolution, most dangerous in their widespread secret societies. However, Lothair becomes infatuated with the mysterious Theodora; parted from her, in a fit of depression he drives about the East End, and gains entrance to a Fenian meeting, whence he is rescued by a mysterious stranger who, presumably, stands for Garibaldi. He is induced, after his brilliant coming-of-age, to finance the invasion of the Papal State in 1867: left for dead on the battlefield, on which Theodora is killed, he is brought to Rome, to his Roman Catholic sweetheart. After a long illness, he is made aware that he is at the centre of a supposed miracle: his life has been saved by the intervention of Our Lady, making Her first visit to Rome. The stir is quite considerable. The Cardinal attempts to convince Lothair that he fell fighting for the Pope: a scene of which it has been said that it "would be a masterly example of high comedy, if it were not intended more obviously for keen satire." (Speare, (1320), p. 107.)

A century later, the machinations of Roman prelates do not appear so sinister as Disraeli pretended. The early arguments of the Cardinal and his chaplains have a power of conviction, in the novel, which is not wholly effaced by the later scenes, where Lothair is virtually kept prisoner in a Roman palace. What was presumably intended to be a devastating satire on unscrupulous Roman methods now seems almost a burlesque melodrama, although there is in the writing sufficient power to carry the reader through without too many misgivings. Lothair escapes, the day before his proposed reception into the Church by Pope Pius IX. Hereafter, the story loses interest. Lothair goes, of course, to Palestine, and meets the inevitable Syrian sage, named Paraclete (!). He also meets the "Aryan" Mr. Phoebus--

who wishes to revive the Olympian worship, and free Europe from Semiticism--a character whose purpose is obscure. Both Phoebus and Paraclete announce their racial theories, but it is noticeable that that of the Syrian, who seems to be treated with a seriousness not accorded to the "Aryan," is startlingly different from all that Disraeli said before, except, less explicitly, in the last part of <u>Tancred</u>,

> The Aryan and the Semite are of the same blood and origin .... Each division of the great race has developed one portion of the double nature of humanity, till after all their wanderings they met again, and, represented by their two choicest families, the Hellenes and the Hebrews, brought together the treasures of their accumulated wisdom and secured the civilisation of man. [Vol. III, ch. 17, p. 184: ch. 77 in later editions--Gladstone himself might have approved this view of the matter.]

Lothair returns to England, and marries the highborn, Anglican, Lady Corisande.

What is to be made of it all? Is it an anti-Roman tract? Is it a warning against the power of the secret societies? Is it to be supposed that the dichotomy, Rome or Revolution, is false?; but the possibility, the Church of England, and, more generally, the English social and political system, is left unexplored. Both Rome and Revolution are painted with surprising sympathy. There is no doubt that Rome, with its vast organisation, surpassing even that of the secret societies, and existing to uphold "an old man on a Semitic throne," exercised a powerful romantic influence on Disraeli. So also did the secret societies: Disraeli seems to have believed in the "conspiracy" theory of history, which is indeed merely a variant on the theory of the Great Man, which Disraeli constantly reiterated. It is even less easy here than in the "trilogy" to see what Disraeli would be at. The "general preface" which he added to the one-volume edition (419) does not advance our understanding greatly: indeed he says "it would be not a little presumptuous for an author thus to be the self-critic of volumes which appeared only a few months ago. Their purport to the writer seems clear enough ...." However, he does there re-state his view of the Church of England in the most uncompromising terms, "the secession of DR. NEWMAN dealt a blow to the Church of England under which it still reels. That extraordinary event has been "apologised" for, but has never been explained. It was a mistake and a misfortune. The tradition of the Anglican Church was powerful. Resting on the Church of Jerusalem, modified by the divine school of Galilee, it would have found that rock of truth which Providence, by the instrumentality of the Semitic race, had promised to St. Peter. Instead of that, the seceders sought refuge in mediaeval superstitions, which are generally only the embodiments of pagan ceremonies and creeds." But there is little of this in Lothair itself, unless it may be linked with the hints of Paraclete, who adheres to Christianity of a tradition older than Rome.

We may hazard that the message was intended to be, neither Rome nor Revolution, but the true religion of the Jews, exemplified by the Church of England. How astounding, that the leader of the traditional "Church party" should have declared in the preface to a set of novels that the Church of England was founded on the Church of Jerusalem, by which is meant Jewry, modified by "the divine school of Galilee." Disraeli had spoken much, perhaps too much, on Church matters in the 1860's, but this remark seems to deepen the suspicion that he did not understand what the Church of England meant. He regarded it as a powerful social and political force, but as the custodian of the Revelation of God in Christ, as the Church of the Incarnation and the Resurrection, he appears to have had only the dimmest idea.

Reviews

370.	Academy,	1, 200-201 (14 May) (H. Lawrenny)
371.	Athenaeum,	no. 2219, 605-06 (7 May)
372.	Atlantic Monthly,	26, 249-51 (August) (Henry James) See 1364
373.	Blackwood's Magazine,	107, 773-96 (E. B. Hamley) See 378, 396
374.	Catholic World,	11, 537-41 (A. F. Hewit)
375.	Christian Observer,	70 , 420-39
376.	Dublin Review,	67, (new ser., 15), 156-78 (Probably by Cashel Hoey) (So in 1586)
377.	Edinburgh Review,	132, 275-89 (R. Monckton Milnes)
378.	Examiner,	no. 3249, 290-91 (7 May); no. 3254, 370-71 (11 June) "Black-

wood on 'Lothair' "
379. Fortnightly Review, 13, 654-67 (F. Harrison)
See 1262
380. Fraser's Magazine, new ser., 1, (81), 790-805
(J. Skelton)
381. Gentleman's Magazine, new ser., 5, 281-305
"Lothair" and the critics.
382. De Gids, 34 (4), 152-75 "Een boek met
raadselen," by S. Vissering.
383. Hours at Home, 11, 256-61 (H. T. Tuckerman)
384. John Bull, 50, 317-19 (7 May)
385. London Quarterly Review, 35, 162-86
386. Macmillan's Magazine, 22, 142-60 (A. Hayward)
387. Month, 12, 727-36 (W. G. Todd)
388. Nation, 10, 372-73 (E. Quincy)
389. New Monthly Magazine, 147, 232-34, and 720-28
(on the "General Preface")
(W. Mackay)
390. North British Review, 52, 453-73 (Richard Simpson)
391. Old and New, 2, 216-19
392. Quarterly Review, 129, 63-86 (attributed to A.
Hayward by Lord Esher (913),
but this is denied in W.I., on
comparison with 386, and the
Quarterly review provisionally
attributed to G. W. Dasent)
393. Revue des deux mondes, n.s. 88, 429-50 (15 July)
(Challemel-Lacour)
394. St. Paul's Magazine, 6, 447-51 "Mr. Disraeli and
the Dukes."
395. Saturday Review, 29, 476 (9 April) "Mr. Disraeli's promised novel"; 29,
611-12 (7 May)
396. The Scattered Nation, 5, 141-45 (C. Schwartz)
(June); 5, 170-72 "Blackwood's
Magazine on 'Lothair' " (July)
397. Sharpe's London Magazine, new ser., 37, 104-05
(August)
398. Spectator, 43, 586-87 (7 May); also 581-
82 (7 May) Mr. Disraeli's hu-
mour; 636 (21 May) Mr. Disraeli on secret societies;
1283-84 (29 Oct.) Mr. Disraeli
on his own teachings (the "General Preface")
399. The Times, 2 May (A. I. Shand)

400.   Tinsley's Magazine, 6, 565-68
401.   Vanity Fair,   3, 290-91, 306, 332-33 (21,
                           28 May; 11 June) The third
                           article is on Goldwin Smith

Pamphlets

402.   Lothair & its author, a lecture by John Ingle.
         London, Hall, 1870

403.   Lothaw or the adventures of a young gentleman
         in search of a religion by Mr. Benjamins (Bret
         Harte), in his Condensed novels, 1871 ed., Boston
         and London, and

404.   separately, published by John Camden Hotten,
         1871.   Pp. (?ii advts.)+ frontis., +(48 unpaged)+
         (8 advts.) See 1266

405.   "Maccallum" (Lothair); or, The peer, the pre-
         late, and the princess, by the Right Hon. B
         D   . Edinburgh, Nimmo, 1871

406.   "Lothair," the "critics," and the Right Hon.
         Benjamin Disraeli's "General Preface to all his
         works." By W. E. London: Edward Truelove
         (1872?)
              Pp. 16 (Verse)

407.   "Lothair:" its beauties and blemishes. By the
         Authoress of "A Woman's Reform Bill for Scolding
         Wives." London, Mackintosh, 1873
              The preface signed "E.G."

408.   Lothair's children, by H.R.H. London, Rem-
         ington, 1890 (By Campbell MacKellar)

409.   The allusions in Lothair, by Goldwin Smith.
         (A four-page pamphlet, "For private circulation,"
         containing the text of a letter from Goldwin Smith
         to the editor of the "Nation," dated 7 April 1905.)

410.   See Nation, 80, 310

411.   N. & Q., 15th ser., 183, 376 (19.xii.1942)
         Disraeli and Goldwin Smith, by F. H. A. Mickle-
         wright

Later editions

412. 1870 New York, Appleton
413-415.   Second, third, fourth editions (The misprint "Capel" for "Catesby" in vol. III p. 254 is corrected in Ed. 2)
416.   "Fifth edition, revised, " with an "Advertisement" dated 13 June 1870
417.   Sixth edition
418.   Seventh edition
419.   Eighth edition. One volume, containing the "General Preface" to the novels; the first volume of Longmans' standard edition. (653)
420. 1957 (Nelson's edition), reissued with an introduction by A. N. Jeffares

Translations

421. French (1870 &c.)
422. Russian (1870 & c.)
423. Hungarian (1871 &c.)
424. Italian, translated and with a preface by Robert Montgomery Stuart, 2 volumes, Florence, 1871-72
425. German (1872)

Later comments

426. Hitchman, F.   : Lothair and Endymion in National Review, 9, 382-94 (1887)
427. Harris, Harold M.   : Heil, Phoebus! in London Mercury, 39, 523-25 (March 1939)
428. N. & Q., 4th ser., 5, 459-60; 6, 25, 231, 291, 401, 436, 558 (1870); 10, 428, 514; 12, 439 (1872-73);
         7th ser., 1, 8, 38 (1.1886);
         9th ser., 6, 407 (24.xi.1900);
         12th ser., 7, 432 (27.xi.1920)
     See 686, 1262, 1266, 1364

Manuscript Hughenden Papers E /I/4
For To the electors of the County of Buckingham, 1874 see 1720

Endymion

429. Endymion by the author of "Lothair" "Quicquid agunt homines" London Longmans, Green, and Co. 1880

Three volumes.   Pp. (iv)+ 331+ (1); (iv)+ 337+ (3); (iv)+
346+ (2 publ. advts.) Half-titles in each volume.
Sadleir, Excursions, 122; XIX C. F., 712
Published 26 November 1880.   No dedication or preface.
Longmans paid £10,000, said to have been the largest
sum ever given for a work of fiction.

Although Endymion was published only after Beaconsfield had ceased to be Prime Minister, a substantial part of
it had been written earlier (462), and another novel (555)
was begun.   However, the world was denied Disraeli's portrait of Gladstone, and Endymion was his last published work.
It is a romance, set in England between 1827 and about 1855,
but it might have been set in fairyland.   It is, allegedly, a
retrospect of the England in which Disraeli had made his way,
centered on Endymion and his twin sister, Myra.   The central pair are quite incredible: their father, who should have
been Prime Minister, commits suicide, and leaves them in
penury.   From this unpromising start, they both rise in the
world, but it is mostly Myra's doing, with the assistance of
assorted ladies of immense wealth and beauty.

The novel is a commentary on the exchange between
Endymion and his future wife,

> "Everything in this world depends upon will."
> "I think everything in this world depends upon
> woman."
> "It is the same thing," said Berengaria. [Vol. II,
> ch. 29, p. 300:   ch. 65 in later editions.]

It is the view already expressed in Lothair, and in earlier
novels, but Endymion is particularly about the relation of
brother and sister.   Endymion's own rise is rapid enough:
he becomes Prime Minister, about the time when Palmerston
actually occupied that place, at the age of 40.   He has been
helped, not merely by the will of his future wife, or an
anonymous gift of £20,000 from another lady of untold wealth,
but by the determination of Myra, who marries the Foreign
Secretary to help her brother's career.   The Foreign Secretary is clearly enough Palmerston, who, however, conven-
iently dies of overwork.   Myra now marries "King Flores-
tan," who is just as clearly Napoleon III, and makes her
triumphal entry into a great European capital, presumably,
though it is oddly placed, Paris.   Even Disraeli's flights of
fancy had never risen so high.   Is he dreaming of what

might have been, of his long-dead Sarah, who eked out a genteel spinsterhood, her fiancé having died in Egypt of smallpox? Romance after so many years, to dull the pain; a sister, not in a Twickenham villa, but reigning in the Tuileries? Alas, alas. But more than this even; our hero has a mother, who dies of grief at being driven from London Society by her husband's ruin, and there is a poignant sentence. "It tortured him to feel that he had often accepted with carelessness or indifference the homage of a heart that had been to him ever faithful in its multiplied devotion." The aged statesman seeks to atone to the shade of poor Maria D'Israeli, between whom and her son there seems to have been so little understanding or sympathy.

The novel is by no means all gloom. It is, indeed, fixed in a past long gone, not without some sardonic references to modern ways, but there is a mellowness, a repose, or is it merely weariness?, which is not to be found in the earlier books. There appear, more or less thinly disguised, other contemporaries, such as Bismarck and Manning, but it is not a roman à clef, nor really a political commentary. It is a picture of a vanished world, recalled with affection tinged with cynicism, and described with wit. It contains an inaccurate account of the Eglinton Tournament of 1839, another visit of discovery to Manchester, and the most remarkable reminder (admittedly placed in 1838) of the legitimist claim of the Duke of Modena to the throne of England. It even contains a description (Vol. III, ch. 32, p. 320: ch. 100 in later editions), of the author's own appointment as Leader of the Commons in 1852. What is most remarkable is that Endymion becomes the Whig Prime Minister, a circumstance on which Queen Victoria remarked. (QVL 2nd ser., iii, 194n.) There is no message, or, if there is, it is that it is all a jest. Endymion contains Disraeli's "last words," for he left no memoirs: the "Impenetrable man" remained impenetrable.

Reviews

430.   Academy,   18, 395-97 (4 Dec.) (Edward
                               Dowden)
431.   American Catholic Quarterly Review, 6, 112-31
                               (John MacCarthy) (1881)
432.   Appleton's Journal, 25, (new ser., 10), 70-76
                               (1881)
433.   Athenaeum,   no. 2770, 701-02 (27 November)
434.   Catholic Progress, 10, 72-76, 103-05, 167-71

		(1881)
435.	Critic,	1, 30-31 (1881) (J. W. Howe: English society and "Endymion")
436.	Dial,	1, 188-89 (1881) (M. W. Fuller)
437.	Dublin Review,	88, (3rd ser., 5), 145-65
438.	Edinburgh Review,	153, 103-29 (Henry Reeve) (Jan. 1881)
439.	Examiner,	no. 3800, 1336-37 (27 Nov.)
440.	Fortnightly Review,	35, 66-76 (1881) (Lord Houghton)
441.	Fraser's Magazine,	102, (new ser. 22) 705-20
442.	Nation,	31, 413-14 (A. G. Sedgwick)
443.	Quarterly Review,	151, 115-28 (Alfred Austin)
444.	Revue des deux mondes,	n.s. 42, 886-907 (15 Dec.) (A. Cucheval-Clarigny)
445.	Revue politique et littéraire	... 2e ser., 12 (no. 23), 539-44 (4 Dec.) (Jeanne Mairet)
446.	Saturday Review,	50, 707-08 (4 Dec.)
447.	Spectator,	53, no. 2735, 1511-12 "Lord Beaconsfield's worldly wisdom" also in Eclectic Magazine, new ser., 33, 329-31 (1881)
448.	Spectator,	53, no. 2735, 1518-19 (27 Nov.)
449.	The Times,	24 Nov.
450.	Vanity Fair,	24, 298-99 (27 Nov.)

Parody

451.   Ben D'Ymion. By the Author of "Loafair," &c. in Punch, 79, 262-64, 266-67, 286-87 (4, 11, 18 Dec. 1880), also in

452.   Lester, H. F.: Ben D'Ymion and other parodies, Swan Sonnenschein, 1887, 1-24. See 1266

Later editions

453. 1880 New York, Appleton
454.   New York, Harper
455. 1881 One-volume edition in Longmans' standard edition, with an anonymous "Memoir"
456. 1905 With a critical introduction on Disraeli's writings, by Edmund Gosse. New York, The Cambridge Society, 1905

Translations

457. Russian (1880 &c.)
458. French (1881)
459. German (1881)
460. Polish (1881-83)

Later comments

461. Grey, Rowland   : Disraeli in Fancy Street in
                          Cornhill, new ser., 66, 102-
                          10 (1929)
462. Blake, Robert   : The dating of "Endymion" in
                          Review of English Studies,
                          new ser., 17, 177-82 (1966)
463. Merritt, James D. : The novelist St. Barbe in
                          Disraeli's "Endymion," re-
                          venge on whom? in N.C.F.,
                          23, 85-88 (1968) (On "Cod-
                          lingsby" (318) &c.: suggests
                          that "St. Barbe" is at least
                          as much Carlyle as Thacke-
                          ray)
464. N. & Q., 6th ser., 2, 484 (18.xii.1880); 3, 10, 31,
      95, 226 ("Key"), 362, 393 (1881);
            12th ser., 11, 251 (23.ix.1922)
      See 426, 799, 1258, 1266

Manuscript Hughenden Papers E/I/5

Works not originally published separately

   * Reprinted in "Tales and sketches," edited by J.
     Logie Robertson (554)

   + Reprinted in "Whigs and Whiggism," edited by W.
     Hutcheon (558)

                          1832

465. * The court of Egypt, a sketch, by Mesr in New
        Monthly Magazine, 34, 555-56 (June)

466. * The speaking Harlequin. The two losses; in one act, ibid., 35, 158-63 (August)

467. * The Bosphorus, a sketch, by Marco Polo Junior, ibid., 35, 242 (September)

468. * Egyptian Thebes, by Marco Polo Junior, ibid., 35, 333-39 (October)

469. (Letter on a speech at Wycombe) in The Times, 13 November

470. * Ixion in heaven, by the author of Contarini Fleming and Vivian Grey in New Monthly Magazine, 35, 514-20 (December), and 37, 175-84 (February 1833)

471. also reprinted with "Popanilla," "The Infernal Marriage" and "Alarcos" in Bryce's uniform edition, 1853; with "Alroy" and other works in Longmans' standard edition, 1871 (125); with "Popanilla" and other works in Guedalla's Bradenham edition, 1926 (663)

472. 1925 "Decorated by John Austen." Cape. Pp. (vi) + 72+ (ii)

473. Spectator, 136, 88 (16 Jan. 1926) (J. St. Loe Strachey)

474. 1927 Ixion in heaven and Endymion   Disraeli's skit and Aytoun's burlesque   London: the Scholartis Press MCMXXVII ("Nineteenth century highways and byways, 1." With a prefatory note by Eric Partridge)
Pp. viii+ (ii)+ 75+ (iii).

475. Thomas, W.: Deux chefs-d'oeuvres de raillerie sociale et politique sous l'inspiration du romantisme anglais (Ixion in heaven, and The infernal marriage) in Revue de l'enseignement des langues vivantes, 53, 345-49, 394-403 (1936)

Manuscript Offered for sale at Christie's, 1881, but withdrawn. The first part offered for sale in 1929.

476. See T.L.S., 25 Feb. 1932, 134

477.   * Ibrahim Pacha, the conqueror of Syria, by Marco
       Polo Junior, in New Monthly Magazine, 37, 153-
       54 (February)

478.   * Walstein; or, A cure for melancholy, by the author
       of "Vivian Grey," "Contarini Fleming" &c. in
       Court Magazine, 3, 3-8 (July)
           also reprinted in Guedalla's Bradenham edi-
           tion, with "Popanilla" and other works, 1926
           (663)

479.   N. & Q., 11th ser., 5, 347 (4.v.1912)

1834

480.   * An interview with a great Turk, from the note book
       of a recent traveller, by the author of Vivian
       Grey &c. &c., in Court Magazine, 4, 11-22
       (January)

481.   * The infernal marriage, by Disraeli the younger,
       author of "Ixion in heaven," in New Monthly
       Magazine, 41, 293-304, 431-40, 42, 30-38,
       139-44 (July-October) Apparently uncompleted.
           also reprinted with "Ixion in heaven" and
           other works in Bryce's uniform edition, 1853
           (471); with "Alroy" in Longmans' standard
           edition, 1871 (125); with "The Young Duke"
           (83), edited by Lord Iddesleigh (see 662);
           with "Popanilla" and other works in Guedalla's
           Bradenham edition, 1926 (663)

482.   1929 with decorations by John Austen, and an intro-
       duction by Eric Partridge. Published by Wil-
       liam Jackson.

483.   T.L.S., 21 Nov. 1929, 953

484.   Translated into French as "Proserpine aux infers,"
       Lille, 1853
           See Sadleir, Excursions, 121; Thomas (475)

485.   N. & Q., 9th ser., 5, 287 (14.iv.1900)

       Manuscript Hughenden Papers E/II/3 (Part I, and the
       beginning of Part III)

486. * The carrier-pigeon, by the author of "Vivian Grey"
      in Book of Beauty for 1835, 128-44
          also reprinted with "Popanilla" and other works in
      Guedalla's Bradenham edition, 1926 (663)

                              1835

487.   Letters between Disraeli and Morgan O'Connell, and
      Disraeli's letter to Daniel O'Connell in The Times,
      6 and 8 May
          The letter to Daniel O'Connell reprinted, 696, 68-
      71
488. + Leading articles in The Morning Post, 22 August to
      7 September. (14 articles). Reprinted in "Whigs
      and Whiggism" with the title "Peers and people."
      Written at the request of Lord Lyndhurst in de-
      fence of the House of Lords. Never acknowledged.

489. * The consul's daughter, by the author of "Vivian
      Grey," in Book of Beauty for 1836, 74-113

490.   Issued separately, and presumably without authority.
      1881/82?

491.   Edward Marshall, N. & Q., 6th ser., 11, 129 (14.
      ii. 1885) and Sadleir, XIX C. F., 710
          Reprinted, with "Popanilla" and other works in
      Guedalla's Bradenham edition, 1926 (663)

492.   Letters to the editor of The Times, 28, 31 Decem-
      ber 1835, 9, 14, January 1836, and, A letter to
      Joseph Hume, in The Times, 12 January 1836, in
      reply to allegations in The Globe about Radical sup-
      port for Disraeli in his early election contests.
          Reprinted in 696, 72-93

                              1836

493. + The Letters of "Runnymede," 19 articles in The
      Times, January to May 1836 and
494. + The Spirit of Whiggism, by Runnymede, ibid., 13,
      16, 27 June, 4, 11, 14 July 1836

495.   An unauthorised edition of 9 of the "Runnymede"
      letters was printed by Cullum, Exeter, 1836 (Sadleir,
      XIX C. F., 717)

496.   The letters of Runnymede. "Neither for shame nor
        fear this mask he wore, That, like a vizor in the
        battle-field, But shrouds a manly and a daring brow."
        London: John Macrone, St. James' Square.
        MDCCCXXXVI.
            Pp. ii(publ. advts.)+ xx+ (ii)+ 234+ vi publ. advts.
            Sadleir, Excursions, 118: XIX C. F. , 717a
            The dedication, to Sir Robert Peel, dated July 27,
            1836. The manuscript of the preface, Hughenden
            Papers, E /II /10a
            This volume contains the 19 letters, and "The
            Spirit of Whiggism," which summarises the argument
            of "Vindication of the English Constitution." Disraeli's
            authorship was never specifically acknowledged.

497.   Review Monthly Review, 1836 part 3, 26-35

498.   1885 with an introduction and notes by Francis
        Hitchman. Published by Bentley.
499.   1923 with an introduction by Francis Bickley.   Pub-
        lished by Chapman & Dodd.
500.   1970 Reprinted by Gregg International Publishers.

501.   Fraser's Magazine, new ser. , 10, 254-68 (1874)
502.   T. L. S. , 3 May 1923, p. 300 (Review of 499)

503.   Leading articles in The Times, 1 and 18 August

504.   + The summary of the session, leading article on
        Lord Lyndhurst's speech, ibid. , 19 August

505.   A new voyage of Sindbad the sailor, recently dis-
        covered, ibid. , 15 December 1836 to 10 February
        1837. 11 articles.

506.   To a maiden sleeping after her first ball, by the
        author of "Vivian Grey" in Book of Beauty for 1837,
        186-87. (Verse)
507.   reprinted in N. & Q. , 7th ser. , 3, 347 (30. iv. 1887),
        and in 676

508.   Calantha, by the author of "Vivian Grey," ibid. ,
        252-55

                        1837

509.   + To the Lord Lieutenant of Ireland, by Runnymede,

                         91

in The Times, 13 February

510. + A character (Spring Rice), by Skelton, Jun., ibid.,
7 March. (Verse)

511. + Open questions, a political eclogue, by Skelton Jun.,
ibid., 9 March

512. + An heroic epistle to Lord Viscount Mel_____e, by
Skelton, Jun., ibid., 20 March

Manuscript Hughenden Papers E/II/5 (incomplete)

513. + To Lord Viscount Melbourne, by Runnymede, ibid.,
17 April (dated 15 April)

514. Review of "England under seven administrations,"
by A. Fonblanque, ibid., 17 May

515. Review of "Society in America," by Harriet Martineau, ibid., 30 May

Manuscript (containing material not printed) Hughenden
Papers E/II/10d

516. * A Syrian sketch, by the author of "Vivian Grey,"
in Book of Beauty for 1838, 249-51

1838

517. + Old England, by Coeur-de-Lion, in The Times, 3
to 15 January. 10 articles.
Said in 1199 to have been thought at the time to
have been by Carlyle.

Manuscript Hughenden Papers E/II/4 (incomplete)

518. Letter (denouncing Austin's allegations, regarding
the Maidstone election, as false) dated 5 June, in
The Morning Post, 6 June and in The Times, 7 June.
See 1078

519. The Portraits of the Honourable Sarah Elizabeth,
Susan Penelope, and Sophia Clarence Copley, daugh-
ters of Lord Lyndhurst. By B. D'Israeli, Esq., M.
P., in Portraits of the children of the nobility ...
edited by Louisa Fairlie, 1st ser., 1838. (Verse)

520.   On the portrait of the Lady Mahon, by B. Disraeli,
         Esq. M. P., in Book of Beauty for 1839, p. 16.
         (Verse)

521.   Reprinted in N. & Q., 4th ser., 1, 388 (25. iv. 1868);
         see ibid., 422 (2. v. 1868); also in 676

522.   On the portrait of the Viscountess Powerscourt, By
         B. Disraeli, Esq. M. P., in Book of Beauty for 1839
         93-94. (Verse)

1839

523. + To Lord John Russell, by Laelius, in The Times,
         6 May

524. + To the Queen, by Laelius, ibid., 13 May

525. + To Lord Melbourne, by Laelius, ibid., 28 May

526. + To the Duke of Wellington (a sonnet) in The Times,
         29 August. Also reprinted N. & Q., 1st ser., 11,
         379 (19. v. 1855), "Oxford Book of Victorian Verse,"
         no. 104, and in 676

527.   N. & Q., 1st ser., 11, 474 (16. vi. 1855); 12, 173
         (1. ix. 1855)

Manuscript Hughenden Papers E/II/10e

528.   The Portraits of the Ladies Sarah Frederica Caro-
         line, Clementina Augusta Wellington, and Adela Cori-
         sanda Maria Villiers, daughters of the Earl of Jersey.
         By B. Disraeli, Esq., M. P., in Portraits of the
         children of the nobility, 2nd ser., 1839. (Verse)

529. * The valley of Thebes in Book of Beauty for 1840,
         3-10

1840

530. * Munich in Book of Beauty for 1841, 13-19
         also reprinted in 829, 494-501

Manuscript Hughenden Papers E/II/7

531. + The state of the case, in a letter to the Duke of
Wellington, by Atticus, in The Times, 11 March

Manuscript Hughenden Papers E /II /6

532. * Eden and Lebanon in Book of Beauty for 1842, 220-
21

1842

533. * The Midland Ocean in Book of Beauty for 1843, 89-
93

1844

534. Fantasia in The Keepsake for 1845, 163-65

Manuscript Hughenden Papers E /II /8

1845

535. * Shoubra in The Keepsake for 1846, 30-34

1853

536. + Coalition. The first leading article in The Press,
7 May. This is the only article which has been reprinted. Buckle (MB. I, 1310, 1314) lists other articles attributed to Disraeli by the 15th Earl of Derby,
who was closely associated with the paper. See also
728 and 739

1855

537. Lines ... to a beautiful mute, the eldest child of
of Mrs. Fairlie, printed in: Madden, R. R. --Lite-
rary life and correspondence of the Countess of Blessington, I, 383-84. The child was Lady Blessington's
great-niece. Reprinted in 676

538. Home letters written by the late Earl of Beaconsfield
in 1830 and 1831 'Absence is often a great element of
charm' Endymion London John Murray, Albemarle
Street 1885
Pp. (x)+ 139+ (1)
Fourteen letters, edited by Ralph Disraeli.

Reviews

539. Athenaeum, no. 3003, p. 625 (16 May)
540. Spectator, 58, 638-39

541. Also published in New York by Harper
542. A "Second edition" (1886?)

543. Lord Beaconsfield's correspondence with his sister
1832-1852 Forti nihil difficile With a Portrait London
John Murray, Albemarle Street 1886
Pp. (ii)+ xiv+ (ii frontis.)+ 269+ (3), advt. on (271)
A further selection, edited by Ralph Disraeli, in reply, as he says, "to the numerous requests I have received for more of my Brother's letters." The preface
hints discreetly that some omissions have been made to
avoid giving offence; in fact, there are wholesale omissions and alterations, rewriting of sentences, and so
much conflation of two or more originals, as to render
the collection quite unreliable as source material. The
dates are frequently inaccurate.

Reviews

544. Academy, 29, 302-03 (H. B. Garrod)
545. Athenaeum, no. 3039, p. 129-30 (23 Jan.)
546. Edinburgh Review, 163, 499-521 (A. I. Shand)
547. Revue des deux mondes, n. s. 75, 681-92 (1 June) (G.
Valbert)
548. N. & Q., 9th ser., 7, 166 (2. iii. 1901)

549. Also published in New York by Harper

550. Lettres de Lord Beaconsfield à sa soeur traduites
avec introduction, notices historiques et notes et pre-
cedées d'une étude sur Lord Beaconsfield et le parti
tory par Alexandre de Haye ... Paris Didier Perrin et
Cie ... 1889
Pp. (vi)+ 460+ (2)
This translation contains substantial prefatory and explanatory matter.

551. Lord Beaconsfield's letters 1830-1852 Forti nihil difficile New edition of 'Home letters' and 'Correspondence
with his sister with additional letters and notes' With a
portrait Edited by his Brother London John Murray,
Albemarle Street 1887
Pp. 14+ (ii frontis.)+ 248+ (2 publ. advts.). Page (176)
numbered 171. Variant states.

552. Quarterly Review, 168, 1-42. (Sir Austen Henry Layard) (1889)
An extremely important, though not necessarily com-
pletely reliable, account of Disraeli's early years. Layard was the nephew of Benjamin Austen, for whose financial dealings with Disraeli see 1028, and, though a
Liberal, appointed Ambassador at Constantinople by
Beaconsfield.

553. Home letters Written by Lord Beaconsfield 1830-1852
With Introduction by The Rt. Hon. Augustine Birrell,
K. C. Cassell & Company Ltd London (&c.)
Pp. 320 (1928)
A reissue of the 1887 edition, with introduction, new
notes and an index, but, unfortunately, no correction of
the texts.

554. Tales and sketches by the Right Hon. Benjamin Disraeli, Earl of Beaconsfield K. G. With a prefatory memoir by J. Logie Robertson, M. A. London William
Paterson & Co. 1891
Pp. xxiii+ (i)+ 389+ (3) ("The Treasure house of tales
by great authors")
Sadleir, XIX C. F., 727
The following are reprinted: 730, 486, 489, 61, 478,
470, 466, 481, 533, 477, 465, 529, 468, 535, 532, 516,
467, 480, 530, 704 (the order in which they appear in
the book)

555. An unfinished novel, known as "Falconet," published
in "The Times," 20, 21 and 23 January 1905. Printed
as an appendix to Monypenny and Buckle's Life, and
with "Endymion" in Guedalla's Bradenham edition. (663)

556. Also published in "New York Times," 22, 29 Jan.,
5 Feb. 1905
A fragment, containing 9 short chapters. The manuscript is in the Museum at Hughenden Manor.
Sadleir, XIX C. F., 730

557. T. L. S., 8 July 1920, 456: a letter identifying the character "Kusinara."

558. Whigs and Whiggism Political writings by Benjamin Disraeli edited, with an introduction, by William Hutcheon with illustrations (Quotation) London John Murray, Albemarle Street, W. 1913
Pp. viii+476, frontis. +1 pl.
The following are reprinted: 136, 611, 488, 151, 493, 494, 509, 513, 523-525, 531, 526, 727, 504, 510-512, 517, 536, 728 (order in which they appear in book)

Reviews

559. Athenaeum, no. 4493, p. 652 (6 Dec.)
560. Fortnightly Review, 101, 655-70 (1914) (W. Sichel)
561. Spectator, 111, 1119-20 (Lord Cromer) see 1295
562. T. L. S., 27 Nov., p. 568 (Disraeli as journalist)

563. A new sheaf of Disraeli letters, hitherto unpublished correspondence with his sister Sarah, by Clarence I. Freed, in American Hebrew, 120, 820-855 passim (15 April 1927)

564. The Letters of Disraeli to Lady Bradford and Lady Chesterfield Edited by The Marquis of Zetland. London: Ernest Benn Limited 1929
Two volumes. Pp. 313+(3), frontis., pl., facs.; 324, frontis., pl., facs.

Reviews

565. Contemporary Review, 137, 253-54 (1930)
566. Criterion, 9, 542-45 (April 1930) (K. Pickthorn)
567. Dublin Review, 191, 28-39 (1932) (G. H. Stevenson: The matchless sisters)
568. Empire Review, 50, 355-60 (Sir H. M. Imbert Terry)
569. English Historical Review, 45, 662-65 (1930) (Gerald Hurst)
570. English Review, 49, 653-54 (Nov.) (G. Le G. Norgate: Disraeli in love)
571. Listener, 2, 649 (13 Nov.) (Kingsley Martin: Disraeli and his women friends)
572. Nation-Athenaeum, 46, (1), 17 (5 Oct.) (Leonard

573.	New Republic,	Woolf) 61, 106-07 (18 Dec.) (R. M. Lovett)
574.	Saturday Review,	148, 375 (5 Oct.) (A.A.B.)
575.	Spectator,	143, 466 (5 Oct.)
576.	T.L.S.,	3 Oct., 763 (Disraeli in love)
577.	Yale Review,	19, 424-27 (Eleanor & Raymond Turner: Disraeli as letter-writer)

578. Published in New York by Appleton

579. Translated into French as "Lettres intimes ...," by Mme. William Laparra, and with a preface by André Maurois. Grasset, 1930

580. Also translated into Czech

581. Letters from Benjamin Disraeli to Frances Anne Marchioness of Londonderry 1837-1861   Edited with an Introduction by the Marchioness of Londonderry   London Macmillan 1938
Pp. (ii)+ xxv+ (i)+ 195+ (1), frontis., pl.

Reviews

582.	American Historical Review,	44, 968-69 (July 1939) (Francis H. Herrick)
583.	New Statesman,	16, 582 (15 Oct.) (Raymond Mortimer: The trowel)
584.	Saturday Review of Literature,	19, no. 3, p. 6 (12 Nov.) (Wallace Notestein)
585.	Spectator,	161, 487 (23 Sept.) (E. F. Benson)
586.	T.L.S.,	10 Sept., 578

587. Benjamin Disraeli on the grotesque in literature, edited by C. L. Cline in Review of English Studies, 16, 68-71 (1940)
Prints a paper from Hughenden (E/V/A/2), which is reproduced in the review of Vivian Grey II in New Monthly Magazine (33). Cline's view is that this part of the review is by Disraeli himself, while Maitre (55) regards it as being by Isaac D'Israeli.

588. The unfinished diary of Disraeli's journey to Flanders and the Rhineland (1824), edited by C. L. Cline in Uni-

versity of Texas Studies in English, 1943, 94-114

589. N. & Q., 15th ser., 186, 279 (3.vi.1944)

590. Rumpel Stilts Kin by B.D. & W.G.M. Printed by
Robert Maclehose & Co Ltd Glasgow for presentation
to members of the Roxburghe Club 1952 (66 copies
printed)
A short play, written by Disraeli and William George
Meredith, probably in 1823. Edited, with an introduc-
tion, by Michael Sadleir.
Sadleir, XIX C. F., 724

591. W. Hutcheon in The Morning Post, 13 January 1914

592. W. F. Prideaux: Disraeli's juvenilia in N. & Q.,
11th ser., 9, 125 (14.ii.1914)
Manuscript Hughenden Papers R/II/A
593. Benjamin Disraeli's letters to Robert Carter (edited
by) Hubert J. Hoeltje in Philological Quarterly, 31, 17-
26 (1952)
Six letters, 1870-1877, are printed in full.

594. Five letters from Benjamin Disraeli to his sister
Sarah (edited by) C. L. Cline in Library Chronicle,
University of Texas, 8, no. 3, 13-18 (Spring 1967)
Letters of 1834-1851

595. Benjamin Disraeli and R. Shelton Mackenzie: unpublished letters (1841-45), by David W. Tutein in VNL 31,
42-44 (1967)

For other miscellaneous writings see 705-712

Speeches

Collections

(For contents, see chronological list of speeches)
At Manchester and Bingley, October 1844. See 715

596. Mr. Gladstone's finance, from his accession to office
in 1853 to his Budget of 1862, reviewed by the Right
Hon. B. Disraeli. London: Saunders, Otley, and Co.
... 1862

Pp. 41+(1). With a short preface

597. "Church and Queen." Five speeches delivered by the
Rt. Hon. B. Disraeli, M. P. 1860-1864. Edited, with
a preface, by a member of the University of Oxford.
London: G. J. Palmer (&) Hamilton, Adams, & Co.
... 1865.
    Pp. xv+ (i)+ 79+ (1)
    Edited by Frederick Lygon, M. P., later Earl Beau-
champ

598. Constitutional reform: five speeches ... (1859-65),
edited (by permission), with an introduction, by John F.
Bulley ... To which is added an appendix ... London
Saunders, Otley and Co., 66, Brook Street, W. 1866.
    Pp. (viii)+ 144
    The appendix is a reprint of the Reform Bill of 1859

599. Parliamentary reform. A series of speeches on that
subject delivered in the House of Commons by the Right
Hon. B. Disraeli (1848-1866). ... Edited by Montagu
Corry ... London: Longmans, Green, and Co. 1867.
    Pp. xi+ (i)+ 478+ (2)

600. The Chancellor of the Exchequer in Scotland being two
speeches delivered by him in the City of Edinburgh on
29th and 30th October 1867 ... William Blackwood and
Sons Edinburgh and London   MDCCCLXVII
    Pp. (iv)+ 44

601. Speeches on the Conservative policy of the last thirty
years, by the Rt. Hon. B. Disraeli, M. P. ... Edited,
with an introduction, by John F. Bulley. London:
John Camden Hotten, 74 & 75, Piccadilly. (1870)
    Pp. 356. Introduction dated 1st Nov. 1869
    Stated by Pope Hennessy (1194) to have been sup-
pressed by Conservatives after Disraeli's death, on account of the views on Ireland expressed in some of the
speeches.

602. Fourth edition, with the addition of the speech at the
Literary Fund dinner, 8 May 1872, published by Chatto
& Windus, 1874.

603. Inaugural address delivered to the University of Glasgow.... Second edition including the occasional speeches
at Glasgow Authorised edition, corrected by the author

100

London   Longmans,   Green,   and Co.   1873
       Pp.   (iv)+ 69+ (3)

604.   Edinburgh Review, 139, 271-88   (1874) (J. A. Hard-
       castle)

605.   Addresses on education, finances, and politics.   By
       The Right Hon. B. Disraeli, on the occasion of his visit
       to Glasgow.   Revised and reprinted.   London: Charles
       Hawksley, 12, Queen Victoria Street, E. C.   1873.
       Pp.   30+ (2)

606.   Selected speeches of the late Right Honourable the
       Earl of Beaconsfield Arranged and edited with introduc-
       tion and explanatory notes by T. E. Kebbel ... Long-
       mans, Green, and Co.   1882
       Two volumes.   Pp.   xx+ 634+ (2); vii+ (i)+ 647+ (1)

607.   Edinburgh Review, 155, 533-67   (Spencer Walpole)
       (with 654 and 676)

608.   Athenaeum, 1882, 1, 211

609.   Spectator, 55, 495-96, 630-31

610.   Tory Democrat two famous Disraeli speeches edited
       by Sir Edward Boyle Bt.   Foreword by the Right Hon.
       Walter Elliot ... Conservative Political Centre (1950)
       Pp.   63+ (1)

Individual speeches

611.   The crisis examined.   By Disraeli the younger.   Lon-
       don: Saunders and Otley, Conduit Street.   1834.
       Pp.   (iv)+ 31+ (1)
       Sadleir, Excursions, p. 117
       The report of a speech at Wycombe, 16 December
       1834.   There is a report in "The Times," 17 Dec.
       1834.
612.   Second edition

613.   The Speech ... at the Anniversary Dinner of The
       Printers' Pension Society, on Tuesday, April the 8th,
       1845.   London: James S. Hodson, 112, Fleet Street.
       Pp.   iv,   (5)-12

614.   The Speech of Mr. Disraeli, in the House of Commons,

on Friday, 15th May, 1846. London: John Ollivier,
59, Pall Mall. 1846.
Pp. 44. See 1080

615. England and Denmark. Speech of Mr. Disraeli in the
House of Commons, the 19th April, 1848, on the Danish
question. London: James Ridgway, Piccadilly. 1848.
Pp. (ii)+ 29+ (1)

616. Second edition

617. Translated as "La Question du Slesvig ...," by L. E.
Borring. Paris, 1848. Pp. 22

618. The New Parliamentary Reform. Mr. Disraeli's
speech. In the House of Commons, on Tuesday, June
20, 1848, On Mr. Hume's motion ... (Church and State
Gazette Office)
Pp. 16. Only the second edition seen.

619. The Parliament and the Government. Mr. Disraeli's
speech on the labours of the Session: delivered in the
House of Commons, on Wednesday, August 30, 1848.
London: William Edward Painter, 342, Strand.
Pp. 32

620. Second edition

621. A Verbatim report of the speech delivered by B.
D'Israeli, Esq., M.P. at the seventh anniversary of
the Hospital for Consumption and diseases of the chest,
Brompton, held at the "Albion" Tavern, Aldersgate
Street, on Wednesday, May 2nd, 1849. London: T. M.
Inchbold ....
Pp. (ii)+ 16+ (2). Yellow wrappers
Dedicated to Jenny Lind.

622. Financial policy. Speech of Mr. Disraeli on the financial policy of the Government, made in the House of
Commons. June 30, 1851. London: Thomas Lewis,
34, Mount Street, Grosvenor Sq. 1851.
Pp. 16

623. Parliamentary reform. The speech of the Right
Honourable the Chancellor of the Exchequer, in the
House of Commons, on Thursday, the 25th March,
1852, on Mr. Hume's motion. London: John Ollivier,

59, Pall Mall.   MDCCCLII.
   Pp. 16

624. The New Budget.   The Financial Statement of the Rt.
      Hon. Benjamin Disraeli, M. P., delivered in the House
      of Commons, on Friday, December 4th, 1852.   London:
      Piper, Brothers & Co., 23, Paternoster Row. (&c. &c.)
      Pp. 36

625. Review Quarterly Review, 92, 236-74. (J. W. Cro-
      ker: cf. The Croker Papers, edited by L. J. Jennings,
      1885, III, 257)

626. Parliamentary Reform.   Speech of the Chancellor of
      the Exchequer, Delivered in the House of Commons Feb.
      28, 1859, on introducing a Bill to amend the representa-
      tion of the people in Parliament.   London: Routledge
      ... 1859.
      Pp. 64

627. Public expenditure. A speech delivered in the House
      of Commons on Mr. Stansfeld's motion, June 3, 1862.
      ... London: Robert Hardwicke, 192, Piccadilly.   1862.
      Pp. 23+ (1)

628. Speech ... At a Public Meeting in aid of the Oxford
      Diocesan Society for The Augmentation of Small Bene-
      fices, held at High Wycombe, on Thursday, October 30,
      1862.   London: Rivingtons, Waterloo Place, 1862.
      Pp. 24

629. Church policy: a speech delivered ... At a Meeting
      of the Oxford Diocesan Society for the augmentation of
      small livings, in the Sheldonian Theatre, Oxford, Nov.
      25, 1864. ... London, Rivingtons ... 1864.
      Pp. 28

630. Review British Quarterly Review, 41, 58-95 (1865)
      (with other works)
         The famous speech in defence of the Church Estab-
      lishment, and attacking the authors of "Essays and Re-
      views." It contains the phrases, "An age of craving
      credulity," and, "I am on the side of the angels."

631. Speech of the Right Honorable B. Disraeli, M. P., on
      the Re-distribution of Seats Bill, which remains un-
      answered by the government.

103

Printed by Harrison and Sons. St. Martins Lane.
(Speech of 14 May 1866)
   Pp. (24), variant states.

632. Speech of the Chancellor of the Exchequer in answer
      to the address presented by the working men of Edin-
      burgh in the Music Hall October 30, 1867   William
      Blackwood and Sons   Edinburgh and London
      MDCCCLXVII
         Pp. 16
         Also issued by E. Head, "British Lion" office,
      275 1/2, Strand, London, W.C.   Pp. 12

633. The Prime Minister on Church and State.   Speech of
      the Right Hon. B. Disraeli, M.P., at the Banquet to
      Her Majesty's Ministers, in the Hall of the Merchant
      Taylors' Company, June 17th.   (1868) (foot of p. (4)
      Abridged, by kind permission, for general distribution,
      by a Graduate of the University of Cambridge.   London:
      William Hunt and Company, Holles Street, Cavendish
      Square.
         Pp. (4)

634. Speech ... at the Free Trade Hall, Manchester,
      April 3, 1872.   Published by W. Tweedie, 337, Strand,
      for the National Union of Conservative and Constitutional
      Associations, 53, Parliament Street, Westminster ...
      (Publications of the National Union, 14.)
         Pp. 27+ (1)
         Another issue has the imprint, Published for the
      National Union of Conservative and Constitutional Asso-
      ciations, 53, Parliament Street, Westminster, S.W.
      Printed by the Central Press Company (Limited), 112,
      Strand.   Pp. 30

635. Re-issued in May 1885 under the title, "A Voice from
      the grave."

636. Watts, Charles A.:   The English monarchy and Ameri-
      can Republicanism, reply to the speech of ... Disraeli
      ... (Manchester, 1872)
         Published Austin, Johnson's Court, London, 1872.
      Pp. 8

637. Speech ... at the banquet of the National Union of
      Conservative and Constitutional Associations.   At the
      Crystal Palace, on Monday, June 24, 1872.   Published

for the Council by R. J. Mitchell and Sons, 52, Parliament Street, Westminster, London, S. W.

Pp. 11+ (1). (Publications of the National Union, 16.) Also printed in Report of the Proceedings at the Annual Conference, and the Proceedings of the Banquet, with other speeches, in National Union Publication, 15.

638. (Another ed.) Speech at the Banquet of the National Union ... at the Crystal Palace ... Commentaries (by) David Daiches, John Holloway, Paul Kluke, Helmut Viebrock ... with a preface by the editor ... Wiesbaden, Franz Steiner, 1968

Pp. xvi+ 88+ (2) (Studies in rhetoric in the nineteenth century, 1.)

(In English and German)

639. Mr. Osborne Morgan's Burials Bill. Speech ... in the House of Commons, March 26, 1873, on moving the rejection of the Bill on its Second Reading. London: Printed for the Church Defence Institution, 25, Parliament Street. 1873.

Pp. 16

640. Inaugural address ... Delivered on Wednesday, November 19, 1873, on the occasion of his installation as Lord Rector of the University of Glasgow Glasgow James Maclehose, 61 St. Vincent Street ... 1873

Pp. 23+ (1)

641. Also published by Longmans, 1873.

Also published by the National Union of Conservative and Constitutional Associations, as Publication 23.

Pp. 13+ (3)

642. Speech ... to the Conservative Association of Glasgow, On Saturday, November, 22nd, 1873. Published for the National Union of Conservative and Constitutional Associations, 53, Parliament Street, Westminster, S. W. November, 1873.

Pp. 16. (Publications of the National Union, 24.)

643. Lord Beaconsfield's speech at Aylesbury ... London: Holmes' Library 1876.

Pp. 23+ (1). 20 Sept. 1876.

644. Apparently also published with "Lord Derby's defence...," under the title, "The Eastern Question."

645. Der Congress vom 13 Juni 1878. 1 Lord Beacons-
fields Rede, Herausgegeben von Rudolph Schramm ...
Leipzig, 1878.
Pp. 19+ (1). In German

646. The agricultural situation. Speech of the Right Hon.
the Earl of Beaconsfield, K.G., at Aylesbury, September
18th, 1879.
Pp. 16 (No printer or publisher)
For miscellaneous speeches see 713-722, and for
election speeches see 1693-1720 passim

Collected editions

647. 1839 Two-volume edition "Works of D'Israeli the
Younger," published by Carey and Hart, Philadel-
phia.
Vol. 1: Vivian Grey, The Young Duke, Contarini
Fleming
Vol. 2: Alroy, Iskander, Henrietta Temple,
Venetia

648. 1850 One volume edition, containing the same works,
published by Harding, Philadelphia.

649. 1853 Uniform edition of the novels, up to and including "Sybil," published by Bryce. Disraeli made
considerable revisions to the earlier novels, particularly "Vivian Grey"

650. 1858 Uniform edition published by Routledge: includes
"Lord George Bentinck" (358), but not (?) "Contarini Fleming" or "Alroy."

651. 1862- Uniform shilling edition, Routledge.
1863 10 volumes

652. 1868 "New edition," five volumes, Warne.
1. The Young Duke, Contarini Fleming
2. Sybil, Alroy
3. Coningsby, Henrietta Temple
4. Venetia, Tancred
5. Ixion in Heaven, with The Infernal Marriage,

Popanilla, and Count Alarcos, Vivian Grey
Vol. 1 contains a preface (pp. (i)-xvi), signed
B., dated Exeter 1866. Each volume contains two
sequences of pagination. It is not clear if this is
the first issue of this edition. Re-issued, dated
1869

653. 1870- Longmans' collected edition. Brown cloth,
1871 green end-papers. 19 cm. The first volume
was the eighth edition of "Lothair" (419), containing the "General Preface." The remaining volumes,
issued at monthly intervals, were:
2. Coningsby
3. Sybil
4. Tancred
5. Venetia
6. Henrietta Temple
7. Contarini Fleming, The rise of Iskander
8. Alroy, Ixion in heaven, The infernal marriage,
Popanilla
9. The Young Duke, The Tragedy of Count Alarcos
10. Vivian Grey
    The volumes in this series were frequently re-
issued, in a slightly smaller format (17.5 cm.),
in a variety of bindings, and not always dated.
"Endymion" was published in the series, 1881
For a review of the 1919 reprint, see 1514

654. 1881 "Hughenden" edition. Longmans. 11 volumes,
in the order of publication of the major novels.
19 cm. Each title-page has an engraving of a
scene connected with Disraeli. Vol. 11, "Endymion," contains a "Memoir." The minor works
with the same novels as in the Collected edition.
    (607) Edinburgh Review, 155, 533-67 (1882)
(Spencer Walpole) (Reviewed with Kebbel's "Selected
speeches," and "Wit and wisdom")

655. Uniform edition of 12 volumes in "Seaside library" series, New York, Munro. 1881.
    Includes, with "Contarini Fleming," an anony-
mous "Life."

656. 1888 "Primrose" edition. Routledge. Paper covers.
8 volumes, "Vivian Grey" to "Sybil"

657.   Sixpenny edition. Ward Lock. Paper covers.
         8 volumes, as above.

658.   1892 "Primrose" edition. Ward Lock. Vivian Grey,
         Young Duke, Henrietta Temple, Coningsby, Sybil

659.   1904 The "Empire" edition. The Works of Benjamin
         Disraeli Earl of Beaconsfield embracing novels,
         romances, plays, poems, biography, short stories
         and great speeches with a critical introduction by
         Edmund Gosse ... and a biographical preface by
         Robert Arnot ... Printed for subscribers only by
         M. Walter Dunne, London and New York. (1904-
         05). 20 volumes. 1244 sets printed.
            The introduction reprinted 1303, 1508
            See 2. cf. 851

660.   1904 "Centenary" edition, edited by Lucien Wolf.
         Only "Vivian Grey" and "The Young Duke" were
         published (q. v.)

661.   1904 "Young England." Uniform edition of Vivian
         Grey, Coningsby, Sybil, and Tancred (qq. v.), edi-
         ted by B. N. Langdon-Davies, illustrated by Byam
         Shaw. 4 volumes. R. Brimley Johnson, 1904

662.   1905- Uniform edition of the novels, up to and in-
         1906 cluding "Tancred," and some minor works,
               edited by the Earl of Iddesleigh.
               9 volumes. John Lane, the Bodley Head.

663.   1926- "The Bradenham edition of the novels and tales
         1927 ..." with introductions by Philip Guedalla. 12
               volumes. Peter Davies.
                  Vol. III contains Popanilla, Ixion in heaven,
               The infernal marriage, The rise of Iskander, The
               carrier-pigeon, The consul's daughter, Walstein,
               and, A true story (qq. v.)
                  Vol. XII contains "Endymion, " and the unfinished
               "Falconet" (555)

664.   Also published by Knopf, New York, 1934

665.   Shanks, Edward: Disraeli the novelist (review
         of "Vivian Grey" and "The Young Duke") in Satur-
         day Review, 142, 732 (11 Dec. 1926)

666.   Swinnerton, Frank: Disraeli as novelist in

Bookman (London), 72, 1-3 (April 1927) (Differs from 1524)

667.   T. L. S., 21 April 1927, 269-70
        Guedalla's introductions are reprinted in 1347.

668.   1927-   Uniform edition.   11 volumes.   John Lane,
        1928   The Bodley Head.

German

669.   1846   B. Disraeli's Sämmtliche Schriften.
                DGK (13. 11647) records an edition of "Contarini
                Fleming" in this series.

Selections from Disraeli's works

        Books and pamphlets consisting wholly of selections
from Disraeli's writings and speeches.

670-   (Publications of the Liberation Society, issued for the
672.   General Election of 1868)

670.   Mr. Disraeli on "The Irish Question" (extract from
        speech of 16 Feb. 1844) Tract 15, and Placard 27. s. s.

671.   "Mr. Disraeli v. Mr. Disraeli" (extracts from Con-
        ingsby, book 7, ch. 2, and speeches of 1868) Tract 17,
        and Placard 38.   s. s.

672.   Mr. Disraeli on the Irish Church.   Leaflet 27.

673.   The best of all good company.   By Blanchard Jerrold.
        A day with the Right Hon. B. Disraeli ... London:
        Houlston and Sons, 7, Paternoster Buildings.   1872.
            Pp. (241)-312.   Part 4 of a series of selections,
        chiefly from contemporary novelists.   Issued separately.
            Includes a biographical sketch, incorporating much of
        the Memoir of Isaac D'Israeli, the General Preface to
        the novels, selections from the novels, and three
        speeches, including that on the death of the Prince Con-
        sort.

674.   Lord Beaconsfield interviewed.   Remarkable statements
        of his Lordship concerning the game of politics; the ori-
        gin and character of political parties; (&c. &c.) ... By
        A. C. Y. and A. G. S.   John Heywood, ... Manchester

(and) London ...
   Pp. 31+ (1).   n. d.   (?1879)   Portrait on front wrapper.
   Editors, Arthur C. Yates, and Arthur G. Symonds.
   (Manchester Public Libraries).

675.   Lord Beaconsfield on What is duty? and What is faith?
   set forth by Henry Brittain ... Malvern, Cyrus E. Brooks
   (and) London, F. Southwell.
      Pp. 12.   n. d.   (?1881)
      The extracts are all from "Tancred."

676.   Wit and wisdom of Benjamin Disraeli Earl of Beaconsfield collected from his writings and speeches   London
   Longmans, Green, and Co.   1881
      Pp. (ii)+ xiii+ (i)+ 382+ (2)

677.   Critic (New York), I, 244-45 (10 Sept.)

(607.)   Edinburgh Review, 155, 533-67 (1882) (Spencer Walpole) (reviewed with Kebbel's Speeches, and Hughenden
   edition)

678.   Nation, 33, 278-79 (reviewed with 1187)

679.   Also published in New York by Appleton

680.   New edition, 1883

681.   Beaconsfield Brilliants: being choice selections from
   the speeches and works of the late Benjamin Disraeli,
   Earl of Beaconsfield ... By Charles Dunlop.   Published
   by Bates, Hendy and Co., 37, Walbrook, London, E. C.
      Pp. 24.   n. d.   (?1881)

682.   The Beaconsfield birthday book (Quotations)   London
   Longmans, Green, and Co.   1884.
      unpaged; with frontis. and illus.   Quotations from
   Disraeli, 3 on each alternate page, the facing pages
   blank, in diary form.

683.   Gleanings from Beaconsfield compiled by H. St. John
   Raikes Marcus Ward & Co Limited   London   Belfast
   & New York
      Pp. (ii)+ 48.   n. d.   (?1886)

684.   Another edition, issued (?) simultaneously.   "People's
   edition, " published by authority of the Primrose League.

Pp. 32

685. Mr. Disraeli on the Irish question in 1843, 1844 and
1868. British Home Rule Association, Tractates, 3.
Pp. 5+ (3). n. d. (? 1886) Extracts from speeches.

686. Lord Beaconsfield (Disraeli). Cliques et coteries.
Masques et portraits. Paris, H. Gauthier, 1892.
Pp. 16. Passages from "Sybil" and "Lothair."

687. Beaconsfield maxims London Arthur L. Humphreys
1906
Pp. (iv)+ 179+ (1)

688. Spectator, 95, 461-62

689. The pocket Beaconsfield being maxims and passages
from the works of the Earl of Beaconsfield compiled by
Alfred H. Hyatt London Chatto & Windus 1907.
Pp. (viii)+ 207+ (3)

690. Wit and Imagination of Benjamin Disraeli London:
Seeley & Co., Limited. MCMVIII.
Pp. 164. ("The Elzevir library") Selected and ar-
ranged by George Sampson.

691. The pocket Disraeli compiled by J. B. Lindenbaum,
M. A., LL. M. Mills & Boon, Ltd., 49 Rupert Street
London, W.
Pp. 141+ (3). (1912)

692. The wisdom of Disraeli or A great policy for a great
party Arranged by T. Comyn-Platt With a preface by
the Marquess of Salisbury, K. G. London "The National Review" Office 43, Duke Street, St. James', S. W. 1.
Pp. xvii+ (i)+ 76+ (2) (1920)
Extracts from the Crystal Palace and other speeches.
The preface emphasises the need for the principles of
Democratic Toryism, while admitting the impossibility
of agreeing with all Disraeli said.

693. A day-book of Benjamin Disraeli Chosen by Mrs.
Henry Head Oxford At the Clarendon Press MDCCCCXX.
Pp. (iv)+ 135+ (1)

694. Outlook, 47, no. 1198, p. 61 (15 Jan. 1921) Disraeli's
wit, by Solomon Eagle (J. C. Squire) See 1313

695. The wit and wisdom of Disraeli (compiled by) Lloyd E.
Smith.   Girard, Kan., Haldeman-Julius Co.
Pp. 64. (1924)

696. The radical Tory Disraeli's political development il-
lustrated from his original writings and speeches   Se-
lected, edited and introduced by H. W. J. Edwards
With a preface by G. M. Young Jonathan Cape Thirty
Bedford Square London
Pp. 320 (1937) See the chronological list of speeches.

697. T. L. S., 13 Nov., 857-58 (The legacy of Disraeli,
Toryism and democracy), 891

698. Benjamin Disraeli   Selections from the Novels Edited
and introduced by Eric Forbes-Boyd   The Falcon Press
Ltd
Pp. 112. (1948)
The chief points of the introduction are that Disraeli
was not a great novelist, and that his political message
is almost wholly out-of-date.

699. Jerusalem by moonlight and The Hebrew race two
excerpts from the writings of Benjamin Disraeli   Poem
by Rose Freeman-Ishill   The Oriole Press   Berkeley
Heights New Jersey U. S. A. 07922 (1965)
Pp. (16) 40 copies printed for private distribution.
Extracts from "Tancred" and "Coningsby."

700. Disraeli and Conservatism (edited by) Robin Grinter
Edward Arnold (Publishers) Ltd.   London
Pp. 64+ 4 facs. Punch cartoons. (1968) ("The Ar-
chive series")
Extracts from writings and speeches

Works edited by Disraeli

701. The life of Paul Jones, from original documents in the
possession of John Henry Sherburne, Esq.   Register of
the Navy of the United States.   London: John Murray,
Albemarle Street.   MDCCCXXV.
Pp. xii+ 320
Sadleir, Excursions, 123

Published September 1825. Disraeli wrote the preface and notes for this abridged edition of the American
original.

702. Literary Gazette, no. 458, 29 Oct. 1825, 690-92

Manuscript, with some notes only in Disraeli's hand,
Hughenden Papers E/II/9

703. Curiosities of literature by Isaac D'Israeli. With a
view of the life and writings of the author. By his son
... Fourteenth edition. Moxon, 1849
Three volumes.
Sadleir, Excursions, 124-25

704. This contains the substantial, but inaccurate, "Memoir"
of his father, dated Christmas 1848. Isaac D'Israeli's
other works were also issued with prefatory notes by
Disraeli (or perhaps by his sister, Sarah), during the
following years. For details, see J. Ogden: Isaac
D Israeli, 210ff. "Memoir" in 554

Miscellaneous letters

705. Mr. Disraeli to Colonel Rathborne. n. d. (1858) Pp. 4
Published by Col. Rathborne, containing 13 letters to
him from Disraeli, dated 1857. See 1092-1095

706. A warning voice. Lord Beaconsfield's appeal to the
people of Great Britain and Ireland. 8 March 1880.
s. s
Beaconsfield's last election "manifesto," in the form
of a letter to the Duke of Marlborough, Lord Lieutenant
of Ireland. The text is printed, and commented on, in
MB. II, 1386-89.

707. Two letters from Disraeli to T. M. Evans, dated 9
May 1830 and 24 Oct. 1832, printed by A. C. Ewald in
Athenaeum, no. 2845, 6 May 1882, 568-69

708. Some early letters of Lord Beaconsfield, by E.
Thomas Cook in Saturday Review, 153, 510, 541-42 (21,
28 May 1932)

709. Unpublished letter to Callendar, on Lady Beaconsfield's death, in Times Literary Supplement, 23 Sept.
1920, 619

710. A letter, hitherto unpublished, from Disraeli to A. F.
W. Montagu, dated 1 Dec. 1873 in The Times, 11 February 1926 (Letter from Lord Wittenham)

711. N. & Q., 13th ser., 150, 127 (20.ii.1926)

712. Disraeli to an agent (Spofforth): confidences by letter:
the Party machine in The Times, 2 Sept. 1931. Letters,
1863-71

For election addresses &c. see 1693-1720 passim

Miscellaneous speeches

(See also the chronological list of speeches)

713. British Prime Ministers of the nineteenth century,
policies and speeches, edited by J. H. Park. New York,
1950, 189-249: the speeches on Chartism (1839), at
Shrewsbury (1843), on Peel (1845), on the Jewish question (1847), on the Second Reform Bill (1867), at Manchester (1872), on Suez (1876), and on Liberal policy
(1881).

714. After the turtle. Thirty-one years' ministerial policy
as set forth at Lord Mayor's Day banquets, from 1848
to 1878. Collected by Richard Seyd. London, Houlston
&c., 1878.
Contains Disraeli's speeches, 1867, 1868, and 1874
to 1878.

715. Addresses delivered by Lord John Manners, M. P.,
At the Birmingham Athenic Institution, August 26th,
1844; B. Disraeli, Esq., M. P., Lord John Manners,
M. P., and the Honourable G. Sydney Smythe, M. P.,
At the Manchester Athenaeum Soirée, Oct. 3rd, 1844;
Lord John Manners, M. P., and B. Disraeli, Esq.,
M. P., At Bingley, Yorkshire, October 11th, 1844 ...
London: Hayward and Adam ... 1845.
Pp. 48+ (2). Title "Young England" on wrapper.

716. Address delivered to the members of the Manchester

Athenaeum, 23 Oct. 1844 in The Importance of literature to men of business: a series of addresses delivered at various Popular Institutions. Revised and corrected by the authors ... Griffin ... 1852, pp. 49-67
The date is wrongly given in the book: the correct date is 3 October.

717. "Mr. Disraeli in Darlington," including a report of a speech at the autumn show of the Darlington Horticultural Society, 21 Sept. 1848 in John Bousfield: Pleasant memories of Darlington and neighbourhood, 1881, 52-56. Referred to, Beaconsfield Quarterly, p. 47

718. Disraeli's reply in defence of his Budget, December 16th 1852 in Famous speeches selected and edited by Herbert Paul, Second series, 1912, 96-132

719. The Nine Hours' Movement for Factory Workers. Mr. Disraeli's visit to Lancashire. Deputation from the factory workers. Revised, with Additions, from the "Manchester Evening News," April 4th, 1872. Manchester: Guardian Steam-Printing Works, Cross-Street.
Pp. 8
(Speeches by the deputation, and Disraeli's reply.)

720. The speech in the House of Lords after the Berlin Congress, 18 July 1878 in Famous speeches selected and edited by Herbert Paul, 1910, 340-360

721. Banquet given to The Earl of Beaconsfield, K. G., and The Marquis of Salisbury, K. G., on their return from Berlin, on the 27th July, 1878 ... London: Harrison and Sons, 1878.
Pp. (ii)+ 35+ (1)
Beaconsfield's speech, in reply to the toast proposed by the Duke of Buccleuch, pp. 16-23; also pp. 34-36

722. Presentation of addresses from the Conservative Associations to the Earl of Beaconsfield, K. G. and the Marquess of Salisbury, K. G. at the Foreign Office, August 6th, 1878. Report of proceedings ...
Pp. 24. (National Union publications, 36, August 1878) Beaconsfield's speech, pp. 16-22. Also includes Salisbury's speech.

For other miscellaneous speeches, see 1693-1720 passim

115

723. Star Chamber. A weekly magazine, published by William Marsh, 145, Oxford Street, from 19 April to 7 June 1826

724. Disraeli was accused, particularly in the Literary Magnet, new ser., 2, 103ff. (Aug. 1826) of starting it to advertise "Vivian Grey."

The editor of the magazine was Peter Hall, a friend of William Meredith, Sarah Disraeli's fiancé, and Disraeli undoubtedly had some connection with it: the evidence appears to be too fragmentary to allow of any definite conclusion. "Vivian Grey" was reviewed in Star Chamber (25), and a so-called "Key" to the novel published. (26) Disraeli is generally regarded as the author of two pieces, "The Dunciad of Today" and "A Modern Aesop." There are manuscripts in the Hughenden Papers (E/II/1) of "A Modern Aesop," and of "The Author of 'Granby,'" which is perhaps also his.

"The Dunciad of Today" was published with "The Revolutionary Epick" in 1904 (149), but the editor did not justify its inclusion.

725. Benjamin Disraeli The Dunciad of to-day a satire and The modern Aesop With an introduction by Michael Sadleir London: Ingpen & Grant 12 Bury Street, W.C.1
Pp. (vi)+ 65+ (3) Edition limited to 750 copies. (1928)
The introduction argues the case for Disraeli's authorship of "The Dunciad of Today," and other papers, chiefly on internal evidence, and affinities with Disraeli's acknowledged work. Too great an emphasis appears however, to be placed on the argument that no other person known to have been connected with Star Chamber was capable of such writing. The case, in my view, remains "not proven." Sadleir's introduction is reprinted, 1350. See also his Excursions, 123-24.

726. T.L.S., 6 Dec. 1928, p. 958

727. Fraser's Magazine: Gallery of literary characters. LXVI. Earl of Mulgrave, 12 (no. 71), 540 (Nov. 1835); LXXII. Sir John C. Hobhouse, 13 (no. 77), 568 (May 1836); LXXVII. Lord Lyndhurst, 14 (no. 82), 457 (Oct. 1836), each article with a portrait. The texts are ascribed to Disraeli by Hutcheon in 558, 386-96. There

are some parallel passages, but, so far as is known, there is no supporting evidence.

728. "Letters to the Whigs," by Manilius, in The Press (Disraeli's paper), 1853. Ascribed to Disraeli by Hutcheon, and printed in 558, 436-69. These letters were shown by Buckle to be by Lytton.
(MB., I, 1312)

729. The obituary of Lord Lyndhurst in The Times, 13 October 1863, by Samuel Lucas; reprinted in his Mornings of the recess ... (a series of papers from The Times), 1864, II, 5-36. Although this was published anonymously, Lucas' authorship was mentioned in the note, in The Times of 2 December 1868, on his death.
M.B., I, 305 implicitly denies that Disraeli was the author, as had been said at the time of its appearance. A. A. W. Ramsay: Sir Robert Peel, 1928, 195 n. 2 affirms Disraeli's authorship, relying on the similarities between the obituary and a passage on Lyndhurst undoubtedly by Disraeli (MB., I, 333). D. Hudson: Thomas Barnes of The Times, 116, "(Barnes) probably wrote the remarkable obituary notice of (Lyndhurst) ... which disclosed details of political scheming behind the scenes in 1835," and see 116 note. Barnes died in 1841, and it is possible that Lucas incorporated his "revelations" in the obituary. Lucas was, or had been, associated with Disraeli: possibly he consulted Disraeli also.

Other writings which have been ascribed to Disraeli

730. "A True story," signed △, in The Indicator, I, 319-20, 12 July 1820. Reprinted by J. L. Robertson (554), and with "Popanilla" and other works in Guedalla's Bradenham edition, 1926 (663). Wolf (45), xviii-xix, states that this "is believed to have been written by him, although the identification rests only on a certain wildness in the style, and the △ with which it is signed." No reason has been discovered for the ascription to Disraeli, nor whether the ascription antedates Robertson's reprint (1891). Angus (1) records, but gives no further information.

731. The present crisis; or, the Russo-Turkish war and its consequences to England and the world. By Coningsby.

London: George Routledge ... 1853.
Pp. 32
The author is unknown, but it is probable that this was a deliberate attempt at deception, by suggesting that it was by Disraeli. Translated into German as

732. "Die gegenwärtige Krisis, " Leipzig, 1854. (D. G. K.)
There is a letter to Disraeli from a German journalist, L. Bucher, who claimed to have exposed the fraud. (Hughenden papers E /VI /O /52.)
The foregoing lists indicate that Disraeli wrote a good deal of material which was published anonymously before his entry into Parliament in 1837, and I have suggested above that there may be items still undiscovered. His known journalistic activities, together with the relative obscurity of his earlier years, gave rise to various conjectures.

733. One example is to be found in "My Autobiography, " by John Timbs, editor of The Illustrated London News, published in The Leisure Hour, no. 1033, 14 October 1871. In a wildly inaccurate paragraph, apparently extensively copied into other papers, he ascribed to Disraeli, not only Star Chamber (which he postdated by four years), but also "A Key to Almack's" (1827), and "A Geographical and Historical Account of the Great World ..." (1829). The sting was presumably in the publisher's alleged remark, "That is young Disraeli, and he will be glad to execute any literary work for a guinea or two"; which, even if apocryphal, was not far from the truth.

734. Disraeli's solicitor, Sir Philip Rose, issued a denial (which appears in The Leisure Hour for 1871 at p. 816), in which he categorically denied Disraeli's authorship of the two latter works, and denied also that he was editor of Star Chamber. On the two books, there seems to be no reason not to accept Rose's denial; on the Star Chamber, as Sadleir points out (725), the question is not whether he was technically the editor, but whether he was the moving force and principal contributor.

735. Disraeli's alleged connection with Murray's "The Representative," 1826
In the summer of 1825 Disraeli became a partner in a venture to launch a daily newspaper with Murray, the publisher, and J. D. Powles, for whom he had written the "Mining pamphlets" (7, 11, 12). He was closely involved in the preparations, but his connection with the

118

paper is generally said to have ceased at the end of
1825, a few weeks before the paper's first appearance,
because he could not find his share of the capital. After
the paper's failure, in the summer of 1826, Murray
blamed Disraeli for having persuaded him to start it.
Disraeli was, however, long said to have been the
editor of, or a writer for, The Representative, and accused of having caused its failure. These
736. allegations were first published in The London Magazine, new ser., 6, 110ff. ("The Private history of the
rise and fall of a morning newspaper") in September
1826, and were repeated from time to time, e.g. in
745. Although Disraeli had earlier denied them, e.g.
1702, the story regained currency about 1869, and a
more formal denial, through his solicitor Rose, became
necessary.

737. In the 1869 issue of Debrett's Illustrated House of
Commons, the Disraeli entry included the statements
(which had not appeared in the 1868 edition) "... in
early life (he) was articled to a firm of solicitors in
Frederick Place, Old Jewry. He was subsequently engaged as a Journalist on the Metropolitan Press, and
afterwards became editor of The Representative newspaper." All this was omitted in the 1870 issue, which
carried a footnote, "As various statements have been
made to the effect that this gentleman once edited the
Representative newspaper, and was otherwise engaged
as a journalist, the editor is authorised to mention that
Mr. Disraeli was never engaged in either of the capaci-
ties mentioned." The ex-Prime Minister would not be
anxious to have the murky episodes of 1825-26 raked
over: the allegations about his connection with the paper
raised the other allegations about Star Chamber (723),
and "Vivian Grey," about which damaging statements had
been made on its publication.
    However, in 1871, the same year that Timbs' fabri-
cations regarding Star Chamber were published (733),
738. James Grant published in "The Newspaper Press" (I,
367), the allegations about The Representative.
    A denial by Rose appeared in The Times on 3rd No-
vember 1871, which referred to the Leisure Hour denial
(734). In both letters, Rose stated that "Mr. Disraeli
has never at any time edited any newspaper, review,
magazine or other periodical publication, and rarely contributed to any, nor has he at any time received or re-

quired any remuneration for anything he has ever written, except for those works which bear his name." In neither, however, was The Representative specifically mentioned. A newspaper correspondence developed, in which R. H. Mair, editor of Debrett's House of Commons, referred to the denials which had led him to insert the footnote in 1870, denials of which Grant, as a newspaper editor, ought to have been aware. Grant could produce no evidence: like Mair, he had relied on heresay. The story had been current for many years, and Disraeli had not denied it. This public discussion ended inconclusively, and, as Rose could deny the grosser errors of Timbs and Grant, the issues of Disraeli's real connections with Star Chamber and The Representative could be glossed over. There is a certain element of disingenuousness in the denials, as Disraeli had written some anonymous pieces for the press (465-536 passim): indeed, he had publicly declared that he was "a gentleman of the press, and bear no other escutcheon [in 1853]." and had himself been a newspaper proprietor. Perhaps he preferred not to risk airing the question of his writing in The Times and The Morning Post in the 1830s; perhaps he did not care what people said, and perhaps he could no longer himself separate the truth from the fiction. The evidence appears to be reasonably conclusive that Disraeli never edited The Representative. The date of his severance with the concern, given by Smiles, II, 206-07 as the end of 1825, is not well attested. The chronology of the weeks at the turn of the year, when he ceased to assist Murray and began to write "Vivian Grey," is obscure. It is possible that Disraeli still had some connection with the paper on its first publication in January 1826, and, although there is no reliable evidence to ascribe anything published in The Representative to him, the possibility cannot entirely be ruled out.

739. The Press
The Press was launched as a Conservative weekly in May 1853. Disraeli's connection with it was not public, and the extent of his writing in it is uncertain. See 536. The editors, Samuel Lucas and D. T. Coulton, clearly wrote under Disraeli's inspiration and advice, as did other associates, such as Lord Stanley and Lytton; articles by Lytton were formerly ascribed to Disraeli (728). Disraeli ceased to control the paper on becoming Chancellor of the Exchequer in 1858. See MB, I, 1305ff.

Disraeli manuscripts

It is not proposed here to attempt to list unpublished writings by Disraeli. The collection at Hughenden contains, besides many unpublished or partly-published letters, a number of very miscellaneous writings of Disraeli's early years, which have not yet been thoroughly examined. It is improbable that any document of literary significance has been overlooked.

740. "Aylmer Papillon" A satirical work, offered in 1824 to John Murray, who declined to publish it. (Smiles, II, 182) See also 61. The manuscript of two chapters, the only part known to survive, is in Hughenden Papers E/V/A/1

741. The manuscript of the Speech on the death of the Duke of Wellington, 15 November 1852, is in B. M. Add. MSS. 37,502. This has not been published other than in Hansard.

742. "Hand list of the Hughenden Papers," prepared by R. W. Stewart. (Published by The National Trust, 42, Queen Anne's Gate, London, S.W.1) Duplicated typescript. First issued 1961. Substantial sections have been added or revised subsequently. The collection includes family and political letters and papers, and the papers of Isaac D'Israeli, of Mary Anne Disraeli, and of her first husband, Wyndham Lewis. The papers, in the possession of The National Trust, are kept at Hughenden Manor, High Wycombe, Buckinghamshire.

WRITINGS ABOUT DISRAELI

Books

1852

743. The Right Honourable Benjamin Disraeli, M. P. A Critical Biography. By George Henry Francis. Reprinted, with additions, from Fraser's Magazine. London: John W. Parker and Son, West Strand. MDCCCLII. Pp. 128
   In series "Critical biographies."
   For the original see 1375-1376

744. Athenaeum, no. 1310, 1324-25 (4 Dec.) (Reviewed with book by Francis on Peel.)
(343.) Edinburgh Review, 97, 420-61 (1853) (Reviewed with "Venetia" and "Lord George Bentinck.")

1854

745. The Right Honourable Benjamin Disraeli, M. P. A literary and political biography. Addressed to the New Generation. (Quotation from Carlyle) London: Richard Bentley, New Burlington Street, ... 1854.
   Pp. (iv)+ 646+ (ii); a "Notice" between last page and end paper.
   There have been various attributions, but this is generally believed to be by Thomas MacKnight, editor of The Northern Whig, Belfast. A bitter and unscrupulous attack.

746. Athenaeum, no. 1366, p. 1584 (31 Dec. 1853)
747. Blackwood's, 75, 255-67 (W. E. Aytoun)
748. Eclectic Review, 5th ser., 7, 257-74
749. The Press, 2, no. 36, 15-16 (7 Jan.) (George Smythe)
   See MB, I, 519
750. Spectator, 26, Supplement 31 Dec. 1853
751. The Times, 17 Jan. See 1235

752. A second edition contains a preface, dated 13 March 1854, in answer to criticisms.

1863

753. Disraeli, the author, orator, and statesman: by John Mill. (Quotation) London: Darton and Hodge, 58, Holborn Hill. 1863.
Pp. (viii)+ 368

754. Athenaeum, no. 1853, 579-80 (2 May)
755. Saturday Review, 15, 608-10 (9 May)

1868

756. The life of Benjamin Disraeli. By John M'Gilchrist. London: Cassell, Petter, and Galpin, La Belle Sauvage Yard, E. C.; and 596, Broadway, New York. n. d. (1868)
Pp. (x)+ 112. 8 pp. publ. advts. (Cassell's Representative Biographies).

1877

757. Benjamin Disraeli Earl of Beaconsfield being forty years and upward of Political Life, from Bradenham House, Buckinghamshire, to Bulgaria. London: Goubaud & Son, 39, Bedford Street, Covent Garden, W. C.
Pp. 44
This pamphlet contains the first two chapters of the following work. Further pamphlets appear to have been published.

758. N. & Q., 5th ser., 9, 397 (18. v. 78)

759. Benjamin Disraeli Earl of Beaconsfield A biography London S. O. Beeton, 39, Bedford Street Covent Garden W. C.
Pp. (viii)+ 745+ (1)+ xiv, frontis. n. d. (1877)

760. Examiner, no. 3613, pp. 526-28 (28 April)
761. Mayfair, no. 20, pp. 10-12 (15 May)
reissued as
762. Benjamin Disraeli Earl of Beaconsfield. Vol. 1. Edited by S. O. Beeton. London: Goubaud & Son, 39 & 40, Bedford Street, Covent Garden, n. d. (1881?) By T. P. O'Connor. Apparently issued with 763

763. Benjamin Disraeli Earl of Beaconsfield a biography
Vol. II. By Algernon Foggo, M.A., Cantab. London
Goubaud & Son, 39 & 40, Bedford Street Covent Garden
n.d. (1881)
   Pp. (viii)+ 676+ xv+ (i)+ (3)-39   Reviews + (vii) publ.
advts. Brown cloth, uniform with 762
   The preface states that much of this was written be-
fore Beaconsfield's death, and part when he was Prime
Minister.

764. Lord Beaconsfield a biography by T. P. O'Connor, M.
A. William Mullan and Son London and Belfast 1879
   Pp. (viii)+ 711+ (1) Green cloth.
   The preface states that 759 was by O'Connor, and
that the material in it was condensed to form the first
part of this work. See 789

765. Second edition, with a new preface. (1879)

766. "People's edition," issued by Bennett Brothers and
W. Stewart & Co., 1880.
   Pp. (iv)+ 292
   The text slightly expanded.

767. A new edition (the sixth), issued by Chatto & Windus,
1884, with a new introduction, describing briefly the
last year of Disraeli's life.
   Pp. xxxvii+ (iii)+ 711+ (1)
768. Seventh edition, 1896.
769. Eighth edition, issued by T. Fisher Unwin, 1905.
770. (Another edition) Collins, n.d. (c.1913)
   Pp. 380+ (?2), frontis.

1878

771. Benjamin Disraeli, Jarl af Beaconsfield. En litterær
charakteristik af Georg Brandes. Kjøbenhavn ... 1878
   Pp. (iv)+ 315+ (1)

772. German translation, Berlin, 1879, reprinted 1901 &c.

773. Lord Beaconsfield. A study. By Georg Brandes.
Authorized translation by Mrs. George Sturge. London:
Richard Bentley and Son ... 1880.
   Pp. iv+ 380

774. Academy, 17, 170-71 (6 March) (Edward Dowden)

775. Catholic World, 31, 410-20, 491-99
776. International Review, 9, 42-50
777. Nation, 30, 420-21 (A. G. Sedgwick)
778. Spectator, 53, 303-05 (6 March)
779. The Times, 25 Feb.

780. Also published in New York, by Scribners.
781.&782. Reprinted 1966, 1968, by Crowell, New York
783. Also translated into Russian (n. d.)

784. La jeunesse de Lord Beaconsfield par Victor Valmont
Paris   Théodore Olmer, ... 1878
    Pp. 71+ (1)
    Disraeli's life to 1839.

1879

785. Bohater wieku. (Lord Beaconsfield).   Szkic z życia
społeczno-politycznego Anglii.   przez J. J. Finkelhausa.
Warszawa.   1879.
    Pp. 140.   Pink wrappers

786. The public life of the Right Honourable the Earl of
Beaconsfield, K. G. etc., etc.   By Francis Hitchman.
(Quotation from North's Plutarch) London: Chapman &
Hall, 193, Piccadilly.   1879.
    2 volumes.   Pp. xxxi+ (i)+ 447+ (1); x+ 487+ (1)+ (4)+ 32
pp. publ. advts. dated Oct. 1878.
    Favourable.   Up to 1874.

787. Academy, 15, 6-7 (4 Jan.)
788. Saturday Review, 46, 819-21 (28 Dec. 1878)
789. Spectator, 52, 1346-49 (25 Oct.) with 764.   See 794
790. Second, revised, edition in one volume.   Sampson,
Low, 1881.

791. Beaconsfield, by George Makepeace Towle.   New York,
1879.
    Pp. 163, frontis, pl.   ("Appleton's New Handy-volume
series").   (Library of Congress catalogue)   Not seen.

1880

792. England under Lord Beaconsfield, the political history
of six years from the end of 1873 to the beginning of
1880 by P. W. Clayden London C. Kegan Paul & Co.,
1, Paternoster Square 1880

Pp. xii+ 542. Preface dated 27 Jan. 1880

793. Third edition, 1891

794. Lord Beaconsfield et son temps par Cucheval-Clarigny
Paris A. Quantin, ... 1880
Pp. (iv)+ 356
Originally in Revue des deux mondes. (1421)
Hitchman (790) alleged that it was plagiarised from
his first edition.

1881

795. Benjamin Disraeli, Earl of Beaconsfield, statesman
and author. A record of his political and literary career. (Quotation) London: Ward, Lock ... n. d. (1881)
Pp. viii, (9)-117+ (1)+ (26) pp. publ. advts.
Anonymous.

796. Memorable men of the nineteenth century. II. The
Earl of Beaconsfield: his life and work. By Lewis Ap-
john. London: The Tyne Publishing Company ... and
Newcastle-on-Tyne.
Pp. 296+ 16 pp. publ. advts., frontis. n. d. (1881)

797. Another edition has imprint, London: Walter Scott,
14 Paternoster Square, and Newcastle-on-Tyne.

798. Two other issues have been seen; one is dated 1887,
the other is undated, but includes an advertisement for
Moore's "Esther Waters," which was published in 1894.
Both give the publisher's address as, London, 24 Warwick Lane, Paternoster Row, but with different word-
order and punctuation; neither has the series on the
title-page, and the photograph facing the title-page differs from that in 796.

799. Disraeli e Gladstone ritratti contemporanei di Ruggero
Bonghi Milano Fratelli Treves, Editori. 1881.
Pp. (viii)+ xvi+ 223+ (1)
Contains, "Disraeli," pp. (3)-84; "Endimione, il ro-
manzo di un uomo di stato," pp. (85)-119.

800. An appreciative life of the Right Hon. the Earl of
Beaconsfield, A Statesman of "Light and Leading."
With portraits of his contemporaries. Edited by Cor-
nelius Brown ... Illustrated with permanent photographs.

London: A. W. Cowan (and) Nottingham: Charles
Wheatley ... MDCCCLXXXI.
2 volumes. Pp. 384; (ii)+ 334+ 34+ 32 pp. publ. advts.,
with (33?) photographs; originally published in fifteen
parts, with the appendix of 34 pages containing "Miscellaneous facts and incidents." Apparently by various
authors.

801. Another edition, London, Harrison, 1882. Some
photographs differ from those in 800.

802. The Right Hon. Benjamin Disraeli, Earl of Beaconsfield, K. G., and his times. By Alexander Charles
Ewald ... London: William Mackenzie, ... 1881.
2 volumes. Pp. 600; 600. Numerous plates. Blue
cloth with gilt decoration. Usually found in five "divisions," the pagination breaking in division 3.

803. Benjameni de Israeli. Who is this uncircumcised
Philistine? By David Œdipus. Contents. The Philistine slain, The sphinx smashed, The Eastern Question
solved, The Asian mystery dissolved, and Ixion in Hell.
London: W. Stewart & Co., The Holborn Viaduct Steps,
E. C. 1881.
Pp. 212
Published anonymously. The Birmingham University
Library copy, which is from the library of Jesse Collings, to whom it was presented by the author, has a
manuscript note ascribing the book to "Christopher Chat-
tock." The character of the work is sufficiently indicated
by the title.

804. The life and political career of the Earl of Beacons-
field, K. G. By Edward Walford ... London Frederick
Warne & Co. Bedford Street, Strand n. d. (1881)
Pp. viii, 192
The publishers' preface dated 22nd April 1881.

805. Second edition, apparently identical

1886

806. Public opinion and Lord Beaconsfield 1875-1880 by
Geo. Carslake Thompson ... London Macmillan & Co.
1886
Two volumes

1887

807. Shelley and Lord Beaconsfield. By Richard Garnett.
London: Printed for private circulation only. 1887.
Pp. 22+ 2 (25 copies printed) See 1279, 1457

1888

808. Life of Lord Beaconsfield. By T. E. Kebbel. London: W. H. Allen ... 1888
Pp. xvi+ 220 ("Statesmen series")

809. Academy, 33, no. 833, pp. 266-67 (21 April) (J. A. Hamilton)

810. Also published in Philadelphia by Lippincott, 1888 ("International statesmen series")

1890

811. Disraeli in outline. Being a biography of the Right Hon. Benjamin Disraeli, Earl of Beaconsfield, K. G., &c., and an abridgment of all his novels; containing lists of principal characters, plots, remarkable passages, criticisms, &c. With full index. By F. Carroll Brewster, LL. D. Cassell ... 1890.
Pp. (iv)+ 394+ (2)

812. Also published in Philadelphia by Allen, Lane and Scott's Printing House.

813. Lord Beaconsfield by J. A. Froude (Quotation) London Sampson Low, Marston, Searle & Rivington ... 1890.
Pp. (ii)+ x+ 267+ (1), frontis. ("The Prime Ministers of Queen Victoria" series)

814. Academy, 38, 605-07 (J. A. Hamilton)
815. Athenaeum, no. 3290, 657-59 (15 Nov.)
816. Blackwood's, 149, 87-102 (1891) (Herbert Cowell)
817. Nineteenth Century, 28, 988-92 (T. E. Kebbel)
818. Quarterly Review, 182, 354-68 (1895) (Rival leaders and party legacies, by T. H. S. Escott)
819. Spectator, 65, 589-90
Frequently reprinted.

820. Issued as No. 666 in "Everyman's Library," 1914,

128

and frequently reprinted.

821.   Also published in New York by Harper, 1890
        "A study of Disraeli from a Carlylean point of view"
        (Dahl).

1891

822.   Disraeli and his day by Sir William Fraser ... Lon-
        don   Kegan Paul, Trench, Trübner & Co., Ltd.   1891
        Pp. (vi)+ 500+ (6)
823.   Second edition

        A collection of anecdotes, others of which are in
824.   his "Hic et ubique, " 1893.   See 1283

√825.   Personal reminiscences of the Right Honourable Ben-
        jamin Disraeli, Earl of Beaconsfield, K. G.   By Henry
        Lake, a member of Mr. Disraeli's committee, and a
        worker with him throughout his first canvass for the
        representation of the County of Buckingham... London:
        Cassell ... n. d. (1891)
        Pp. (viii) including portraits and a facsimile+ viii+ 104
        +(20) pp. publ. advts.
        Dedicated to the Primrose League.   Chiefly concerned
        with the election campaign of 1847.

1892

826.   Benjamin Disraeli's Dichtungen.   I.   Disraeli's Leben
        und Jugendschriften.   von Ph. Aronstein.   Offenbach ...
        1892
        Pp. xv+ (i)+ 48.   All published (?)
        Reprint of 1591.   See 1470

1900

827.   The Earl of Beaconsfield   By Harold E. Gorst ...
        London   Blackie ... 1900
        Pp. 2+ x+ 232.   ("The Victorian era" series)
        Favourable.

1902

828.   Ministres et hommes d'état Disraëli par Maurice
        Courcelle   Paris   Félix Alcan ... 1902
        Pp. (iv)+ 180+ (8)+ 16 pp. publ. advts.

829.   Benjamin Disraeli   An unconventional biography   By
        Wilfrid Meynell ... London: Hutchinson & Co. Pater-
        noster Row   1903
            2 volumes.
            Pp. xiv+ (ii)+ 290, frontis. , pl. ; vi+ 291-597+ (1),
        frontis. , pl.

830.   Academy, 65, 320-22 (3 Oct.)
831.   AHR, 9, 595-97 (1904) (W. Roy Smith)
832.   Athenaeum, no. 3962, 445 (3 Oct.)
833.   Blackwood's, 174, 684-91 ("Musings without method")
834.   Bookman, 25, 94-97 (L. Melville)
835.   Dial, 35, 461-62 (P. F. Bicknell)
836.   Nation, 78, 115-16 (1904) (A. G. Sedgwick)
837.   Spectator, 91, 654-55

838.   Also published in New York by Appleton, 1903.

839.   (Another edition) The Man Disraeli   A revised edi-
        tion of "Benjamin Disraeli: An Unconventional Biogra-
        phy" By Wilfrid Meynell ... Hutchinson ... (1927)
            Pp. xiii, 288, frontis. , pl.

840.   Also published in Toronto by Ryerson Press, 1927.
            A collection of anecdotes, letters and some of Dis-
        raeli's ephemeral pieces; the arrangement in the second
        edition is better.

1904

841.   Disraeli a study in personality and ideas by Walter
        Sichel ... Methuen ... 1904
            Pp. (viii)+ 335+ (1)+ frontis. + 40 publ. advts. , dated
        May 1903.

842.   Academy, 66, 375 (2 April)
843.   Athenaeum, no. 3987, 398-99 (26 March)
844.   Nation, 79, 182-83 (A. G. Sedgwick)
845.   Spectator, 92, 603

846.   T. L. S. , 1 April, 98-99

847.   Also published in New York by Funk and Wagnall,
        1904.

848. Beaconsfield by Walter Sichel with twelve illustrations
Methuen & Co   36 Essex Street   W.C.   London   1904
Pp. xvi+212, frontis., pl. ("Little biographies"
series)

849. Athenaeum, no. 3991, 529 (23 April)

850. (Another edition) has no date on the title-page, but
"New and Cheaper Issue" after "London": on verso of
title-page dated 1905.
The series is titled "The Oxford biographies"

851. The Earl of Beaconsfield, K. G.   Keys to the famous
characters delineated in his historical romances, with
portraits and biographies, supplemented by a critical ap-
preciation of Lord Beaconsfield by Dr. H. Pereira
Mendes, and miscellaneous addenda by Robert Arnot,
M.A., New York and London, M. W. Dunne (1904).
Pp. x, 11-100, frontis., illus. (Library of Congress
catalogue) Not seen.   Recorded in NCBEL (1969) as
"Mendes, H. P.   Key to Vivian Grey.   1904" Recorded
in 1047.   Cf. 659

1907

852. (Howes, R. W.:   Disraeli, a key to the characters
with notes and portraits.   New York, 1907) Not seen.
Recorded in NCBEL (1969) as "Key to Vivian Grey."
Recorded in 1047

1910

853. The life of Benjamin Disraeli Earl of Beaconsfield.
By William Flavelle Monypenny Volume I.   1804-1837.
With portraits and illustrations Read no history, nothing
but biography, for that is life without theory. --Contarini
Fleming.   London: John Murray, Albemarle Street,
W. 1910.
   I.   (1804-1837) Pp. x+400   Oct. 1910
   II. (1837-1846) Pp. x+420   Nov. 1912
   III. (1846-1855) Pp. x+589+ (1)   Nov. 1914
   Though described as "By William Flavelle Monypenny
and George Earle Buckle," volume III is, with the ex-
ception of a few passages, by Buckle.   The title-pages
of volumes IV to VI read "By George Earle Buckle in
succession to W. F. Monypenny"

IV.   (1855-1868) Pp. viii+ 608   May 1916
V.   (1868-1876) Pp. x+ 560   June 1920
VI.   (1876-1881) Pp. vii+ (i)+ 719+ (1) June 1920
Volume VI. contains an index to the whole work.

Reviews

1910

854.   Blackwood's,   188, 685-700 ("Musings without
                            method").
855.   Bookman,   39, 129-33 (Scimitar and broads-
                            word: Disraeli and Bright, by
                            Walter Sichel).
856.   Fortnightly,   94, 1014-26 (L. Melville)
857.   Nation,   91, 521-22 (R. Ogden)
858.   Nineteenth Century, 68, 821-40 (W. Sichel)
859.   N. & Q., 11th ser., 2, 398-99 (12 Nov.)
860.   Spectator,   no. 4296, 693-94 (29 Oct.)
861.   T.L.S.,   27 Oct., 397-99 (J. Morley)

1911

862.   AHR   16, 627-28
863.   Contemporary Review, 99, Literary Supplement 40,
                            6-9
864.   Dial,   50, 13-16 (L. M. Larson)
865.   Dublin Review,   148, 1-23
866.   Edinburgh Review,   214, 196-217
867.   North American Review, 193, 221-28

1912

868.   Blackwood's,   192, 860-74 ("Musings without
                            method")
869.   Nation,   95, 562-64 (R. Ogden)
870.   Spectator,   109, 810-12
871.   Spectator,   109, 889-91, 952-54 (Lord
                            Cromer. See 931)
872.   T.L.S.,   14 Nov., 501-03 (J. C. Bailey.
                            See 1308)

1913

873.   AHR   18, 585-87
874.   Contemporary Review, 103, 22-31 (G. W. Russell)
875.   Dial,   54, 235-37 (L. M. Larson)

876. Dublin Review,   152, 1-20, 217-31 (W. Ward.
                          See 1297)
877. Fortnightly,   99, 478-90 (M. Woods)
878. Nineteenth Century, 73, 133-55 (W. Sichel)
879. North American Review, 197, 268-74
880. Quarterly Review,   218, 208-29 (A. Cecil)

1914

881. Blackwood's,   196, 849-56
882. Spectator,   113, 748-50
883. T. L. S.,   26 Nov., 521-22 (J. C. Bailey.
                          See 1308)

1915

884. AHR   20, 635-38 (Edward Porritt)
885. Contemporary Review, 107, 117-18
886. Dial,   58, 308-09 (15 April)
887. Dublin Review,   157, 38-54 (B. Holland)
888. Nation,   100, 51-52 (R. Ogden)
889. Nineteenth Century,   77, 168-93 (W. Sichel)

1916

890. Blackwood's,   199, 839-49
891. Bookman,   50, 95-98 (W. Sichel)
892. Contemporary Review, 109, 794-96
893. Dublin Review,   159, 194 (July)
894. Edinburgh Review,   224, 23-42 (Lord Cromer)
895. Fortnightly,   105, 997-1004 (Baumann: "Dis-
                          raeli's meridian." See 1324)
896. London Quarterly Review, 126, 136-37
897. Nation,   103, 83-84 (R. Ogden)
898. New Republic,   9, Supplement, 30-32 (H. J.
                          Laski)
899. Nineteenth Century,   80, 350-70 (W. Sichel)
900. Quarterly Review,   226, 508-31 (A. Cecil)
901. Spectator,   no. 4585, 606-07 (13 May)
902. T. L. S.,   11 May, 217-18 (J. C. Bailey.
                          See 1308)

1917

903. AHR   22, 374-77 (Edward Porritt)

133

1920

904.	Athenaeum,	no. 4707, 72-73 (16 July)
905.	Blackwood's,	208, 236-47 (C. Whibley)
906.	Bookman,	58, 171-72 (Walter Sichel)
907.	Contemporary Review, 118, 290-93
908.	Dublin Review,	167, 193-218 (A. Cecil)
909.	Edinburgh Review,	232, 233-55 (W. Sichel)
910.	Fortnightly,	114, 226-36 (A. Baumann)
911.	De Gids,	84, (3), 468-81, 84, (4), 142-57 (P. Geyl)
912.	Plain English,	no. 2, 34-35, 17 July (S. M. Ellis. See 1321)
913.	Quarterly Review,	234, 1-21 (Lord Esher)
914.	Spectator,	no. 4799, 829-30 (19 June)
915.	T. L. S.,	17 June, 373-74 (J. C. Bailey. See 1308)
916.	Woman's Leader,	16 July. (L. Strachey. See 1339)
917.	Yale Review,	new ser., 9, 600-19 (W. C. Abbott: An Accidental Victorian. See 1318)

1921

918.	AHR	26, 672-82 (J. Bryce)
919.	London Quarterly Review, 135, (5th ser., 21), 1-16 (J. Telford)
920.	Nation,	112, 555-56 (13 April)

1923

921.	Preussische Jahrbücher, 193, 129-54, 257-68, 194, 1-22 (Emil Daniels)

1925

922.	Finsk Tidskrift,	99, 210-40 (Rolf Pipping) in Swedish

1929

923.	English Review,	49, 768-70 (Dec.)
924.	T. L. S.,	26 Sept., 729-30 (The past and present of Toryism, by K. Feiling. See 1329)

925.   Saturday Review of Literature, 6, 1185-86 (12 July)
                 (Wallace Notestein)
    See 1289, 1309

926.   The life of Benjamin Disraeli Earl of Beaconsfield
    By William Flavelle Monypenny and George Earle Buckle
    New and revised edition in two volumes ... Murray ...
    1929
    Pp. xi+ (i)+ 1668; vii+ (i)+ 1622+ (2)

927.&928. Both editions were also published in New York
    by Macmillan.

929.   An Italian translation of Vol. I (only?), by L. Villari,
    1911.

930.   New edition reprinted, New York, Russell & Russell,
    1968.

1912

931.   Disraeli by the Earl of Cromer   Macmillan ... 1912
    Pp. v, 40
    The review of the first two volumes of Monypenny,
    871; reprinted 1290

932.   Blackwood's, 193, 270-76 (1913)

1911

933.   Oscar A. H. Schmitz Die Kunst der Politik 1911   Bei
    Meyer & Jessen   Berlin
    Pp. 470+ (2)
    Subsidiary title-page: "Lord Beaconsfield (Benjamin
    Disraeli)"
934.   (Second edition) München, 1914
935.   (Another edition) Oscar A. H. Schmitz   Englands
    politisches Vermächtnis an Deutschland München 1916
    bei Georg Müller
    Pp. 454+ (2)
    Half-title: "Schmitz Englands politisches Vermächtnis
    an Deutschland durch Benjamin Disraeli, Lord Beacons-
    field. Der Kunst der Politik dritte Auflage."

1912

936. On a Dictum of Mr. Disraeli's And other Matters An Address Delivered before the University of Glasgow on December 5th, 1912   By the Right Hon. Augustine Birrell ... London   Arthur L. Humphreys, 187 Piccadilly W   1912
       Pp. 22+ (2)

1923

937. (Lord Beaconsfield, 1804-1832, by Alexander Külischer. Berlin, Rimon-Verlag, 1923).   In Hebrew.
       Pp. 227

1925

938. Disraeli & Gladstone   A Duo-Biographical Sketch By D. C. Somervell   Jarrolds ... 1925
       Pp. 310+ (2)

939. Empire Review, 43, 127-35 (1926) (Disraeli and Gladstone, by Augustine Birrell.   Reviewed with 948.)
940. English Review, 42, 125-27 (1926) (G. Le Grys Norgate)
941. Nation-Athenaeum, 38, (8), 292 (21 Nov.) (Leonard Woolf.   Reviewed with 948.)
942. Spectator, 136, 458-60 (H. Perry-Robinson.   Reviewed with 948.)
943. T. L. S., 15 Oct., 664

944. Published in New York by George H. Doran, 1926, and by
945. Garden City Publishing Company, 1929.
946. Published by Faber, 1932.   (The Faber Library, 8.)
947. Translated into German, 1926.

948. Disraeli: the alien patriot by E. T. Raymond ... Hodder and Stoughton ...
       Pp. (iv)+ 361+ (3) frontis. + pl. n. d. (1925)
       The author's real name was Edward Raymond Thompson.

       Empire Review see 939
       Nation-Athenaeum see 941
949. New Republic, 46, 147-48 (24 March 1926) (R. M. Lovett)
950. Saturday Review, 140, 591-92 (21 Nov.) (The tragedy

of Disraeli, by Edward Shanks)
951. South Atlantic Quarterly, 26, 201-02 (April 1927)
(Lewis Patton)
Spectator see 942
952. T. L. S., 5 Nov., 729

953. Also published in New York, by Doran, 1925.

1926

954. Benjamin Disraeli the romance of a great career 1804-
1881 By the Rt. Hon. Sir Edward Clarke, K. C.
London John Murray, Albemarle Street, W. 1926
Pp. ix+ (i)+ 308+ (2 publ. advts.), frontis. & pl.

955. Saturday Review, 142, 37-38 (10 July) ("A. A. B. ")
956. Saturday Review of Literature, 3, 71 (28 Aug.) (Walter
S. Hayward)
957. Spectator, 137, 61 (J. St. Loe Strachey)
958. T. L. S., 24 June, 427

959. Also published in New York, by Macmillan.

1927

960. La vie de Disraëli par André Maurois (Paris, Galli-
mard) 1927
Pp. (iv)+ 340+ (4) (Vies des hommes illustres, 8.)
Frequently reissued.
961. Also published in Revue Paris, 15 February-15 April
1927

962. Disraeli A Picture of the Victorian Age by André
Maurois Translated by Hamish Miles London John
Lane The Bodley Head Ltd (1927).
Pp. x+ (iv)+ 334+ (2 publ. advts.), frontis., 1 pl.
Frequently reissued.
963. Also published in serial form in The Forum, 78 (Oct.
1927-March 1928)

964. Bookman (N. Y.), 67, 92-93 (March 1928) (The Puck
of English politics, by Rose Lee)
965. Central Literary Magazine, 30, 26-35, 41-51 (1931)
(A résumé of Maurois, by Harry Grindle)
966. English Review, 46, 63-71 (1928) (A new French interpretation of Disraeli, by C. Sarolea)
967. Independent (N. Y.), 120, 188 (25 Feb. 1928) (An un-

Victorian Victorian, by J. Bakeless)
968.   Nation, 126, 456-58 (18 April 1928) (J. Salwyn Schapiro)
969.   New Republic, 54, 73-74 (29 Feb. 1928) (R. M. Lovett)
970.   Nouvelle Revue Française, 29, 101-03 (July 1927)
(Jean Schlumberger)
971.   Quarterly Journal of Speech, 14, 576-78 (1928) (Edwin
H. Paget)
972.   Revue Bleue, 65, 408-11 (Lucien Maury)
973.   Saturday Review of Literature, 4, 625, 629 (25 Feb.
1928) (Wallace Notestein)
974.   Spectator, 139, 736 (29 Oct.) (John Strachey)
975.   T. L. S., 10 Nov., 802; and 1 Dec., 910 (Letter from
G. F. Bosworth on Disraeli's schooldays at Walthamstow)

976.   Also published in New York by Appleton, 1928
977.   Issued by Penguin Books, 1937
978. &979.   Translated into Russian, and Czech.

980.   Disraeli by D. L. Murray   London: Bouverie House
Ernest Benn Limited   MCMXXVII
Pp. ix+ (i), 11-298+ (2) ("Curiosities of politics")

981.   Bookman (N. Y.), 65, 326-27
982.   Saturday Review, 143, 383 (12 March) ("A. A. B.")
983.   Saturday Review of Literature, 4, 20 (6 Aug.) (Ama-
bel Williams-Ellis)
984.   T. L. S., 3 March, 137

985.   Also published by Little, Brown, Boston.

For The Man Disraeli, by Wilfred Meynell, 1927 see 839

1930

986.   Benjamin Disraelis Orientalismus von Boris Segalo-
witsch.   Verlag "Kedem" Berlin 1930
Pp. vii+ (i)+ 139+ (1)
See 1605

987.   Revue Anglo-Américaine, 8, 362-63 (April 1931) (L.
Cazamian)

1933

988.   Die Romankunst Disraelis von Hildegard Seikat   1933
Verlag der Frommannschen Buchhandlung (Walter Bieder-

mann) Jena
Pp. 78 (Forschungen zur englischen Philologie, 3.)

1935

989. Disraelis Imperialismus und die Kolonialpolitik seiner
Zeit (by) Hans Rühl Mayer & Müller, Leipzig, 1935
Pp. xvi, 168 (Palaestra, 196.)

990. Archiv ..., 169, 258-59 (Karl Brunner) (1936)
991. Beiblatt zur Anglia, 47, 22-25 (1936) (Heinrich Wenz)
992. English Studies (Amsterdam), 20, 77-79 (April 1938)
(C. A. Bodelsen)

993. Disraeli, Gladstone, and the Eastern Question, a
study in diplomacy and party politics, by R. W. Seton-
Watson. Macmillan, 1935.

1936

994. Disraeli by Harold Beeley   Great Lives   Duckworth,
3 Henrietta Street   London   W. C. 2 (1936)
Pp. 144 ("Great lives" series, 65.)

995. Sunday Times, 17 May 1936: Disraeli then and now,
how his contemporaries regarded him (G. M. Young).
See 1348
996. T. L. S. , 23 May, 427
(The best short account.)

1941

997. Benjamin Disraeli Von Rudolf Craemer   Hanseatische
Verlagsanstalt Hamburg 1941
Pp. 226, frontis. , pl.
See 1549

998. Pfeffer, K. H. : Zur Geschichte der Judenfrage:
Benjamin Disraeli in Historische Zeitschrift, 166, 311-18
999. &1000.   Translated into French, Czech.

1943

1001. Sir R. George Stapledon Disraeli and the new age.
Faber and Faber Ltd London (1943)
Pp. 177+ (3)

1002. Quarterly Review, 282, 249 (1944)
1003. T. L. S., 8 April 1944, 176

1004. Also published in New York by Transatlantic, and in
1005. Toronto by Ryerson Press.

1946

1006. (Lord Beaconsfield's plan for a Jewish state, by N.
M. Gelber. Tel-Aviv, Leinmann, 1946/47). In Hebrew.
Pp. 111 (National Union Catalog).
1007. (English translation of 1006, by T. H. Gaster, noted
in 1018.) Not traced.

1951

1008. Dizzy The Life and Nature of Benjamin Disraeli ...
by Hesketh Pearson ... Methuen ... (1951)
Pp. xi+ (i)+ 284, frontis., pl.

1009. Arnold, Carroll C. in Quarterly Journal of Speech,
38, 94
1010. Fulford, R. in The Listener, 1 Nov., 46
1011. Hanna, Paul L. in AHR 57, 730-31 (1952)
1012. Maitre, R. in Etudes anglaises, 5, 260
1013. Schuyler, R. L. in Political Science Quarterly, 68,
294-97 (1953) (with 1018)
1014. Taylor, A. J. P.: Lost, a Prime Minister in New
Statesman, 42, 412 (13 Oct.)
1015. T. L. S., 23 Nov., 751

1016. Also published in New York by Harper,
and by
1017. Grosset and Dunlap in the series, "Biographies of
distinction."

1952

1018. Benjamin Disraeli Earl of Beaconsfield by Cecil Roth
Philosophical Library New York (1952)
Pp. viii+ (vi)+ 178
The leading account of the Jewish element in Disraeli.

1019. Booth, B. A. in NCF 7, 232
1020. Clinchy, E. R. in American Academy of Political
and Social Science, Annals, 285, 212-13 (1953)
1021. Hall, Walter P. in AHR 58, 686 (April 1953)
Schuyler see 1013

1953

1022. Peacocks and primroses   A Survey of Disraeli's
 ‾‾Novels by Muriel Masefield   London   Geoffrey Bles
 MCMLIII
 Pp. 319+ (1), frontis.
 An introduction to the novels, with copious extracts.

1023. Maitre, R. in Etudes anglaises, 7, 127
1024. Listener, 49, 571
1025. T. L. S. , 22 May, 332 (Day-dreams of a Prime Minister)

1956

1026. (Benjamin Disraeli, by B. Jaffe, Tel-Aviv 1956).   In
 ‾‾Hebrew.

1959

1027. "The Monstrous Clever Young Man" The Novelist
 ‾‾Disraeli and His Heroes by Arthur H. Frietzsche   Utah
 State University Press Logan, Utah ... December, 1959
 Pp. 60
 (Utah State University Monograph series, vol. 7, no.
 3.)

1960

1028. The young Disraeli   B. R. Jerman   Princeton, New
 ‾‾Jersey Princeton University Press   London: Oxford
 University Press   1960
 Pp. xiv+ 327+ (3)

1029. Blake, R. in History Today, 11, 361
1030. Bryden, R. in Spectator, 205, 1050 (30 Dec.)
1031. Cline, C. L. in NCF 15, 265-68
1032. Clive, J. in JMH 33, 206-07 (1961)
1033. Costigan, G. in AHR 66, 785-86 (1961)
1034. Fulford, R. in The Listener, 64, 999
1035. Gash, N. in EHR 77, 397-98 (1962)
1036. Graubard, S. R. in VS 4, 177-78
1037. Johnson, P. in New Statesman, 17 Dec. , 975
1038. Smith, S. M. in MLR 57, 308 (1962)
1039. T. L. S. , 23 Dec. , 823; 13 Jan. 1961, 25
 See 1614

141

1040. Beaconsfield and Bolingbroke by Richard Faber   Faber and Faber   24 Russell Square   London (1961)
Pp. 107+ (5), pl.

1041. Christie, I. R. in The Listener, 66, 739
1042. Sampson, R. V. in VS 6, 288-89
1043. T. L. S., 27 Oct., 768 (with 1045)

1044. Disraeli's religion The Treatment of Religion in Disraeli's Novels by Arthur H. Frietzsche ... Utah State University Press   Logan, Utah ... December, 1961
Pp. 46+ (2)
(Utah State University Monograph series, vol. 9, no. 1.)

1045. Disraeli   By Paul Bloomfield   Published for the British Council and the National Book League by Longmans, Green & Co. (1961)
Pp. 39+ 1, frontis.   (Writers and their work, 138.)
T. L. S., see 1043

1963

1046. Disraeli, by M. Komroff, New York, Messner, 1963.
Not seen.

1047. Raymond Maitre ... Disraeli homme de lettres La personnalité La pensée L'oeuvre littéraire Études anglaises 14 Didier 1963
Pp. (iv)+ 463+ (5)
See 1620

1966

1048. Nottingham University Miscellany no. 2   Mr. Disraeli's readers   Letters written to Benjamin Disraeli and his wife by nineteenth-century readers of "Sybil; or the Two Nations" Edited with an introduction by Sheila M. Smith ... Sisson and Parker   Ltd. for the University of Nottingham   1966
Pp. (ii)+ 65+ (5), frontis.

1049. Haddakin, Lilian in MLR 62, 321 (1967)
1050. McCord, N. in N. & Q., 212, 72 (Feb. 1967)
1051. NCF 21, 300-01

1052. T. L. S., 9 June, 512

1053. Disraeli by Robert Blake   Eyre & Spottiswoode
       London   (1966)
       Pp. (ii)+ xxiv+ (ii)+ 819+ (1), frontis., pl.

1054. Annan, Noel in NYRB 8, no. 6, p. 14-16 (6 April
       1967)
1055. Cline, C. L. in NCF 22, 407-10 (1968)
1056. Curtis, L. P. in VS 11, 237-40 (1967)
1057. Fido, Martin in Oxford Review, no. 4, 81-85 (1967)
1058. Fraser, P. in History, 54, 116-17 (1969)
1059. Gash, N. in EHR 83, 360-64 (1968)
1060. Graubard, Stephen R. in AHR 73, 139 (1967)
1061. James, R. R. in Spectator, 21 Oct., 520-21
1062. Lichtheim, George: The illusionist in Partisan Re-
       view, 34, 132-35
1063. Pitt, H. G. in Listener, 76, 618 (27 Oct.)
1064. Taylor, A. J. P.: The Wrecker in New Statesman,
       72, 589-92 (21 Oct.)
1065. T. L. S., 20 Oct., 949-50
1066. 1065 reprinted, "Dizzy heights, a prospect of Beacons-
       field" in "T. L. S., " 5, (1966), 1967, 1-8

1067. Also published in New York by St. Martin's Press.

1967

1068. 1867: Disraeli, Gladstone and revolution, the passing
       of the second Reform Bill, by Maurice Cowling. Cam-
       bridge University Press, 1967.

1069. Jan Pilát: Benjamin Disraeli. Nakladatelstvi Svo-
       boda. Praha 1967
       Pp. 257+ (3). (Portréty, 25.)

1070. Disraelian Conservatism and social reform, by Paul
       Smith. London, Routledge, and University of Toronto
       Press, 1967.

1968

1071. Disraeli, Democracy and the Tory Party, Conserva-
       tive leadership and organization after the Second Reform
       Bill, by E. J. Feuchtwanger. Oxford, Clarendon Press,
       1968.

1072. Benjamin Disraeli By Richard A. Levine ... Twayne
Publishers, Inc. New York (1968)
  Pp. 183+ (9) (Twayne's English Authors series, 68.)

1073. The Boy Disraeli Olga Somech Phillips Illustrated
by Denise Brown Max Parrish. London (1968)
  Pp. 120

1969

1074. Disraeli by Robert Blake Oxford University Press
1969
  Pp. 64 (The Clarendon Biographies, 23.)

1075. T. L. S., 10 April, 398

1076. Disraeli and Gladstone Robert Blake ... The Leslie
Stephen Lecture 1969 Cambridge at the University Press
1969
  Pp. (ii)+ 35+ (3)

1077. Benjamin Disraeli, Prime Minister extraordinary, by
Neil Grant. New York, F. Watts, 1969. ("Juvenile
literature") Not seen.

Pamphlets and ephemera

For Key to Vivian Grey. 1827. See 36

1838

1078. The case of The Queen v D'Israeli, with an argument
in vindication of the practice of the Bar. By Joseph
Stammers ... London: Richard Pheney ... 1838.
  Pp. 24
  Disraeli was accused of libelling Charles Austin, who
appeared for the petitioners in the Maidstone election
petition of 1838, and who, Disraeli alleged, had falsely
accused him of bribery. Disraeli also attacked the pro-
fession, in the Morning Post, 6 June 1838 (518). He
was obliged to apologize in Queen's Bench.

1079. Benjamin Disraeli, Esquire, M. P. Portrait by
Chalon. With 4 pp. text. Folio. (1841). In series,
"Portraits of eminent Conservatives and statesmen with
genealogical and historical memoirs. Second series."

For Anti-Coningsby. 1844. See 235
For Key to the characters in Coningsby. 1844. See 232
For Strictures on Coningsby. 1844. See 234
For A new key to the characters in Coningsby. 1845.
See 233.

1846

1080. A letter to Benjamin D'Israeli, Esq. M. P. upon the
subject of his recent attack upon the Minister by a bar-
rister London William Pickering 1846
Pp. 15+ (i) Dated 26 May 1846. See 614
A bitter and unscrupulous attack.

1848

1081. The Italian question. A second letter to Lord Palmerston ... with a refutation of certain misrepresentations
by Lord Brougham, Mr. D'Israeli, and the Quarterly Review, respecting the rights of Austria and the Lombardo-
Venetians ... By A. B. Granville ... London: James
Ridgway, 160 Piccadilly. 1848.
Pp. 63+ (1), map facing p. 39
The reference is to Disraeli's speech of 16 Aug.
1848. "It may well excite amazement that (he) ...
should have proved so keen in seizing hold of the first
opportunity that offered of disparaging and casting obloquy
on the countrymen of his nearest ancestors."

1849

1082. Burthens on land. Speech of the Right Hon. Sir
Charles Wood, Bart. Chancellor of the Exchequer, in
the House of Commons, Wednesday, March 14th, 1849,
on the motion of Mr. Disraeli, on local taxation. London: James Ridgway, Piccadilly. 1849.
Pp. 50

1083. Speech of the Chancellor of the Exchequer, on Mr.
D'Israeli's motion, July 2, 1849, on the state of the

nation. London: James Ridgway, Piccadilly. 1849.
Pp. (ii)+ 76. By Sir Charles Wood.

1851

1084. A letter to Benjamin D'Israeli, Esq. M. P. suggesting
an adequate mode of repelling the late Papal Aggression.
By the Rev. Francis Merewether ... London, Rivington
(&c.), 1851.
Pp. 31+ (1)

1085. The case of the farmer and labourer stated, in a
letter to Benjamin D'Israeli, Esq., M. P. London:
James Ridgway, 169, Piccadilly. 1851.
Pp. 50

1852

1086. How should an income tax be levied? Considered in
a letter to the Right Hon. Benjamin Disraeli, M. P.
Chancellor of the Exchequer. By John Gellibrand Hub-
bard, Esq. London: Longman, Brown, Green, and
Longmans. 1852.
Pp. 55+ (1)
Noticed in 343

1087. The true policy for the artisans. A letter to the
Right Hon. Benjamin Disraeli, ... on the means of bet-
tering the condition of the artisans of England. By Iron
Hand. London: C. Mitchell, Red Lion Court, Fleet
Street. MDCCCLII.
Pp. 16

For Mr. D'Israeli's opinions, political and religious ...
1852 See 351
For An answer to some of the opinions and statements
respecting the Jews ... in ... "Lord George Bentinck."
1852. See 352
For The Bank Charter Act in the crisis of 1847; with an
examination of certain passages in Mr. Disraeli's life
of Lord George Bentinck. 1854 See 353

1856

1088. A letter to the Right Hon. Benjamin Disraeli, M. P.
for the County of Buckingham, on the culture of the
field. By Agricola. "Pulverize your soils deeply."

London: Lovell Reeve, Henrietta Street, Covent Garden. 1856.
Pp. 35+ (1)
"These pages are addressed to you, because you have always been the consistent advocate of Agriculture."

1089. Second edition, enlarged. 1860.
Pp. (ii)+ 46

1857

1090. Flaccus-cum-Whimsicalus: being an Account of the supposed mysterious Birth, Travels and Adventures, Sayings and Doings, in Parliament and out of it, of the Right Hon. Benjamin Disraeli. By Hi-Bealdarc-Benali. (Archibald Belaney) London: Hall, 1857.
(Publishers Circular, 1857) Not seen.

1091. The rebellion of India. 1.--Mr. Disraeli's speech reviewed. (&c.) By D. Urquhart. London: D. Bryce, 48, Paternoster Row. 1857.
There are apparently two versions, one of Pp. 31+ (1), containing a second section, Illegality of the acts abolishing native customs...; the other, of Pp. 45+ (1), containing additionally a third section, The wondrous tale of the greased cartridges. Section 1 occupies pp. (3)-22.

1860

1092. Mr. Disraeli and the "Unknown envoy." A letter to the Right Hon. the Lord Viscount Palmerston, ... By Colonel Rathborne ... London: Charles Westerton, 20, St. George's Place, Hyde Park Corner. 1860.
Pp. 30+ (2); colophon on p. (31)

1093. Another edition.
Pp. 31+ (1); colophon on p. (32)

1094. Mr. Disraeli, Colonel Rathborne, and the Council of India. A letter addressed to (list of names) ... in explanation of a petition for enquiry, presented from Colonel Rathborne, on the 9th August, 1859. (For distribution to the Members of the House of Commons.) ... London: 1860.
Pp. (ii)+ 88

147

1095. Supplement to Mr. Disraeli, Colonel Rathborne, and
the Council of India ... London: Charles Westerton ...
1861
Pp. 24

For Disraeli's letters to Rathborne see 705

1863

1096. Fiscal oppression   A letter to the Right Hon. Benjamin Disraeli, M. P. on the operation of the high spirit-
duties William Blackwood and Sons Edinburgh and London   MDCCCLXIII
Pp. 24. Signed "A Scotch distiller."

1865

1097. Disraeli: a lecture delivered in the theatre of the
Medical College, to the educated youth of Bengal.   The
13th April 1865.   By Major G. B. Malleson, Bengal
Staff Corps.   Calcutta: O. T. Cutter, Military Orphan
Press.   1865.
Pp. (iv), 33+ (1).   Buff wrappers

1867

1098. Church rates the patrimony of the poor; being an at-
tempt to set the subject in a new point of view.   A let-
ter to the Right Hon. Benjamin Disraeli, M. P., ... By
Philip Freeman ... London: Joseph Masters ...
MDCCCLXVII
Pp. 16

1099. Gladstone and Disraeli, and the Whig and Tory parties
A lecture delivered in the Assembly Rooms, Leith, By
Magnus C. Rendall, on the 18th November, 1867.   "Not
this man, but Barabbas. Now, Barabbas was a robber."
St. John xviii.   40.   Reprinted from the Leith Burghs
Pilot.
Pp. (ii)+ 6
Liberal.

1100. Letter to the Right Hon. Benjamin Disraeli, M. P.
Chancellor of the Exchequer.   By Edward Romilly, late
chairman of the Board of Audit.   London: William
Ridgway, 169, Piccadilly. W. 1867.
Pp. 48

1101. The Life of the Right Hon. Benjamin Disraeli, M. P. Chancellor of the Exchequer. Containing the triumphant carrying of the Great Reform Bill, 1867 ... Printed and Published by Diprose & Bateman, 13 and 17, Portugal Street, Lincoln's Inn Fields. 1d (1867).
Pp. 8

1868

1102. Pamphlet, page (1) headed, "Mr. Dilke on Mr. Disraeli's manifesto."
Pp. 8. A speech at an election meeting, Chelsea, 21 October 1868.

1103. A letter to the Rt. Hon. Benjamin Disraeli, First Lord of the Treasury. By W. Palmer, Homerton. London: Published by Houlston & Wright, 65, Paternoster Row. (1868)
Pp. 20. Only the second edition seen.

1104. A second letter addressed to the Right Hon. Benjamin Disraeli, First Lord of the Treasury. By W. Palmer, Homerton. (Published by Houlston & Wright, London, n. d. 1868.)
Pp. 16
Chiefly about the Irish Church.

1105. Religious equality in Ireland not inconsistent with the maintenance of our constitution in Church and State. A letter to the Right Hon. B. Disraeli, M. P. by C. G. Prowett ... London: C. Perry, Great Portland Street. MDCCCLXVIII.
Pp. 15+ (1)

1106. Benjamin Disraeli the past and the future   A letter to John Bull, Esq. By a democratic Tory William Blackwood and Sons Edinburgh and London MDCCCLXVIII.
Pp. 35+ (1). By John Skelton

1107. The Irish Church question considered in a letter addressed to the Right Hon. B. Disraeli, M. P. By a Winchester churchman. London: Simpkin, Marshall, & Co. Winchester: Jacob and Johnson, and J. Pamplin.
Pp. 43+ (1). Dated 10 August 1868.

1108. Letter on the present wine duty addressed to the

Right Hon. Benjamin Disraeli, First Lord of the Treasury, by a Portuguese wine grower. London, August 28, 1868.
Pp. (4)

1109. The "No Popery" premier and the Irish people. By an Irish Catholic. "He says--'Follow me.' Follow him! Who is to follow him? or why is anybody to follow him? or where is anybody to follow him to?" Speech of Mr. Disraeli (attacking Sir R. Peel) ... Dublin: sold by Thomas Richardson & Son, 9, Capel-Street, and all booksellers. (1868)
Pp. 40
Disraeli in office recanted the opinions he had previously held about Ireland, and is determined to maintain the Protestant ascendancy. Disraeli is referred to as "the greatest public impostor since the days of Cagliostro."

1110. A word to the clergy, on Mr. Disraeli's letter to the Earl of Dartmouth on the Irish Church Question. To which are added, brief considerations on the subject of mental conversion, and confession of error, viewed in relation more especially to the present age, as an age of transition. ... London: E. Stanford, Charing Cross. 1868.
Pp. (iv)+ 51+ (1). Signed W. S. H.
An attack on the alleged insincerity of Disraeli's declaration of 24 March 1868.

1870

1111. (wrapper) Our Prime Ministers. By Percy Le Clerc London: E. Truelove, 256, High Holborn. 1870
(title-page) Our Prime Ministers. Gladstone Disraeli (Quotation from Carlyle. Chartism.)
Pp. (ii)+ 32+ (2). Only the second edition seen.

For Lothair & its author, by J. Ingle. 1870 see 402
For Lothaw or the adventures of a young gentleman in search of a religion, by Bret Harte. 1871 see 403-404
For "Maccallum" (Lothair) ... 1871 see 405
For The English monarchy and American Republicanism, reply to the speech of Disraeli, by C. A. Watts. 1872 see 636
For "Lothair," the "critics," and the Right Hon. Benjamin Disraeli's "General Preface ..." 1872? see 406

For "Lothair:" its beauties and blemishes. 1873 see
407

1874

1112. A Letter to the Right Hon. B. Disraeli, in reply to
certain statements contained in his speech July 15, 1874,
on "The Public Worship Regulation Bill," as reported
in "The Standard." By the Rev. C. S. Grueber ...
Oxford and London: James Parker and Co. 1874.
Pp. 19+ (1). Dated 21 July 1874
A "Ritualist" point of view.

1113. Second edition

1114. The Public Worship Regulation Bill. Abolish the
Mass; or, "The Mass in masquerade."--Vide Mr. Disraeli's Speech on Second Reading. By the Rev. Robert
Linklater, M.A. London: The Church Printing Company, 13, Burleigh-Street, Strand, W.C.
Pp. 8 n.d. (1874)
"I charge Mr. Disraeli with deliberately using an am-
biguous and unpopular term, likely to inflame the religious hatred and ignorant prejudices of the uninformed,
and using this term for party purposes against his own
better knowledge."

1115. Mrs. Brown and Disraeli. By Arthur Sketchley ...
London: George Routledge and Sons, The Broadway,
Ludgate. n.d. (1874)
Pp. (ii)+ 154. Pictorial boards, with title, "Mrs.
Brown on 'Dizzy.'"
By George Rose.

1875

1116. The Westmeath Coercion Act. Letter addressed by
Dr. Nulty, Bishop of Meath, to Benjamin Disraeli. Dub-
lin, 1875.
The Roman Catholic Bishop.

1117. The quarrel between Mr. Merrypebble & Mr. Bull
showing how Mr. Benjamins became the manager of the
St. Stephen's Co-operative Stores. London: Elliot Stock,
62, Paternoster Row. 1875.
Pp. 16 (?). Pink wrappers
"Mr. Merrypebble," nickname for Gladstone.

1118. The Right Hon. Benjamin Disraeli, Earl of Beaconsfield. Exeter: Printed by C. J. Bellerby, "Flying
Post" Office, Little Queen Street. 1876.
   Pp. (ii)+ 19+ (1). Signed "Ismaël," dated August 22,
1876.
   The copy in the Hughenden Papers, E/VIII/7, has a
manuscript note ascribing it to "Christopher Harris."

1119. By the author of "Ginx's baby." The Blot on the
Queen's Head; or, how little Ben, the head waiter,
changed the sign of the "Queen's Inn" to "Empress Ho-
tel, Limited," and the consequences thereof. By a
guest. London: Strahan & Co., 34, Paternoster Row.
1876.
   Pp. 32. Blue wrappers
   "Advertisement" inserted between wrapper and p. 1,
dated March 25th, stating that this was written and
printed within eleven hours, the author "feeling a deep
repugnance to the Royal Titles Bill, and seeing how
rapidly it was being forced through Parliament."
   By John Edward Jenkins, M. P. The format and
colour of the wrapper vary. The later issues are illustrated. A copy with the legend "100th Thousand" has
been seen.

For a reply see 1201

1120. By the author of "Ginx's baby." Ben changes the
motto a sequel to "The blot on the Queen's Head." By
a guest. Illustrated by Linley Sambourne. Vizetelly &
Co., 10, Southampton Street, Strand. n.d. (1879?)
   Pp. 31+ (1)
   See 1145-46

1121. (Privately printed pamphlet, with MS. note on cover)
Mr. Disraeli's duel with Sir Robert Peel, 1843 to 1846.
Compiled (for private recreation) by Colonel Malleson.
   Printed, Calcutta. 1876?
   (A copy in Hughenden Manor.)

1122. Benjamin D_____ his little dinner. Illustrated by
"Whew." London: Weldon & Co., 15, Wine Office
Court, Fleet Street, E. C. 1876.
   Pp. (vi)+ x+ (ii) advts. + 71+ (ii)advts, 73-76+ (iv) advts.
   Four illus.

1123. Second edition, with (iv) prelims, and illus. differently placed.

1124. Les mystères de M. Disraeli Genève--Bale--Lyon Librairie   H. Georg   1876
   Pp. 8.   Green wrappers.   Signed "Th. de M." Dated 6 Août 1876.

1877

1125. England's policy and peril: a letter to the Earl of Beaconsfield. By Alfred Austin. London: John Murray, Albemarle Street. 1877.
   Pp. 32.   Dated Dec. 7.

1126. The Earl of Beaconsfield. Part I. Novelist. Part II. Politician and statesman. By Matthew Seton ... Reprinted from "Colburn's New Monthly Magazine." London: E. W. Allen, 1877
   Pp. 36.   See 1410

1127. The Earl of Beaconsfield and the Conservative Reform Bill of 1867.   A lecture, Delivered at the Cambridge Reform Club, on Monday, November 13, 1876, by Sedley Taylor ... preceded by a letter to the author from Professor Fawcett, M. P.   Printed and published by the National Press Agency (Limited), 106, Shoe Lane, London, E. C.   1877.
   Pp. 31+ (1)
1128. Second edition
1129. Third edition

1130. Great state trial of Great Britain versus Benjamin Beaconsfield and others before Lord Chief Justice Rhadamanthus and a national jury.   In the supreme court of public opinion, sitting at the Assize town of Ubivis.   Price Sixpence.   Printed from the Notes of the Authorised Reporter of the Court.
   Pp. 24   n. d.   (1877)

1878

1131. The Beaconsfield policy.   An address delivered in connection with the Victoria Street Church Literary Society, Derby, December 11th, 1878.   Also in connection with the Zion Church Young Men's Society, Atter-cliffe, Sheffield, December 16, 1878, by William Crosbie,

153

M. A., LL. B. Published by request. "The Government
of the World is carried on by Sovereigns and Statesmen."
(?)--Earl Beaconsfield. "Kings and Prime Ministers
and all manner of persons, in public and private, diplo-
matising or whatever else they may be doing, should
walk according to the Gospel of Christ, and understand
that this is the law, su-preme over all laws."--Thomas
Carlyle. London: Simpkin, Marshall and Co., Stationers' Hall Court. Derby: Francis Carter, Iron Gate.
Pp. 18+ (2). Dated Dec. 1878

Beaconsfield is attempting to tamper with Constitutional Government, and convert it to "bastard Imperialism" by exalting the sovereign's power. The Act of
1867 was insincere and immoral. Crosbie denounces
the Afghan War as unchristian, and its being carried on
without consulting Parliament as unconstitutional.

1132. De Morgan's tracts for the times. A letter to the
Right Hon. Earl Beaconsfield, Showing the means by
which the lawyer's clerk became Prime Minister, Giving
numerous extracts from the novels of Disraeli, In which
he advocated revolution and republicanism As the only
remedy for a nation's grievances. By John De Morgan,
Twice a State Prisoner in 13 months for advocating the
cause of the oppressed. ... London: 13, Booksellers'
Row, Strand; and all Newsagents.
Pp. 14+ (2). Introduction dated Queen's Prison, Holloway, February, 1878.

1133. Sixth edition. Leeds: Printed and published by De
Morgan & Co., 11, Market Place, Briggate.
Pp. 15+ (1) n. d. (1880)

1134. The impending crisis. Shall we go to war? Pro-
posal for the impeachment of Disraeli. Six millions to
be added to the taxes. The duty of the people. By
John De Morgan, state prisoner. Holloway Castle Gaol,
Jan. 29th, 1878. One penny. Printed and published by
Geo. Howe, 13, Booksellers' Row, Strand, London.
Pp. 6+ (2). Leeds City Libraries.

1135. Lord Beaconsfield. A paper read by T. T. Hayes,
Junr., before the members of the Leigh Liberal Club.
Printed by request. "My Lord, I am on the side of the
Angels." Speech by Mr. Disraeli, at Oxford Price One
Penny. Leigh: The Journal Steam Printing Works: Of-
fice, 3, Market-Place. (Second edition)

154

Pp. 20. See 1161

1136. Third edition. Leigh

1137. Another: London: John Kempster & Co., Limited,
9 & 10, St. Bride's Avenue, Fleet Street, E.C. 1878.
The B.M. copy headed "One hundred and seventy-fifth
thousand."
(There are slight differences in the text of 1135 and
1137. Another Leigh issue (fortieth thousand) known,
and there are probably other variants.)
" 'Vivian Grey' is an excellent guide ... to the principles which have governed Mr. Disraeli's political life
..."

1138. The Beaconsfield sermon preached by the Rev. E.
Paxton Hood, at Cavendish Street Chapel, Manchester,
Sunday, November 18th, 1878. Manchester: Tubbs and
Brook, 11, Market Street.
Pp. 14+ (2)

1139. Second edition
Disraeli's statement that "Sovereigns and statesmen
rule the world" is denounced as a political danger and a
religious fallacy.

1140. The Beaconsfield sermons. No. 2. Act the citizen.
Preached by the Rev. E. Paxton Hood, at Cavendish
Street Chapel, Manchester, Sunday, November 25th,
1878. Manchester: Tubbs and Brook, 11, Market
Street.
Pp. 16
Answers critics of the first sermon: the Christian
minister must necessarily be a political teacher. De-
nounces the Afghan War and the misgovernment of India.
Beaconsfield is "best delineated by himself in 'Vivian
Grey.' " The Queen must be told to get rid of him.

1141. Who is Your Leader? and Whither is He Leading
You? A lecture delivered before the members of the
Liberal Club, Moss Side, Manchester. Peter Spence,
Esq., J.P., in the chair. By the Rev. Paxton Hood.
Manchester: Tubbs and Brook, 11, Market Street. A.
Heywood & Son, Oldham Street. London: A. Heywood
& Son, 12, Holywell Street, Strand.
Pp. 16 n.d. (1879)
Another vigorous attack.

1142. Breakers ahead! or the doomed ship, the determined

captain, and the docile crew. A review of Lord Bea-
consfield's policy. Dedicated, by permission, to the
Right Hon. W. E. Gladstone, M. P. London: G. J.
Palmer, 32, Little Queen Street, W. C. Birmingham:
Martin Billing, Son, & Co., Livery Street.
  Pp. 12. Preface signed H. H. J. (Jenkins), dated
May 1878.
  A violent attack. Disraeli is denounced as a traitor
more interested in maintaining Jewish financial power in
the Ottoman Empire than in the preservation of peace
and justice. "Lord Beaconsfield has ever shown himself
the inveterate foe to freedom, in every shape and form."

1143. Political stone broth: how a clever cook concocted it;
or, Lord Beaconsfield's manipulation of the Tory party.
A Lecture delivered by Archibald Maccullagh to the
Members of St. John's Liberal Club, Manchester, May
6th 1878. J. A. Beith, Esq., President of the Club,
in the Chair. "Oh Politics, thou splendid juggle." Vivian Grey. Abel Heywood & Son, 56 & 58, Oldham Street,
Manchester; and 4 Catherine Street, Strand, London, E. C.
  Pp. 32
  Beaconsfield is not and "never can have been" a Tory,
a statement supported by reference to "Vivian Grey,"
the Wycombe election and his maiden speech. The unprecedented act of bringing Indian troops to Europe is
denounced, and the author hints that Beaconsfield is
seeking a crown for himself.

1144. (wrapper) O Bekonsphild kai oi pelatai tou Beacons-
field et ses clients. Upo Oth. S. Pularinou Ant.
Chaloulos (Ekdotes). En Athenais, ek tou tupographeiou
Nikolaou Rousopoulou. 1878.
  (title-page) O Beskonsphild kai oi pelatai tou
  Pp. 16

1145. Bendizzy's vision: disclosing his secret reasons for
changing the name of the "Queen's Inn." Price threepence. London: Smart & Allen, London House Yard,
E. C.
  Pp. 12 n. d. (1878?)
  A sequel to 1120, but perhaps not also by J. E. Jenkins. Supposed to be written after a Conservative defeat; Beaconsfield regrets having "changed the name."

1146. Ben's dream about the "Schemers of Philistia" and
"Ishmael's noble sons;" with my Lord John Bull's rude

156

remarks. Price threepence. London: Smart & Allen,
London House Yard, E. C.
Pp. 12   n. d. (1878)
Stated to be by the same author as 1145. The Rus-
sians appear as the "Philistines," India as "Goshen" and
the Turks as "Ishmaelites." "John Bull" knows, despite
Beaconsfield, that "the noble sons of Ishmael are the
dirtiest, laziest, vilest set of rascals under the sun,"
friendly only from self-interest, and the maintenance of
whom is too high a price even for the road to India.

1147.   Constantinople, and who is to have it? The great
question answered. A Letter to the Right Hon. the Earl
of Beaconsfield, K. G., by a Conservative watchman.
(Quotation) London: William Ridgway, 169, Piccadilly,
W. 1878.
Pp. 13+ (3). Dated Sept. 1878
Liberal critics are captious, with their mean objec-
tions to the £6m. vote, and Gladstone is traitorous and
seditious. The answer to the question is, "England":
Beaconsfield alone can do it, and put an end to Russian
expansion. Is this meant to be satirical?

1148.   Earl Beaconsfield: a political sketch. (Quotation
from Noctes Ambrosianae) Price one penny. Published
by request. The All Saints' Ward Liberal Association,
Birmingham. 1878.
Pp. 20
The text of a speech. Signed "J. C." The Birming-
ham City Library copy is attributed to the Rev. John
Cuckson.

1149.   Impeachment of Lord Beaconsfield. Two petitions
from the Foreign Affairs Committees against the cession
to Russia of the Sound and the Dardanelles. "There is
no State where one alone commands." Sophocles in An-
tigone. London: Office of the "Diplomatic Review," 31,
Essex-Street, Strand. --September, 1878.
Pp. 8+ 8.   Yellow wrappers

1150.   A letter to Lord Beaconsfield. No publisher; n. d.
(1878)
Pp. 12
A vigorously anti-Russian pamphlet, dealing with
Khiva, Russian massacres of subject peoples, and forced
conversions in Poland, atrocities of which Gladstone
took no notice, though they occurred at the same time

157

as the Bulgarian massacres.

1151. The life of the Earl of Beaconsfield, K. G. "I sit
down now, but the time will come when you will hear
me."--Mr. Disraeli, in 1837. "The Californian Address
to Lord Beaconsfield, recognising his brilliant qualities
as a statesman, illustrates an opinion that prevails over
the whole world."--The Times, in 1878. By a London
journalist. London: Haughton & Co., 10, Paternoster
Row. Price One Penny.
    Pp. (16), paged 4 to 16, the last page unnumbered.
n. d. (1878)

1152. Two imperial policies. London: William Ridgway,
169, Piccadilly, W. 1878.
    Pp. 23+ (1)
    Dated 14 Sept. 1878. The policies are those of Bis-
marck and Beaconsfield.

1153. Weldon's Christmas annual. Fifth season. Dizzi-
ben-Dizzi; or, The orphan of Bagdad. Contents: Intro-
ductory and dedicatory. Dimod the genie; or, the third
catch. The orphan's adventures in the cavern of peril.
Ben-Dizzi's education; or, the first lesson. Albione and
Caledon; or, the enchanted country. Ursa major; or, the
great bore. The seed and its fruit; or, the new revolu-
tion. The black palace of Ebene; or, Agib the evil one.
Dimod and the harridan; or, the missed opportunity.
With five full-page and numerous other illustrations.
London: Weldon & Co., 9, Southampton Street, Strand,
W. C. 1878.
    Pp. x+ 62, pl.

1879

1154. Lord Beaconsfield and the Irish Catholic University
scheme; or, An Alliance between Conservatism and Ul-
tramontanism considered as a Party Move and an Imperial Policy. A letter addressed to the Right Hon. the
Earl of Beaconsfield by the Rev. Leslie Marlborough
Carter ... "Et tu Brute." Dublin: Hodges, Foster,
and Figgis ... 1879.
    Pp. 8. Blue wrappers

1155. Portraits comparés des hommes d'état contemporains
I Mr Gladstone & Lord Beaconsfield par J. -H. du
Vivier. Bruxelles Gay et Doucé, éditeurs. 1879

Pp. vi+ 28+ (2)

1156. Lord Beaconsfield and his foreign policy. By Alexander Rumer... London: Abel Heywood and Son, 4, Catherine Street, Strand. Manchester: 56 and 58, Oldham Street. 1879.
Pp. (ii)+ 8+ (2). Grey wrappers
"The advent of the present Ministry brought forward a policy the chief feature of which was a promulgation of Personal, Imperialistic, and Autocratic Government."

1157. The book of Benjamin. Appointed to be read in households. London: Charles Watts, 84, Fleet Street, E. C.
Pp. 31+ (1). Grey wrappers n. d. (1879?)
By A. Capel Shaw.
H. & L., VI, 296

1158. (Another issue) containing a "Preface to fifth and revised edition," dated Birmingham, February 6th, 1879. This refers to the "rapid sale of four editions." The sub-title is, Appointed to be read by the electors of England; this phrase appears on the wrapper of the first edition.
The British Museum has a "Seventh edition," with the Preface, dated Feb. 1879, to the fifth edition.

1159. The second book of Benjamin. A record of things past, present, and to come. "Benjamin shall ravin as a wolf."--Gen. XLIX. 27. London: Charles Watts, 84, Fleet Street, E. C.
Pp. 23+ (1). Blue wrappers n. d.

1160. Whom to follow William Ewart Gladstone, M. P. "I never did repent for doing good Nor shall not now" Merchant of Venice or the Earl of Beaconsfield, K. G. "O Eastern Star! Peace! Peace!" Antony and Cleopatra Edinburgh: Andrew Elliot London: Simpkin, Marshall, & Co. 1879
Pp. (ii?)+ 132
Liberal. Life of Gladstone by George Smith; Life of Disraeli by Sir George Adam Smith. (H. & L., VI, 232)

1161. Lord Beaconsfield: a lecture delivered by Joseph Snape, Esq., at the Cheetham Conservative Club, Manchester, March 14th, 1879 ... Salford: Printed and

Published by the Salford Steam Printing Company, 54, Chapel Street.
Pp. 37+ (3). An answer to 1135

1162. Grocers' licences: a letter to the Right Hon. the Earl of Beaconsfield K. G. , giving the evidence and opinions of Chief Constables and Superintendents of Police. By James Taylor, General Secretary to The National Union for the Suppression of Intemperance. November, 1878. Manchester: Samuel M. Strong, Printer, 84, Market Street.
Pp. 15+ (1)
(Another issue), dated January 1879, published from National Union Offices: 40, Victoria Street, Manchester.

1163. Words of Warning for Englishmen. No. XVI. The Truth about the Wreath. Lord Beaconsfield on his trial before the working men of England. A Letter Addressed to the Working Classes by the Chairman of the People's Tribute. (Quotation) Recipients of this Pamphlet are requested to promote its distribution among the Working Classes. The profits are allotted to Charities. Price One Penny. Published by Abel Heywood & Son, Manchester and London.
Pp. 16+ (4). Dated Ryde, Aug. 1879
The author, Edward Tracy Turnerelli, had collected 52, 800 pennies from the working classes to present a gold laurel wreath to Beaconsfield. This was purchased and exhibited, but Beaconsfield refused to accept it, insinuating that Turnerelli had been badgering him for political preferment. Turnerelli denies this, stating that he had worked for the Conservative cause for many years at great expense without expecting reward. See his "Memories of a life of toil, " 1884, 184-231.

1164. Words of warning to Englishmen. Seventeenth and last. Tracy's death and burial. His last will, his portrait, and a photo of The Beaconsfield wreath. A postmortem memento. Edited by one of his executors ...
Pp. 18+ (2)
Contains extracts from "The Times, " 11 April 1879, on the gold laurel wreath, and other press extracts. Turnerelli was not, in fact, dead.

1165. The apparition of the late Lord Derby to Lord Beaconsfield. By Politicus. Manchester: Tubbs and Brook, 11, Market Street. Price One Penny. n. d. (1879?)

Pp. 16

Derby (the 14th Earl, who died in 1869), is supposed
to appear to Beaconsfield, who is reading an optimistic
despatch from Constantinople. Beaconsfield boasts that
he could make the Commons vote its own abolition, and
create an absolute monarchy; that he preserves the shad-
ow of liberty to keep the people happy. He is sick of
irresponsible chatter about the Constitution, especially
from the present Lord Derby; the trade depression is
cyclical, not the fault of the government. Derby's ghost
denounces a vacillating Eastern policy, the destruction of
confidence and trade, high taxation and the poverty resulting from the government's policy.

1166. Lord Beaconsfield: a sketch. With an account of
his quarrels with O'Connell, Hume, Peel, etc. Dash
the proud trickster in his gilded car; Bare the mean
heart that lurks beneath a star.--Pope. Price Twopence.
Published by Charles Watts, 84, Fleet Street, London,
E. C.
Pp. 32   n. d. (1879)

1167. (Another), with the quotation, "He asked me what was
my prinserpuls? 'I hain't got enny,' said I--'not a prin-
serpul. Ime in the Show Bizniss.' "--Artemus Ward.

1168. The Premier's defence of his administration. An Appeal to the Justice of the British Nation. Descends du
haut des cieux, auguste Vérité! Répands sur mes écrits
ta force et ta clarité: * * * C'est à toi de montrer aux
yeux des nations Les coupables effets de leurs divisions.
Voltaire. John Hodges, 24, King William Street, Charing
Cross, W. C.   1879.
Pp. 31+ (1)
An ironic review of the ministry.

1169. Squire Bull, and his bailiff, Benjamin. A political
allegory. Abel Heywood & Son, 56 & 58, Oldham Street,
Manchester; and 4, Catherine Street, Strand, London.
Pp. 15+ (1). Blue wrappers   n. d. (1879)

1880

1170. How Ben behaved himself. "Which things are an Al-
legory." By F. Bickerstaffe Drew ... London: W.
Ridgway, 169, Piccadilly, W.   1880.
Pp. 32

161

"Lady Gengulpha" advertises for a new bailiff. Mr.
Ben Dizzy, a youthful sixty, appreciates the beautiful--
in the peerage, and compliments Gengulpha on "Our
strife in the Islands" as second only to the Bible. He
did nothing about the land, ignored business, and passed
an unsatisfactory "Bill to put down Ritualism"; he revelled
in Turkish atrocities, but refused to attack Russia. His
administration "had been a childish, vulgar game of loud
talking, swagger and idleness."

1171. Beaconsfield the immaculate. A reply. "The Won-
derful Juggler."--Kirke White. "What a fool Honesty
is! and Trust, his sworn brother, a very simple gentleman!" Winter's Tale. London: F. E. Longley, 39,
Warwick Lane, E. C.
Pp. (32). n. d. (1880). By J. P. Stafford. (H. &
L., I, 182)
None previous to fourth edition seen.
The Preface consists of extracts from a bitterly hostile article in the Contemporary Review for December
1879. (1419). There are 12 caricatures, each with
comments opposite, referring to various episodes, including Burma, Zululand, the Turnerelli wreath, and
Conservative finance.
"To the jaundiced eye of the Tories, every foreign
potentate is but the puppet of the Russian power. We
might even suppose, according to their perverted view,
that Russian emissaries provoked the Zulu war ... Lord
Beaconsfield closely resembles the mad-brained Don
Quixote, who, led away by his wild imagination, was
continually discovering evil where none existed, and
fighting against fancied foes."
A "reply" to "New gleanings from Gladstone," by G.
Stronach, published 1879. See also Stafford's "The battle of the genii" (1736).

1172. Fifth edition

1173. Bits of Beaconsfield   A new series of Disraeli's
Curiosities of literature. "People have declined to
think of morality in connection with him." Fortnightly
Review   Abel Heywood & Son, Manchester and London.
Pp. (32).   Brown wrappers   n. d. (1880)
Satirical plates, with prose and verse fragments.

1174. Watts' political series. No. 1. Lord Beaconsfield's
Imperialism: a trial and sentence. "When vice prevails

and impious men bear sway, The post of honour is a
private station." London: Watts & Co., 84, Fleet
Street, E. C.
    Pp. 24   n. d.   (1880)   Blue wrappers

1175.   Lord Beaky's lies, and England's allies.   By Jif.
    (Quotations) London: Charles Watts, 84, Fleet Street.
    Pp. 8   n. d.   (1880)
    A bitter attack, especially on foreign and colonial
    policy.   Includes "An appeal to Dean Stanley not to al-
    low the erection of a memorial to Prince Louis Napoleon
    in Westminster Abbey."

1881

1176.   Lessons from the life of the Earl of Beaconsfield,
    K. G.   A funeral sermon Preached on April 24th, 1881,
    at St. John's Church, Longsight, by the Rev. J. A.
    Atkinson ... Manchester: John Heywood, Excelsior
    Buildings, Ridgefield; and 11   Paternoster Buildings,
    London.   1881.
    Pp. 12
    Text, Esther, ix. 4.   Various characteristics of Dis-
    raeli--Perseverance, Imperturbable good temper, Singu-
    lar self-control, Power of influencing others, and Influ-
    ence in the Commons--are taken to point a sermon
    chiefly concerned with an attack on immorality, particu-
    larly in dance halls and political clubs.

1177.   A sermon preached on Sunday, April 24, 1881, on
    occasion of the death of Lord Beaconsfield.   By the Rev.
    Horatio Bentley ...   London: Richard Bentley and Son
    ... 1881.
    Pp. 16

1178.   The life and career of the Earl of Beaconsfield: a
    paper Read before the New Southgate and Friern-Barnet
    Conservative Association.   By Arthur Hancock, (One of
    the Vice-Presidents).   "Circumstances are beyond the
    control of man, but his conduct is in his own power."
    Benjamin D'Israeli, 1832.   Printed at the Request and
    for the Benefit of the Association.   1881.
    Pp. 28.   Dated June, 1881.   Red wrappers

1179.   A sketch of the public career of the late Right Hon.
    Earl of Beaconsfield, K. G., by Frederick Arthur Hynd-
    man, ... (Quotations) London: W. H. Allen & Co., 13

Waterloo Place. 1881.
 Pp. iv+ 83+ (1). Pink wrappers
 "Dedicated to the Conservative working man. "

1180. Im Vaterhause Lord Beaconsfield's. Von Dr. Ad.
 Jellinek. Wien, 1881.
 Pp. 33+ (1)

1181. Some personal recollections of the later years of the
 Earl of Beaconsfield K. G. Reprinted, with additions
 from 'The Times' William Blackwood and Sons Edinburgh and London MDCCCLXXXI.
 Pp. 37+ (3). Purple wrappers
 By Lady Janetta Manners, later Duchess of Rutland.
 Dedicated to the Queen.
1182. Third edition
1183. Fourth edition

1184. The late Earl of Beaconsfield's First Constituency.
 Early Speeches and Incidents of the Contest. (Reprinted
 from the "Maidstone and Kent County Standard" of April
 23rd, 1881.) Maidstone: "Standard" Office, 94, Week
 Street.
 Pp. 14

1185. The life and work of Benjamin Disraeli (Earl of Bea-
 consfield). Reprinted from the "Times" London: 8,
 Falcon Court, 32, Fleet Street, E. C.
 Pp. 16. (Portrait on front cover)

1186. A memoir of the Earl of Beaconsfield reprinted from
 'The Times' by permission London Longmans, Green
 and Co. 1881
 Pp. 83+ (1). Blue wrappers
 See 1270

1187. Memorials of Lord Beaconsfield. Reprinted from
 "The Standard. " With a portrait. London: Macmillan
 and Co. 1881.
 Pp. (viii)+ 248+ (6 advts.), frontis.
 (678) Nation, 33, 278-79 (Reviewed with 676)

1188. Police News Edition. Life and death of the Earl of
 Beaconsfield (portrait). Price One Penny London: G.
 Purkess, 286, Strand, W. C.
 Pp. 16

164

1189. The late Lord Beaconsfield. His life and career.
Leeds: printed and published by the Yorkshire Conser-
vative Newspaper Company, Albion Street. 1881.
   Pp. 48. Leeds City Libraries.

1882

1190. Lord Beaconsfield. A sketch. By Captain Richard
F. Burton.
   Pp. 12   No publisher, n. d. (1882)
   Attacks the pro-Turkish policy.

1191. The Life of the Earl of Beaconsfield, author, statesman, premier. (Ward & Lock's penny books for the
people. Biographical series, no. 2.) (1882). Signed
G. R. E. Not seen.

1883

1192. This is the Tree that Ben Raised: a political satire.
(Illustrated) Dedicated (without permission) to "The G.
O. M. " by J. F. T. W. Price sixpence. London: Simpkin,
Marshall and Co. Chelmsford: "Essex Weekly News"
office. And of all booksellers.
   Pp. 32. Pictorial wrapper   n. d. (1883)
   Pro-Disraeli

1884

1193. An incredible story, originally told in a letter to The
Right Hon. the Earl of Beaconsfield, K. G., then Prime
Minister of England. Re-written and further continued.
(Quotation) Fourth edition. 1884.
   Pp. 30+ (2). No publisher or printer.
   City of London Guildhall Library. Ascribed to Sir
Thomas James Nelson, the City Solicitor. No other
edition seen. On the London sewage question in the
1870s.

1885

1194. Lord Beaconsfield's Irish policy   Two essays on
Ireland by Sir John Pope Hennessy, K. C. M. G.   These
pages are inscribed with his permission to the Right
Hon. Lord Randolph Churchill, M. P. London   Kegan
Paul, Trench & Co., 1, Paternoster Square   1885
   Pp. (iv)+ 86+ (2). Grey wrappers
   Reprinted from 1452

1195.   (On p. (3)) Lord Beaconsfield's ghost: a political
colloquy between Lord Beaconsfield & Lord Dolly Windbag.
Lord Dolly Windbag is clearly meant for Lord Randolph Churchill.
(On wrapper) Lord Beaconsfield's ghost: (Caricature,
Churchill and the ghost) by G. W. Norma.   Author of
"A political humbug. "   "There is no act of treachery or
meanness of which a political party is not capable; for
in politics there is no honour. "--Lord Beaconsfield.
(Vivian Grey, iv. , 1) "Discriminations between wholesome
and unwholesome victories are idle and unpractical.   Ob-
tain the victory, leave the wholesomeness or unwhole-
someness to critics ...   Certainly any political victory
in which Whigs bear a part must be to the last degree
unwholesome and scrofulous. "--Lord Randolph Churchill.
(Fortnightly Review, May, 1883) "Get money--honestly
if you can--but get money. "--Old Saying.   Manchester:
Abel Heywood & Son, 56 & 58, Oldham Street.   London:
Henry Darbyshire & Co. , 9, Red Lion Court, Fleet
Street.
Pp. 20+ (4)   n. d. (1886)
1196.   Second edition

For Ben D'Ymion and other parodies, 1887 see 452
For Lothair's children, 1890 see 408

1895

1197.   Lamartine et Lord Beaconsfield Étude politique par
Alexandre de Haye Extrait de la Nouvelle Revue Inter-
nationale.   Paris   Librairie Cotillon ... 1895
Pp. 22.   Green wrappers.   See 1464

1899

1198.   Lord Beaconsfield, K. G. , (Disraeli), as a writer,
from a political view.   Specially inscribed to Members
of the Primrose League ... By J. A. P.   Beverley ...
Pp. 52   n. d. (1899)
By J. A. Pitman.   Apparently a lecture frequently
delivered under the auspices of the Primrose League.

1199. (P. 1) Disraeli. By J. A. Lovat-Fraser, M. A.,
Barrister-at-Law. (foot of p. 8) "Barry Docks News,"
Barry Docks.
Pp. 8   n. d.   (1901)

For The Earl of Beaconsfield, K. G.   Keys to the famous
characters delineated in his historical romances ...
1904 see 851
For The allusions in Lothair, 1905 see 409

Verse

1200.   A letter to the Right Hon. Benjamin Disraeli, M. P.
Forti nihil difficile.   London: John Camden Hotten, 74
& 75, Piccadilly.   1869.
Pp. 28+ (4), including wrappers: paged 8-28
By Mortimer Collins.   (H. & L., III, 309)
"Born Tories to astound and Whigs to enrage."

For "Lothair," the "critics," and the Right Hon. Benjamin Disraeli's "General Preface ...," 1872? see 406

1201.   Ginx's "blot" removed; or, "Queen-Empress" vindi-
cated.   Showing how Big Billy, after demolishing the
Irish Church, laid violent hands on the British State.
By J. M. (Redivivus).   London: Hardwicke & Bogue,
192, Piccadilly, W.   1876.
Pp. 24

1202.   Third edition
See 1119

1203.   Beaconsfield: a mock-heroic poem, and Political
Satire.   London: Abel Heywood & Son, Catherine Street,
Strand.   Manchester: Oldham Street.   MDCCCLXXVIII.
Pp. 51+ (1).   Dedicated to Bright.

1204.   (Noted in Westminster Review, 110, 566)

1205.   The premier's dream: a poem, by "Alguien."   Price,
Two-pence.   London: E. W. Allen, Ave Maria Lane.

Pp. 22+ (2)

1206. The Pretty Little Coronet and Great Big B! (1878).
A single folded sheet, c. 140x9 cm., with 10 drawings
and satirical verses on one side. "When I was a youth
I plied my pen."

1207. Imperial Ben. A Jew d'Esprit. By James George
Ashworth. London: Remington and Co., 5 Arundel
Street, Strand, W. C. 1879.
   Pp. (viii)+ 88. Blue cloth

1208. "Contarini Fleming." A psychological satire. Dedicated to the Right Hon. the Earl of Beaconsfield, Premier of England, sine permissu. By Isaac McTimon.
"Ridendo mores castigat." (London) John Hodges (&c.)
1879.
   Pp. 22+ (2)
   "No apology need be offered for borrowing this title
from Lord Beaconsfield. His Lordship cannot reasonably
object, seeing that the 'borrowing' is fairly acknowledged.
This is more than novel-writing, panegyric-pronouncing
statesmen at all times do."

1209. Beaconsfield ballads, or Dover's powders in delect-
able doses for digestions disordered by "Liberal" diet.
A collection of political lyrics, ballads, and epigrams.
Price threepence   Dover: Published at the office of
the "Dover Standard" ... 1880 ...
   Pp. 12. Green wrappers. Attributed to the Rev. J.
B. McCaul.

1210. Dissolution of Parliament. A statesman's adventures
in search of a majority: A Political Squib. A. W. G.
E. & S. Livingstone, Edinburgh. William Porteous &
Co., Glasgow. Abel Heywood & Son, Manchester.
   Pp. 37+ (1). Yellow wrappers   n. d. (1880)

1211. Ben-dizzy the bold! A Retrospect, in Verse. By a
true Briton. Dedicated to the electors of England. "It
is not Radicalism, it is not the revolutionary spirit of
the Nineteenth Century, which has consigned 'another
place' to illustrious insignificance: it is Conservatism
and a Conservative Dictator." Disraeli--1845. B.
Buckmaster, 46 Newington Butts, S. E.
   Pp. 16   n. d. (1880)

1212. Jingo Bolero! Or, the Tory idol. A satirical poem
by P. Clarke. One Penny. London: J. Heywood,
Paternoster Square. Manchester: J. Heywood, Ridge-
field, John Dalton Street. Ashton-under-Lyne: Griffin
& Sheard, Printers and Stationers, 130, Stamford Street.
Pp. 7+ (1). n. d. (1880?) Manchester City Libraries.
See 1234

1213. On Lord Beaconsfield, the Queen, and Time. Com-
posed by Thomas Baker. Brighton (1881) s. s. Verses,
beginning with an acrostic on "Lord Beaconsfield."

1214. (Another edition). Spontaneous thoughts ... on Lord
Beaconsfield, the Queen, and Time. (1890?)

1215. In Memoriam Benjamin Disraeli, Earl of Beaconsfield (by) Samuel K. Cowan. Raphael Tuck & Sons. A
card [see illustrations, from either side of a card
measuring 16 1/2x11 cm.].

1216. In Memoriam. (Verses on) The Earl of Beaconsfield (By Edwin Drew) (London, 1881, Ptd., Welham &
Gillingham, 282, Kentish Town Road). A card.

1217. Beaconsfield. Buried at Hughenden, April 26th, 1881.
Published by the author, 17, Oxford Street. Signed T.
G. P. (Potter) s. s.
"At Hughenden to-day, King Death doth keep/High
Court. There lamentations true and deep/Prevail; and
of all that vast mournful host/Not one will lack regret
for Statesman lost ..."

1218. Poetic biographical sketches of Lord Beaconsfield.
By Leinad. Under the patronage of Chas. Stuart Wort-
ley, Esq., M. P. Copyright. Published by Leonard &
Son, Sheffield.
Pp. 112. (1882?) Sheffield City Libraries.

1219. Poetic Biographical Sketches of Earl Beaconsfield.
By Daniel Bryan. Under the patronage of Charles
Stuart Wortley, Esq., M. P. Copyright. Published by
Messrs. Pawson and Brailsford, Sheffield. London:
Simpkin, Marshall & Co.
Pp. (iv)+ 112. Red cloth. Preface dated Jan. 1882.

1220. Primroses An elegy in four cantos written in memory
of the late Earl of Beaconsfield, K. G. with which are

IN MEMORIAM
BENJAMIN DISRAELI, EARL OF BEACONSFIELD.
Died April 19TH 1881.

This and opposite page (see entry 1215);

Honour and Peace! With both his spirit now
Is crowned: from his beloved England's heart
When shall the honour of his name depart
Or Time remove one laurel from his brow?
O great and gentle spirit! such as thou
Know not of Death: Death is but honoured peace
When warrior souls from glorious warring cease
And to his call, like heroes calmly bow!
Even as thy grave is wreathed with immortelles,
Twined by thine Indian Empress, England's Queen,
So in our hearts thy name immortal dwells
And grateful England keeps thy memory green:
And year by year, thine honoured grave above
Lays the first springtide primrose of her love!

COPYRIGHT.   SAMUEL K. COWAN. M.A

Two sides of a memorial card, 16 1/2 x 11 cm.

incorporated 'The songs of the people' Griffith and
Farran West corner of St. Paul's Churchyard, London
1884
Pp. (ii)+ xii+ 122

1221. Saturnalia or Beaconsfield at the vote of censure by
U. P. London: W. H. Allen & Co., 13 Waterloo Place,
Pall Mall. S. W. 1885.
Pp. 14

1222. The Beaconsfield Acrostic. 1886. In Memoriam.
A card with verses on "Benjamin Disraeli," and a photograph, published by S. Newbold, Liverpool.

1223. Beaconsfield: a national poem. Price Threepence.
Published by Joseph Boulton & Co. Limited, Finsbury,
E. C.
Pp. (4). Dated April 19, 1890.

1224. Benjamin Disraeli. Earl of Beaconsfield, K. G. In
Upwards of 100 Cartoons from the Collection of "Mr.
Punch." Punch Office, 85, Fleet Street, London.
(1878).
29 cm., (112) pp.

1225. (a new edition, with 113 cartoons, 1881.)
28 cm., 128 pp.
"Punch" was generally anti-Disraeli.

1226. Benjamin Disraeli through the eyes of Punch, by M.
P. York. Corby Historical Society, 1969.
Pp. (iv)+ 38+ (2)

1227. The Right Hon. Benjamin Disraeli, Earl of Beacons-
field, K. G., from Judy's point of view, as shewn in her
cartoons during the last ten years. London: "Judy"
Office, 99 Shoe Lane, Fleet Street, E. C.
Pp. 150. Cartoons, 41x27 cm. March 1880.
Very pro-Disraeli.

Nos. 1228-1233 are noted from copies in the Gladstone papers in the British Museum. The Add. MSS. numbers are given.

1228. (4) pp. "Sold by G. W. Mee, Bookseller, 3 High
Street, High Wycombe. Printed at the "Guardian Office,"
Wycombe." c. 1864 (44, 403 f. 118)

P. (1) headed "Mr. Disraeli," has the story of his radical candidature in Wycombe in 1831 (sic). Disraeli made a speech from the figure of a lion above the portico of the "Red Lion." "About a month ago ... the lion's head fell off from sheer decay." On pp. (2) and (3), verses, "Dizzey & the Wycombe lion, who has lost his head ..."

1229. A crudely printed broadsheet headed "Dizzy's lament," with verses,
> "Oh dear! oh dear! what shall I do?
> They call me saucy Ben the Jew..."
n. d. (1868) (44, 421 f. 229)

1230. A single sheet, headed "Imperium et libertas." Verses, signed "J. R., Glasgow, 19th March, 1880." Anti-Disraeli (44, 462 f. 215)

1231. A single sheet, headed "The song of King Benjamin: a ballad for the times."
Verses, signed "An Ipswich elector," with MS. note "Rob. Seager." (1880)
Anti-Disraeli (44, 462 f. 229)

1232. A single yellow sheet, headed "The despot, Lord B. Air--'Bonnie Dundee.'"
Verses, with MS. note, "With the Author's respects (aged 16)." (1880) (44, 462 f. 299)

1233. A single sheet, "In Memoriam 19th April 1883." Signed "G. G. P., Conservative Club, Cheltenham." (44, 480 f. 204)

> "Disraeli! loving genius--Sovereign servant--man's master,
> Thy spirit lives through time and space--eternal;
> And Wisdom claims thee as her brightest son.
> E'en when time ends and vast eternity begins,
> Thy name on Angels' lips shall ever pass along!
> Duty--thy sphere! whilst yet another left her path,
> Hath made the page of History beam with loving light.
> Bent on thy country's good with noble enterprise,
> Thy name stands forth in purest radiance bright,
> And thy opponent, in his old age, sinks to destruction."

Perhaps the most extravagant claim made for Disraeli's enduring fame.

1234. Great peace song, by Peter Clarke, of Bolton, as op-
posed to the great war song, by Mr. Williams, of London. J. Mather, Steam Printer, Bookbinder, &c., 111,
Deansgate, Bolton.
s. s. (1878?) Manchester City Libraries.
It seems likely that this is by the same author as
1212.

Articles in books

1854

1235. Gilfillan, George: Benjamin Disraeli in A third gallery of portraits, Edinburgh, 1854, 402-16, and in
Galleries of literary portraits, Edinburgh, 1856, I,
326-33
(Review of Tancred and of 745)

1856

1236. Thackeray, William Makepeace: Codlingsby, by D.
Shrewsberry, Esq. in Miscellanies, prose and
verse, II, 1856, 429-41 (in series of papers
"Novels by eminent hands"), and frequently re-
printed.
See 318

1858

1237. Jeaffreson, John Cordy: The Right Hon. Benjamin
Disraeli in Novels and novelists, 1858, II, 221-61

1859

1238. Maddyn, Daniel Owen: Mr. Disraeli in Chiefs of
parties, 1859, II, 219-41

1861

1239. Ritchie, J. Ewing: The Right Hon. Benjamin Disraeli in Modern Statesmen, 1861, 56-69, and, with
minor alterations, in British senators, 1869, 12-25

1240. Kebbel, Thomas Edward: Mr. Disraeli, May 1860 in
Essays upon history and politics, 1864, 326-62

1868

1241. Kebbel, Thomas Edward: Mr. Disraeli in English
statesmen, 1868, 153-74. (Differs from 1240). A
revised version of 1381.

1869

1242. Althaus, Friedrich: Benjamin Disraeli in Englische
Charakterbilder, Berlin, 1869, I, 87-164

1870

1243. Friswell, J. Hain: The Right Hon. B. Disraeli in
Modern men of letters, 1870, 195-240

1872

1244. Reid, Sir Thomas Wemyss: Mr. Disraeli in Cabinet
portraits, 1872, 1-16

1873

1245. Hill, Frank Harrison: Mr. Disraeli in Political portraits ... reprinted from "The Daily News, " 1873,
22-38

1246. Maginn, William: Benjamin Disraeli in A Gallery of
illustrious literary characters (1830-1838) ... re-
published from "Fraser's Magazine" ..., 1873,
98-100. With portrait. The original text (1373)
is reprinted, and "Notes, " by the editor, William
Bates, added. The book is dedicated to Disraeli.
See 1259

1247. Cartoon Portraits and Biographical Sketches of men
of the day. The drawings by Frederick Waddy.
London, Tinsley, 1873, 38-45, with a cartoon.
(Second edition, 1874) From Once a week.

1874

1248. "The National Portrait Gallery" (Cassell), 1874, I, 9-16. (With portrait.)

1875

1249. Higginson, Thomas Wentworth: Mr. Disraeli in English statesmen, New York, 1875, 35-70

1876

1250. Stephen, Sir Leslie: Mr. Disraeli's novels in Hours in a library, 1876, II, 344-93. See 1405

1877

1251. Yates, Edmund H.: The Earl of Beaconsfield at Hughenden in Celebrities at home, 1st ser., 1877, 69-76. (Reprinted from The World.)

1879

1252. Collins, Mortimer: The literary character of Mr. Disraeli in Pen sketches, 1879, II, 1-50. See 1394

1880

1253. Reid, Sir Thomas Wemyss: Lord Beaconsfield in Politicians of today, 1880, I, 37-52 (differs from 1244).

1254. Towle, George M.: Beaconsfield in Certain men of mark, Boston, 1880, 95-123. See 1428

1881

1255. Bagehot, Walter: Mr. Disraeli as a member of the House of Commons in Biographical studies, 1881, 364-68. See 1369, 1406

1882

1256. Bauer, Bruno: Disraeli's romantischer und Bismarck's socialistischer Imperialismus. Chemnitz, 1882. Chapters IV and V are particularly concerned with Disraeli.

1257. Greg, William Rathbone: The great twin brethren (Disraeli and Napoleon III), in Miscellaneous essays, 1882, I, 149-60. (Probably written in 1866.)

1258. Scherer, Edmond: Endymion in Études sur la littérature contemporaine, v. 7, 1882, 70-83, and translated in Essays on English literature, 1891, 208-20

1883

1259. Bates, William: Benjamin D'Israeli in The Maclise portrait-gallery of "Illustrious literary characters," with memoirs ... 1883, 164-72. See 1246. With the same portrait, but the original text (1373) is not reprinted; the 1883 text is an expanded version of the "Notes" in 1246.

1260. Las Alménas, F. X. de Palacio y García de Velasco, count de: Benjamin Disraeli in Los grandes caractéres políticos contemporáneos, Madrid, 1883, I, 1-102

1261. Skelton, Sir John: Disraeli in Essays in history and biography, 1883, 240-59

1886

1262. Harrison, Frederic: The romance of the peerage: Lothair in The choice of books, 1886, 147-71 and in Modern English essays, edited by Ernest Rhys, 1922, I, 190-215. See 379

1263. Kebbel, Thomas Edward: Lord Beaconsfield in A History of Toryism ... 1886, 333-401. See 1455

1264. Smith, G. Barnett: The Earl of Beaconsfield in The Prime Ministers of Queen Victoria, 1886, 287-332

1889

1265. Geffcken, F. H.: Beaconsfield in The British Empire ..., translated by S. J. Macmullan, 1889, 237-66

1266. (Parodies of Disraeli's novels) in Hamilton, Walter, editor: Parodies of the works of English and

American authors, vol. 6, 1889, 238-42. (Of Lothair, Tancred (3), Sybil (2) and Endymion) see 403-404, 318, 323-324, 284-285, 451-452

1267. Philipson, David: Disraeli's "Coningsby" and "Tancred" in The Jew in English fiction, Cincinnati, 1889, 103-21

1890

1268. Henley, William Ernest: Disraeli in Views and reviews, 1890, 20-32

1893

1269. Espinasse, Francis: Lord Beaconsfield and his minor biographer in Literary recollections and sketches, 1893, 407-26. See 1467

1270. "Lord Beaconsfield": The Times obituary and leading article, April 20, 1881 in Eminent persons, biographies reprinted from "The Times," II, 1893, 292-324, and the leading article in History through "The Times," selected by Sir James Marchant, 1937, 264-68. See 1186

1894

1271. Gregory, Sir William: Disraeli in Autobiography, 1894, 90-105

1895

1272. Harrison, Frederic: Benjamin Disraeli in Studies in early Victorian literature, 1895, 91-111. Reprints 1468 with verbal revisions.

1273. Skelton, Sir John: Mainly about Disraeli in Table-talk of Shirley, 1895, 241-60

1896

1274. Esher, Reginald Brett, 2nd Viscount: The Queen and Lord Beaconsfield in The yoke of empire, 1896, 117-51

1275. Russell, George W. E.: Lord Beaconsfield in Collections and recollections, by one who has kept a diary, 1898, 295-306. Reprinted from The Manchester Guardian, 1897; frequently reprinted.

1276. Zangwill, Israel: The primrose sphinx in Dreamers of the ghetto, 1898, 383-87

1900

1277. Clarke, Sir Edward: Lord Beaconsfield and the Tory Party in Public speeches, 1890-1900, 1900, 288-92

1278. Whibley, Charles: Disraeli the younger in Pageantry of life, 1900, 239-69

1901

1279. Garnett, Richard: Shelley and Lord Beaconsfield in Essays of an ex-librarian, 1901, 101-25. See also 807, 1457

1280. Muret, Maurice: Lord Beaconsfield, un homme d'état israélite in L'Esprit juif, essai de psychologie ethnique, Paris, 1901, 135-68

1903

1281. Bryce, James: Benjamin Disraeli, Earl of Beaconsfield in Studies in contemporary biography, 1903, 1-68. (Revision of 1445).

1282. Cazamian, Louis: Disraeli, le torysme social in Le roman social en Angleterre, 1830-1850, 1903, 315-79

1905

1283. Birrell, Augustine: Disraeli ex relatione Sir William Fraser in In the name of the Bodleian, 1905, 150-56, and in Collected essays and addresses, 1880-1920, I, 1922, 382-88. See 822

1906

1284. Lord, Walter Frewen: Lord Beaconsfield in The
       mirror of the century, 1906, 203-30

1285. "Melville, Lewis": Benjamin Disraeli in Victorian
       novelists, 1906, 19-51. See 1484

1907

1286. Kebbel, Thomas Edward: Lord Beaconsfield in Lord
       Beaconsfield and other Tory memories, 1907, 1-70.
       Reprinted, with revisions, from The Standard.

1287. Walpole, Sir Spencer: Mr. Disraeli in Studies in
       biography, 1907, 91-140

1909

1288. Jackson, Holbrook: Benjamin Disraeli in Great Eng-
       lish novelists, 1909, 181-214

1912

1289. Russell, G. W. E.: The Young Disraeli in After-
       thoughts, 1912, 115-26. Review of Monypenny,
       vol. I, from Daily News.

1913

1290. Cromer, Evelyn Baring, Earl of: Disraeli in Politi-
       cal and literary essays, 1st ser., 1913, 177-203.
       See 931

1291. "Grierson, Francis": Benjamin Disraeli in The In-
       vincible alliance and other essays ... 1913, 186-
       92

1292. Lowell, James Russell: D'Israeli as a novelist in
       The Round table, 1913, 83-120. Review of "Tan-
       cred." See 317

1293. Samuel, Horace B.: The psychology of Disraeli in
       Modernities, 1913, 50-69. See 1491

1294. Butler, Sir George Geoffrey G.: Disraeli in The
       Tory tradition, 1914, 60-102

1295. Cromer, Evelyn Baring, Earl of: The young Disraeli
       in Political and literary essays, 2nd ser., 1914,
       63-69. See 561

1296. Vincent, Leon H.: "Vivian Grey" and its author in
       Dandies and men of letters, 1914, 255-76

1297. Ward, Wilfrid: Disraeli and Lord Cromer on Dis-
       raeli in Men and matters, 1914, 1-43; 44-69. See
       876, 1499

1915

1298. Meester, Marie E. de: Disraeli's "Tancred" in
       Oriental influences in English literature of the
       nineteenth century, Heidelberg, 1915, 58-60.
       (Cursory)

1299. More, Paul Elmer: Disraeli and Conservatism in
       Aristocracy and justice (Shelburne essays, 9th ser.),
       London and Boston, 1915, 149-189. (A slightly
       revised version of 1503)

1916

1300. Russell, George W. E.: Lord Beaconsfield in Por-
       traits of the seventies, 1916, 25-46

1917

1301. Whibley, Charles: The Corn Laws, a group (the in-
       troduction to 362 reprinted with minor revisions)
       in Political portraits, (1st ser.), 1917, 254-311

1918

1302. Russell, George W. E.: Benjamin Disraeli in Prime
       Ministers and some others, 1918, 35-41

1919

1303. Gosse, Sir Edmund: The Novels of Benjamin Disraeli

in Some diversions of a man of letters, 1919, 151-78. See 659, 1508

1920

1304. Carré, Jean Marie: Disraeli in Goethe en Angleterre, étude de littérature comparée, Paris, 1920, 215-21, in chapter " 'Wilhelm Meister' et les jeunes romanciers (1825-1835)," deals with Vivian Grey.

1305. Guedalla, Philip: Mr. Disraeli, statesman; novelist; journalist (3 articles) in Supers and supermen, studies in politics, history and letters, 1920, 155-75 (first two articles also in 1347).

1306. Scott, Ernest: Disraeli and Conservatism in Men and thought in modern history, Melbourne, 1920, 244-58

1307. Taylor, G. R. Stirling: Benjamin Disraeli, Earl of Beaconsfield in Modern English statesmen, 1920, 175-215

1921

1308. Bailey, John Cann: The political life of Disraeli (4 parts) in Some political ideas and persons, 1921, 45-118. See 872, 883, 902, 915

1309. Gosse, Sir Edmund: The last years of Disraeli in Books on the table, 1921, 3-9. (A review of volumes 5 & 6 of Buckle, from The Sunday Times.)

1310. Lucy, Sir Henry W.: Benjamin Disraeli, Earl of Beaconsfield, and Enter Lord Beaconsfield in Lords and Commoners, 1921, 18-33, 142-46. The first article is from 1502.

1311. Walkley, Arthur Bingham: Disraeli and the play in Pastiche and prejudice, 1921, 149-54. From The Times, 7 July 1920, p. 12. Disraeli as a play-goer.

1922

1312. Bigham, Clive: The Conservatives: Disraeli in The Prime Ministers of Britain, 284-99

1313. Squire, Sir John Collings: Disraeli's wit in Essays at large, by Solomon Eagle, 1922, 191-95. See 694

1923

1314. Guedalla, Philip: Mr. Disraeli, poet in Masters and men, 1923, 163-74, and in 1347

1315. Murry, John Middleton: Disraeli on love (Henrietta Temple) in Pencillings, little essays on literature, 1923, 138-46, from The Times, 28 July 1922, p. 13 (see also a letter from Edward Clarke, 4 August 1922).

1316. Walkley, Arthur Bingham: Corinthianism (Henrietta Temple) in More prejudice, 1923, 232-36. See 182

1317. Whibley, Charles: Benjamin Disraeli in Political Portraits, 2nd ser., 1923, 108-229

1924

1318. Abbott, Wilbur Cortez: An accidental Victorian: Benjamin Disraeli in Conflicts with oblivion, New York, 1924, 35-70. See 917

1319. Sherman, Stuart Pratt: The Disraelian irony in Points of view, New York and London, 1924, 291-323. See 1519

1320. Speare, Morris Edmund: The political novel, its development in England and America, New York, 1924. (Chapters 1 to 6 are wholly or mainly about Disraeli.)

1925

1321. Ellis, Stewart Marsh: Disraeli, the human side in Mainly Victorian, 1925, 366-69. See 912

1322. Quiller-Couch, Sir Arthur: Disraeli in Charles Dickens and other Victorians, 1925, 180-98

1926

1323. Hearnshaw, Fossey John C.: Disraeli in The political principles of some notable Prime Ministers of
the nineteenth century, 1926, 177-228

1927

1324. Baumann, Arthur A.: Disraeli's meridian in The
last Victorians, 1927, 41-57 and in Personalities,
1936, 217-31. See 895

1928

1325. Hagberg, Knut: in Medmänniskor, Stockholm, 1928,
translated as Disraeli and the fair sex in Personalities and powers, 1930, 15-29

1326. Roberts, Richard Ellis: Waistcoats and wit in Reading for pleasure, 1928, 158-63

1929

1327. Murray, Robert H.: Disraeli the novelist-statesman
in Studies in the English social and political think-
ers of the nineteenth century, 1929, I, 206-43

1328. Taylor, G. R. Stirling: Benjamin Disraeli, Earl of
Beaconsfield, 1804-1881 in Seven nineteenth century
statesmen, 1929, 204-36. (Differs from 1307.)

1930

1329. Feiling, Keith: Monypenny and Buckle's "Disraeli"
in Sketches in nineteenth-century biography, 1930,
169-81. See 924

1330. Howe, Susanne: On the side of the angels: Benjamin
Disraeli in Wilhelm Meister and his English kins-
men, New York, 1930, 178-201

1331. Lazaron, Morris S.: Benjamin Disraeli in Seed of
Abraham; ten Jews of the ages, New York and
London, 1930, 259-88

1931

1332. Hagberg, Knut: Disraeli och det sociala problemet
in Burke, Metternich, Disraeli, Stockholm, 1931,
131-77

1333. MacCarthy, Desmond: Disraeli in Portraits, I, 1931,
79-91. (New ed., 1949.)

1932

1334. Baker, Joseph Ellis: Disraeli: "Young England" in
religion in The novel and the Oxford Movement,
Princeton, 1932, 45-53. (Princeton Studies in
English, 8.)

1335. Baumann, Arthur A.: Benjamin Disraeli in The
great Victorians, edited by H. J. and H. Massingham, 1932, 173-83

1336. Edler, P. J.: Disraeli in Engelska statsmän under
de senaste hundra åren, Stockholm, 1932, 81-147

1933

1337. Brinton, Crane: Disraeli in English political thought
in the nineteenth century, 1933, 130-48

1338. Marriott, Sir John Arthur R.: Benjamin Disraeli,
Earl of Beaconsfield--the Conservative revival in
Queen Victoria and her ministers, 1933, 120-42

1339. Strachey, Giles Lytton: Dizzy in Characters and
commentaries, 1933, 269-72 and in Biographical
Essays, 1948, 264-67. See 916

1934

1340. Cook, E. Thornton: The Rt. Hon. Benjamin Disraeli
(first Earl of Beaconsfield) in What manner of
men?, 1934, 201-15

1341. Hayward, John: Benjamin Disraeli, Earl of Beaconsfield in Twelve Jews, edited by Hector Bolitho,
1934, 41-61

1342. Russell, A. J.: Disraeli in Their religion, 1934,

185

135-56.

1343. Somervell, D. C.: Benjamin Disraeli in Great demo-
       crats, edited by Alfred Barratt Brown, 1934, 227-
       39

1935

1344. MacMunn, Sir George Fletcher: Benjamin Disraeli
       in Leadership through the ages, 1935, 299-311

1936

1345. Rosa, Matthew Whiting: Disraeli in The Silver-fork
       school, novels of fashion preceding "Vanity Fair,"
       Columbia U. P., 1936, 99-115

1346. Toledano, André and Daniel: Disraeli in Hommes
       d'Etat, Paris, 1936, III, 589-700

1937

1347. Guedalla, Philip: Mr. Disraeli, statesman; novelist;
       poet (3 chapters, "The Primrose path") in Idylls
       of the Queen, 1937, 159-217. "Novelist" from
       1305, and the introductions to 663. "Statesman,"
       from 1305. "Poet," from 1314.

1348. Young, George Malcolm: B.A. Kohnfeldt ("as the
       street humorists of Berlin called him") in Daylight
       and champaign, essays, 1937, 52-58, and in Vic-
       torian essays, 1962, 162-67. See 995

1939

1349. Modder, Montagu Frank: The Disraelian era in The
       Jew in the literature of England, Philadelphia,
       1939, 192-216

1944

1350. Sadleir, Michael: Disraeli, The Star Chamber and
       The Dunciad of Today in Things past, 1944, 248-
       63. (The Introduction to 725.)

1351. Thomas, Henry and Thomas, D. L.: Disraeli in
       Living biographies of famous men, New York, 1944,

1945

1352. Saintsbury, George: Disraeli, a portrait in George
Saintsbury, the memorial volume, a new collection
of his essays and papers ... 1945, 154-60. Also
published as "A Saintsbury miscellany," New York,
1947. See 1456

1946

1353. Pritchett, V. S.: Disraeli in The living novel, 1946,
66-72. See 1556

1948

1354. Aldington, Richard: The lustrous world of young Disraeli in Four English portraits, 1801-51, 1948, 51-
100

1949

1355. Colson, Percy: The young Disraeli, a study in am-
bition in Their ruling passions, 1949, 163-202

1951

1356. Apt, I. R.: Benjamin Disraeli in Sixteen portraits
of people, whose houses have been preserved by
the National Trust, edited by L. A. G. Strong,
1951, 55-65

1952

1357. Biggs-Davison, John: Disraeli--and after in Tory
lives, 1952, 113-45

1953

1358. Cecil, Algernon: Lord Beaconsfield in Queen Victoria and her Prime Ministers, 1953, 191-219

1359. Holloway, John: Disraeli in The Victorian sage,
1953, 86-110. (A revised form of 1565.)

1360. Magnus, Sir Philip: Disraeli in British Prime Minis-

ters, edited by A. Duff Cooper, 1953, 108-22.
See 1564

1954

1361. Briggs, Asa: Benjamin Disraeli and the leap in the
dark in Victorian people, 1954, 276-308

1955

1362. Thackeray, William Makepeace: Coningsby, Sybil in
Contributions to the Morning Chronicle, edited by
G. N. Ray, 39-50, 77-86. See 222, 277

1956

1363. Taylor, Alan John P.: Dizzy in Englishmen and
others, 1956, 65-69. See 1569

1957

1364. James, Henry: Lothair by Lord Beaconsfield in
Literary reviews and essays, edited by Albert
Mordell, New York, 1957, 303-08. See 372

1960

1365. Moers, Ellen: Disraeli in The Dandy, Brummell to
Beerbohm, 1960, 84-104

1961

1366. Graubard, Stephen R.: Benjamin Disraeli, the romantic egoist in Burke, Disraeli, and Churchill:
the politics of perseverance, Harvard, 1961, 89-
171

1367. Medlicott, W. Norton: Bismarck and Beaconsfield
in Studies in diplomatic history and historiography,
edited by A. O. Sarkissian, 1961, 225-50

1964

1368. Blake, Robert: The Rise of Disraeli in Essays in
British history presented to Sir Keith Feiling,
edited by H. R. Trevor-Roper, 1964, 219-46

1369. Bagehot, Walter: Mr. Disraeli (1859), Why Mr. Disraeli has succeeded (1867), Mr. Disraeli's administration (1868), and Mr. Disraeli as a member of the House of Commons (1876) in Historical essays, edited with an introduction by Norman St. John-Stevas, New York, 1965, 276-95. See 1255, 1379, 1380, 1382, 1406

1370. Harris, Leon A.: Benjamin Disraeli in The fine art of political wit, New York, 1964, and London, 1965, 40-64

1371. McCabe, Bernard: Benjamin Disraeli in Minor British novelists, edited by Charles Alva Hoyt, Southern Illinois U. P. , 1967, 79-97

1372. Brasher, N. H.: Disraeli, statesman or charlatan? in Arguments in history, Britain in the nineteenth century, 1968, 127-55

Articles in periodicals (excluding reviews of books in this list)

Items in Notes and Queries are listed separately, 1628-1659.

1373. (Maginn, William)   : Gallery of literary characters. XXXVI. Benjamin D'Israeli in Fraser's Magazine, 7, 602. (With portrait) See 1246, the introduction ascribes, by implication, to Maginn, and 1259

1374. New Monthly Magazine: Memoir of Disraeli, 49,
532-34. (With the D'Orsay
portrait.)

1847

1375. Francis, George Henry: Literary legislators. I. B.
Disraeli in Fraser's Magazine,
35, 79-95, 193-208. See 1376

1852

1376. Francis, George Henry: Mr. Benjamin Disraeli as
leader and legislator in Fra-
ser's Magazine, 45, 127-41.
With 1375 published as 743

1377. Fraser's Magazine : The new curiosities of literature by the Right Hon. Benja-
min Disraeli, M. P., with
notes and illustrations, 46,
637-43 (Dec.) (The plagiarisms
from Thiers and others.)

1378. Illustrated London News: (Disraeli's speech at) The
Buckinghamshire election, 21,
63-64 (24 July).

1859

1379. Bagehot, Walter : Mr. Disraeli in The Economist,
17, 725-26 (2 July) See 1369

1867

1380. Bagehot, Walter : Why Mr. Disraeli has succeeded in The Economist, 25,
1009-10 (7 Sept.) See 1369

1381. Kebbel, Thomas Edward: Mr. Disraeli in The
People's Magazine, I, 617-18
(7 Sept.) See 1241

1382. Bagehot, Walter : Mr. Disraeli's administration in The Economist, 26, 1414-15 (12 Dec.) See 1369

1383. Cracroft, Bernard : Mr. Disraeli, the novelist in Fortnightly Review, 10, 146-59, and reprinted, abridged, ibid., 180, 265-70 (Oct. 1953).

1384. Gleig, G. R. : The Right Honourable Benjamin Disraeli in Blackwood's Magazine, 104, 129-44, 369-84, 491-508

1385. London Society : The Premier novelist, 13, 385-99

1386. Towle, G. M. : Disraeli, Prime Minister of England in Hours at Home, 7, 309-20

1387. St. James' Magazine: Mr. Disraeli's premiership, new ser., 1, 119-26

1388. St. Paul's Magazine : The Conservative premier, 3, 14-31, 185-201

1869

1389. St. James' Magazine: Cabinet photographs. II. Mr. Disraeli and Mr. Gladstone, new ser., 3, 385-400

1390. Sheppard, Nathan : Benjamin Disraeli in Western Monthly (Lakeside Monthly), 1, 338-47

1391. (Trollope, Anthony) : Mr. Disraeli and the Mint in St. Paul's Magazine, 4, 192-97 (May) (Attribution doubtful, see Sadleir, M.: Trollope, a bibliography, 229.)

1870

1392. Appleton's Journal : Disraeli the novelist, 3, 604-07

1393. Bundy, J. M. : Disraeli as statesman and novelist in Putnam's Monthly Magazine, new ser., 6, 87-95

1394. Collins, Mortimer : The literary character of Mr. Disraeli in British Quarterly Review, 52, 121-51. See 1252

1395. Leisure Hour : Benjamin Disraeli, 19, 294-98

1396. New Monthly Magazine: Carlyle and Disraeli, 147, 118-22. (Numbered "I," but apparently no sequel.)

1397. White, Richard G. : The styles of Disraeli and of Dickens in Galaxy, 10, 253-63

1871

1398. London Society : The author of "Vivian Grey" and "Lothair," 19, 427-40. Reprinted in Appleton's Journal, 5, 703-06

1399. Reede, Frank : Disraeli in New Era, 1, 376-81, 423-27, 453-58

1872

1400. Dublin University Magazine: Benjamin Disraeli, 80, 511-15. (By W.T.D.)

1401. Holbeach, Henry : Literary legislators. I. Mr. Disraeli in St. Paul's Magazine, 10, 30-42

1402. Hopkins, John Baker: Disraeli, a political study in Gentleman's Magazine, new ser., 8, 695-702

1873

1403. Jennings, L. J.   : Benjamin Disraeli in Atlantic Monthly, 32, 641-55

1874

1404. Illustrated London News: Mr. Disraeli, 64, 149-50 (14 Feb.) (With full-page portrait)

1405. Stephen, Sir Leslie : Mr. Disraeli's novels in Fortnightly Review, 22, 430-50. See 1250

1876

1406. Bagehot, Walter   : Mr. Disraeli as a member of the House of Commons in The Economist, 34, 969-70 (19 Aug.) See 1255 and 1369

1407. British Quarterly Review: Political career of Mr. Disraeli, 64, 147-79

1408. Lucy, Sir Henry W. : Vivian Grey, Lord Beaconsfield in Gentleman's Magazine, 239 (new ser., 17), 689-707

1409. McCarthy, Justin   : Vivian Grey grown old in Galaxy, 21, 325-32

1410. Seton, Matthew   : The Earl of Beaconsfield in New Monthly Magazine, new ser., 10, 387-96, 511-32. See 1126

1877

1411. Canadian Monthly   : Schoolboy days of Lord Beaconsfield, by D. F., 12, 154-59

1412. Nadal, E. S.   : Benjamin Disraeli in Scribner's Monthly, 14, 190-94

1413. Fortnightly Review : The political adventures of
                            Lord Beaconsfield, 29, 477-
                            93, 691-709, 867-88, 30, 250-
                            70. (This has been attributed
                            to Frank Hill, of the Daily
                            News (N. & Q., 11th ser., 2,
                            268, 317 (1910) and to Gold-
                            win Smith (1567).)

1414. Fraser's Magazine : The policy of Lord Beacons-
                            field's government, new ser.,
                            17, 135-41

1415. Laugel, A. : A French estimate of Lord
                     Beaconsfield in Nation, 27,
                     209-10 (3 Oct.)

1416. Motley, J. L. : Personalities of the House of
                       Commons. I. Mr. Disraeli
                       in New Monthly Magazine,
                       new ser., 13, 419-22

1417. Southern Quarterly Review: Benjamin Disraeli--the
                                  Jew, new ser. (Baltimore),
                                  24, 373-84

1879

1418. Contemporary Review: Lord Beaconsfield: why we
                            follow him, by a Tory, 36,
                            665-81

1419. Contemporary Review: Lord Beaconsfield: why we
                            disbelieve in him, by a Whig,
                            36, 681-96

1420. These two articles are also in Eclectic Magazine,
                             new ser., 31, 129-51 (1880).

1421. Cucheval-Clarigny, A.: Lord Beaconsfield et son
                             temps in Revue des deux
                             mondes, n.s., 35, 481-513,
                             787-824; 36, 129-69 (1, 15
                             Oct., 1 Nov.) See 794

1422. Kebbel, Thomas Edward: The political novels of
Lord Beaconsfield in Nineteenth
Century, 6, 504-28

1423. Sullivan, Margaret : Lord Beaconsfield in Lippincott's Magazine, 23, 197-204

1424. Time : Unexplored passages in the
life of Lord Beaconsfield, 1,
129-36

1425. Valbert, G. : Lord Beaconsfield et la dissolution du Parlement in Revue
des deux mondes, n. s., 34,
698-709 (1 Aug.)

1880

Eclectic Magazine see 1420

1426. Laugel, A. : The French popularity of
Beaconsfield in Nation, 30,
345-46 (6 May)

1427. Time : Half-mast at Hughenden, 2,
428-38. (A "prophecy" of the
effects of Disraeli's death).

1428. Towle, George M. : Certain men of mark. 7.
Beaconsfield in Good Company,
5, 193-201. See 1254

1881

1429. Athenaeum, no. 2791, 557-60 (23 April)
(Obituary).

1430. Austin, Alfred : At his grave (Hughenden, May
12th 1881) in Contemporary
Review, 39, 1015-18. (Verse).

1431. Bryce, James : Beaconsfield in Nation, 32,
331-32 (12 May)

1432. Bryce, James : Lord Beaconsfield in Congregationalist, 10, 416-27 (Not
signed).

1433. Cowell, Herbert : The Earl of Beaconsfield (Obittuary) in Blackwood's Magazine, 129, 674-82

1434. Illustrated London News: Obituary, 78, 401-25

1435. London Society : Lord Beaconsfield's florin, by J. M'L. C., 40, 313-17

1436. MacColl, Malcolm : Lord Beaconsfield in Contemporary Review, 39, 991-1014

1437. Noyes, George C. : Lord Beaconsfield in Dial, 2, 1-3

1438. Potter, P. M. : Lord Beaconsfield in Scribner's Monthly, 22, 262-65

1439. Saturday Review, 51, 507-08 (23 April) (Obituary); 541-42 (30 April) (Funeral); 609-10 (14 May) (The Monument to Lord Beaconsfield.)

1440. Sichel, Walter : Wit and humour of Lord Beaconsfield in Macmillan's Magazine, 44, 139-48

1441. Skelton, John : A last word on Disraeli in Contemporary Review, 39, 971-990

1442. Spectator, no. 2756, 528-29 (23 April) (Obituary).

1443. Stoddard, R. H. : The Earl of Beaconsfield (with portrait frontispiece to issue), Critic, I, 110-11 (23 April).

1444. Times : Lord Beaconsfield's novels, 3 August.

1882

1445. Bryce, James : Lord Beaconsfield in Century Magazine, 23 (new ser., 1), 729-44. See 1281

1446. Lazarus, Emma   : Was the Earl of Beaconsfield
a representative Jew? in Century Magazine, 1, 939-42

1883

1447. Churchill, Lord Randolph: Elijah's mantle: April
19th, 1883 in Fortnightly Review, 39, 613-21 (see H. E.
Gorst, The Fourth party,
240.)

1448. Leisure Hour   : Hughenden and Lord Beaconsfield, 32, 33-38

1449. Saturday Review   : Lord Beaconsfield's statue,
55, 485-86 (21 April)

1450. Spectator   : Lord Beaconsfield's statue,
56, 504

1451. Temple Bar   : Lord Beaconsfield's character,
69, 178-95

1884

1452. Hennessy, Sir John Pope: Lord Beaconsfield's Irish
policy in Nineteenth Century,
16, 663-80. See 1194

1885

1453. Blind, K.   : A meeting with Mr. Disraeli
in Time, new ser., 1, 514-30

1454. Bryce, James   : The Earl of Beaconsfield, a
study in Temple Bar, 74,
402-13

1455. Kebbel, Thomas Edward: Tory Prime Ministers.
VIII. Lord Beaconsfield in
National Review, 6, 414-31.
See 1263

1886

1456. Saintsbury, G.   : Benjamin Disraeli, Earl of

197

Beaconsfield in Magazine of
Art, 9, 221-27. See 1352

1457. Garnett, R.   : Shelley and Lord Beaconsfield,
                                  a lecture in The Shelley So-
                                  ciety's Papers, 1, 122-37.
                                  See 807, 1279

1888

1458. Gerard, Morice   : A lapsed copyright (of the
                                  earlier novels) in Temple Bar,
                                  83, 422-28

1459. Gerard, Morice   : Disraeli's womankind, ibid.,
                                  84, 97-104

1460. Pierrepont, Edwards: Lord Beaconsfield and the
                                  Irish question in North Ameri-
                                  can Review, 147, 669-79

1461. Sichel, Walter   : Lord Beaconsfield as a land-
                                  scape painter in Time, new
                                  ser., 7, 533-42

1889

1462. Kidd, Joseph   : The last illness of Lord Bea-
                                  consfield in Nineteenth Cen-
                                  tury, 26, 65-71

1463. Lucy, Sir Henry W. :   Mr. Disraeli in Temple Bar,
                                  85, 515-29, 86, 49-65

1891

1464. De Haye, Alexandre :   Lamartine et Lord Beacons-
                                  field in Nouvelle revue inter-
                                  nationale, 23, (1), 185-92.
                                  See 1197

1465. Farrer, J. A.   : Was Lord Beaconsfield the
                                  sun?, a lecture in the year
                                  3000 in Gentleman's Magazine,
                                  271, 254-59

1466. Salmon, Edward : Lord Beaconsfield, after ten years in National Review, 17, 262-74

1893

1467. Espinasse, Francis : Lord Beaconsfield and his minor biographer in Bookman, 4, 140-41, 171-73. See 1269

1894

1468. Harrison, Frederic : Studies of the great Victorian writers: III--Disraeli's place in literature in Forum (New York), 18, 192-203. See 1272

1469. Robbins, Alfred F. : Lord Beaconsfield as a phrasemaker in Gentleman's Magazine, 276, 302-12

1895

1470. Aronstein, Philipp : Benjamin Disraeli's Leben und dichterische Werke. I. Disraeli's Leben in Anglia, 17, 161-98. II. Disraeli's Dichtungen, 261-395. The first chapter of I and the first book of II are a revised version of the pamphlet 826. This account deals with all Disraeli's novels. See 1591

1896

1471. Greenwood, Frederick: Characteristics of Lord Beaconsfield in Cornhill, new ser., 1, 589-604

1472. Hoste, James W. : Disraeli on national education in Fortnightly Review, 65, 808-17

1897

1473. Greenwood, Frederick: Disraeli vindicated in Blackwood's Magazine, 161, 426-43

1898

1474. Colquhoun, A. H. U.: Disraeli, the man and the
minister in Canadian Magazine,
11, 273-82

1475. Whibley, Charles : Disraeli the younger in Blackwood's Magazine, 163, 583-97

1900

1476. Sichel, Walter : Disraeli and the colonies in
Blackwood's Magazine, 167,
492-95

1901

1477. Vogüé, vicomte Eugène de: La littérature impéria-
liste--les romans de Benjamin
Disraeli ... in Revue des deux
mondes, n. s., 3, 196-212 (1
May).

1478. Russell, George W. E.: Lord Beaconsfield's novels
in New Liberal Review, 2,
37-44

1902

1479. Academy : The decline of oratory, and
the Disraeli tradition, 62,
675-76 (11 Jan.)

1480. Gower, Lord Ronald : Lord Beaconsfield, reminiscences in Magazine of Art,
1902, 207-09

1481. Hellman, George S. : Benjamin Disraeli, Earl of
Beaconsfield in Bookman (New
York), 16, 386-99

1482. Sichel, Walter : The prophecies of Disraeli in
Nineteenth Century, 52, 112-
24

1483. Iddesleigh, Walter Stafford Northcote earl of: Lord
Beaconsfield's novels in Month-
ly Review, 13, (2), 87-102
(Nov.)

1904

1484. "Melville, Lewis"   : Benjamin Disraeli's novels in
Fortnightly Review, 82, 861-
73. See 1285

1485. Meynell, Wilfrid   : Newman and Disraeli in Bookman, 26, 45-50

1905

1486. Blackwood's Magazine: Musings without method--Dis-
raeli's first and last novels,
177, 287-89

1487. Blackwood's Magazine: Mr. Balfour and Lord Beaconsfield, 177, 704-11

1488. Friswell, Laura   : Benjamin Disraeli, a pen and
ink sketch in Temple Bar,
132, 230-37

1489. Macmillan's Magazine: Benjamin Disraeli, 91, 229-
40

1490. Saltus, Edgar   : Benjamin Disraeli in Munsey's
Magazine, 33, 159-62

1491. Samuel, Horace B.   : The psychology of Disraeli in
Fortnightly Review, 83, 224-
36. See 1293

1492. Seccombe, Thomas   : Benjamin Disraeli in Bookman,
27, 237-43

1907

1493. Bruce, J. D.   : Disraeli as a novelist in
Sewanee Review, 15, 353-69

1494. Lucas, Reginald   : Lord Beaconsfield's novels in Quarterly Review, 207, 153-73

1495. Russell, George W. E.: Lord Beaconsfield's portrait gallery in Cornhill, new ser., 22, 27-46

1496. Stronach, George   : Beaconsfield as plagiarist in Academy, 72, 632-33

1909

1497. Lethbridge, Roper   : Lord Beaconsfield as a tariff reformer in Nineteenth Century, 66, 934-48

1913

1498. The Beaconsfield Quarterly, edited by Frederick J. Harrics.
Published at the "County Times" Offices, Cardiff. "A Magazine established for the purpose of promoting a wider study of the life and works of Benjamin Disraeli ..."
Four issues were published, April 1913 to January 1914.

1499. Ward, Wilfrid   : Disraeli in Dublin Review, 152, 1-20, 217-31. See 1297

1915

1500. Escott, T. H. S.   : Dropped stitches in Disraelian biography in Contemporary Review, 107, 76-84

1501. Escott, T. H. S.   : Lord Beaconsfield in society in Fortnightly Review, 103, 431-42

1502. Lucy, Sir Henry W. : Disraeli ... personal notes in Chambers' Journal, 7th ser., 5, 135-37 (Feb.) See 1310

1503. More, Paul Elmer : Disraeli and Conservatism in
Atlantic Monthly, 116, 373-85.
See 1299

1916

1504. Escott, T. H. S. : Disraeli's young men in Contemporary Review, 110, 487-
93

1505. Hugins, Roland : Disraeli's doctrine of Toryism
in South Atlantic Quarterly,
15, 241-49

1506. Sadler, Hugh : Contrasts: Benjamin Disraeli
and Abraham Lincoln in Nine-
teenth Century, 79, 409-15

1918

1507. Baumann, Arthur A. : Was Disraeli a democrat? in
Fortnightly Review, 109, 71-
79

1508. Gosse, Sir Edmund : The novels of Benjamin Disraeli in Transactions, Royal
Society of Literature, 2nd
ser., 36, 61-90. (The general introduction to the "Empire" edition of the works,
see 659, 1303.)

1920

1509. Architect : Disraeli and London, 104 (no.
2, 690), 20-21 (9 July)

1510. Edmonds, Edward : Disraeli's novels in New
World, 2, 344-50

1511. Morison, J. L. : The imperial ideas of Benjamin Disraeli in Canadian His-
torical Review, 1, 267-80

1512. National Review : Disraeli and the racecourse,
by "Newmarket," 76, 228-40

203

1513. Spectator   : Disraeli on the secret societies
                               and the Jews, 124, 750-51,
                               782-83   (5, 12 June)

1514. Times Literary Supplement: The novels of Disraeli
                               (review of 1919 reprint of col-
                               lected edition), 8 July, 429-30

1515. Times Literary Supplement: (Letters, including "The
                               Phrases of Disraeli," from J.
                               A. Lovat-Fraser, on his pla-
                               giarisms), 18 Nov., 758 and
                               25 Nov., 779

1921

1516. Escott, T. H. S.   : Lord Beaconsfield's Surrey
                               houses in Fortnightly Review,
                               115, 73-80

1922

1517. Baumann, Arthur A. : Lord Salisbury and Disraeli
                               (review of Cecil's Life of
                               Salisbury) in Fortnightly Re-
                               view, 116, 84-94

1518. Britten, James   : The primrose and Primrose
                               Day in Month, 139, 303-10
                               (April)

1519. Sherman, Stuart P. : The Disraelian irony in Book-
                               man (New York), 55, 238-46,
                               381-85. See 1319

1924

1520. Bain, F. W.   : Disraeli in The Criterion, 2,
                               143-66   (Feb.)

1521. George, R. E. Gordon: The novels of Disraeli in
                               Nineteenth Century, 96, 668-
                               76

1925

1522. Spectator   : Disraeli and Mr. Baldwin,

1927

For La Vie de Disraëli, by A. Maurois, in Revue Paris, and in The Forum, see 961, 963

1523.   Trevelyan, Sir George Otto: Recollections of Disraeli in Saturday Review, 143,
515-16 (2 April)

1928

1524.   Swinnerton, Frank   :   Disraeli as novelist in London
Mercury, 17, 260-72 (Jan.)
and in Yale Review, 17, 283-
300.   (Differs from 666.)

1525.   Fisher, H. A. L.   :   The Political novel (Disraeli
and Trollope) in Cornhill, 64,
25-38

1929

1526.   Clarke, A. H. T.   :   The genius of Disraeli, a pen
portrait in Fortnightly Review,
131, 98-111

1527.   Gretton, R. H.   :   Disraeli and the making of an
Opposition in The Listener, 2,
43-45 (10 July)

1930

1528.   Lock, D. R.   :   The Victorian era and Disraeli in Socialist Review, new
ser., 2, 140-44

1529.   Lovat-Fraser, J. A.:   With Disraeli in Italy in Contemporary Review, 138, 192-
99

1530.   Stevenson, Lionel   :   Stepfathers of Victorianism
(i.e., Disraeli and Bulwer
Lytton) in Virginia Quarterly
Review, 6, 251-67

1931

1531. Buckle, George Earle: Statesman and prophet in The Times, 18 April

1532. Jennings, Sir Ivor : Disraeli and the constitution in Journal of Comparative Legislation and International Law, 13, 182-98

1533. Temperley, Harold : Disraeli and Cyprus in English Historical Review, 46, 274-79, 457-60

1932

1534. Caro, Joseph : Benjamin Disraeli, Juden und Judenthum in Monatsschrift für Geschichte und Wissenschaft des Judenthums, 76, 152-66, 217-29

1535. Modder, Montagu Frank: Young Disraeli in Scotland in London Quarterly and Holborn Review, 156 (6th ser., 1), 295-306

1536. "Paston, George" : The young Disraeli and his adventures in journalism in Cornhill, new ser., 73, 385-99

1537. Somerville, H. : Disraeli and Catholicism in Month, 159, 114-24

1933

1538. Berman, Harold : Novels of Benjamin Disraeli in Open Court, 47, 398-408

1934

1539. Hirsch, Leo : Disraeli-Lassalle: Versuch über einen politischen Typus in Der Morgen, 9, 493-96 (March)

1540. Irvine, Bryant : "Dizzy's dictum": Toryism in search of a leader in Saturday Review, 157, 64-65 (20 Jan.)

1541. Modder, Montagu Frank: The alien patriot in Disraeli's novels in London Quarterly and Holborn Review, 159, (6th ser., 3), 363-72

1542. Polson, Sir Thomas A.: The voice of Disraeli in Saturday Review, 158, 238 (13 Oct.)

1935

1543. Haworth, Sir Lionel : Baldwin and Disraeli in Saturday Review, 159, 459-60 (13 April)

1937

1544. Aldag, Peter : Benjamin Disraeli über die Juden-und Rassen-frage in Hochschule und Ausland, 15, 170-73

1545. Hudson, Ruth Leigh : Poe and Disraeli in American Literature, 8, 402-16

1938

1546. Hentschel, Cedric : Disraeli and Lassalle in German Life and Letters, 2, 93-106

1939

1547. Cline, Clarence Lee : Disraeli and Peel's 1841 Cabinet in Journal of Modern History, 11, 509-12

1941

1548. Cline, Clarence Lee : Disraeli and John Gibson Lockhart in Modern Language Notes, 56, 134-37

1549. Craemer, Rudolf : Benjamin Disraeli in Forschungen zur Judenfrage (Ham-
burg), 5, 22-147. See 997

1550. James, Stanley B. : The tragedy of Disraeli in
Catholic World, 152, 414-19

1942

1551. Cline, Clarence Lee : Disraeli at High Wycombe in
University of Texas Studies in
English, 22 (1942), 124-44

1552. Temperley, Harold and Henderson, G. B.: Disraeli
and Palmerston in 1857 in
Cambridge Historical Journal,
7, 115-26

1943

1553. Cline, Clarence Lee : Disraeli and Thackeray in
Review of English Studies, 19,
404-08

1554. Willcox, W. B. : The Tory tradition in American Historical Review, 43,
707-21

1945

1555. Gordon, Wilhelmina : Disraeli the novelist in Dalhousie Review, 25, 212-24

1556. Pritchett, V. S. : Books in general in New
Statesman, 30, 111 (18 Aug.)
See 1353

1557. Shahani, Ranjee G. : Some British I admire. I.
Disraeli in Asiatic Review,
new ser., 41, 92-95

1947

1558. Arnold, Carroll C. : Invention in the Parliamentary
speaking of Benjamin Disraeli,
1842-1852 in Speech Mono-
graphs, 14, 66-80. See 1611

1559. Arnold, C. C.   : Speech style of Benjamin Dis-
                               raeli in Quarterly Journal of
                               Speech, 33, 427-36

1949

1560. Robertson-Scott, J. W.: Who secured the Suez Canal
                                shares? in Quarterly Review,
                                287, 336-47

1950

1561. Cecil, Algernon   : The novels of Disraeli, a
                               revaluation in The Listener,
                               43, 29-31 (5 Jan.)

1562. Forbes-Boyd, Eric   : Disraeli, the novelist in Es-
                               says and Studies, new ser.,
                               3, (1950), 100-17

1951

1563. Kapur, Anup Chand   : Disraeli's forward policy on
                               the North-West Frontier of
                               India, 1874-77 in Panjab Uni-
                               versity Research Bulletin,
                               Arts, 1951, no. IV.

1564. Magnus, Sir Philip : Benjamin Disraeli in History
                               Today, 1, (9) 23-30 (Sept.)
                               See 1360

1952

1565. Holloway, John   : Disraeli's "view of life" in
                               the novels in Essays in Criti-
                               cism, 2, 413-33. See 1359

1566. Kirk, Russell   : The social imagination of Dis-
                               raeli in Queen's Quarterly
                               (Kingston, Ont.), 59, 471-85

1567. Rieff, Philip   : Disraeli, the chosen of his-
                               tory. Uniting the Old Jerusa-
                               lem and the New in Commen-
                               tary, 13, 22-33 (also a letter
                               by Rabbi H. A. Fine on "Dis-

209

raeli and Jewish emancipation,"
ibid., 187.)

1954

1568. Jerman, B. R.   : Disraeli's fan-mail: a curiosity item in NCF 9, 61-71

1955

1569. Taylor, A. J. P.   : Books in general in New Statesman, 49, 108-09 (22 Jan.) See 1363

1956

1570. Jerman, B. R.   : Disraeli's audience (Sarah Disraeli) in South Atlantic Quarterly, 55, 463-72

1957

1571. Riggs, R. E.   : Peel and Disraeli, architects of a new Conservative Party in Western Humanities Review, 11, 183-87

1960

1572. D'Avigdor-Goldsmid, Sir Henry: Disraeli's novels in London Magazine, 7, (10), 45-48

1573. McIntyre, W. D.   : Disraeli's colonial policy, the creation of the Western Pacific High Commission in Historical Studies, Australia and New Zealand, 9, 279-94

1961

1574. Lewis, Clyde J.   : Theory and expediency in the policy of Disraeli in VS 4, 237-68

1575. McIntyre, W. D.   : Disraeli's election blunder: the Straits of Malacca issue

in the 1874 election in Renaissance and Modern Studies, 5,
76-105

1962

1576. Lewis, Clyde J.   : Disraeli's conception of divine
                             order in Jewish Social Studies,
                             24, 144-61

1577. Tucker, Albert   : Disraeli and the natural aris-
                             tocracy in Canadian Journal
                             of Economics and Political
                             Science, 28, 1-15

1964

1578. Duerksen, R. A.   : Disraeli's use of Shelley in
                             VNL 26, 19-22

1579. Jerman, B. R.   : The production of Disraeli's
                             trilogy in Papers of the Bib-
                             liographical Society of Ameri-
                             ca, 58, 239-51

1580. Painting, D. E.   : Thackeray v. Disraeli in
                             Quarterly Review, 302, 396-
                             407

1965

1581. Cowling, Maurice   : Disraeli, Derby and fusion,
                             October 1865 to July 1866 in
                             Historical Journal, 8, 31-71

1582. Stembridge, Stanley R.: Disraeli and the millstones
                             in Journal of British Studies,
                             5, 122-39

1966

1583. Blake, Robert   : Disraeli the novelist in Essays
                             by Divers Hands, new ser.,
                             34, 1-18

1584. Blake, Robert   : Disraeli's political novels in
                             History Today, 16, 459-66

211

1585. Blake, Robert   : Disraeli, the problems of a
                             biographer in Cornhill, 175,
                             (no. 1049), 295-307

1586. Painting, David E. : Disraeli and the Roman Catho-
                             lic Church in Quarterly Re-
                             view, 304, 17-25

1967

1587. Arnold, Beth R.   : Disraeli and Dickens on Young
                             England in Dickensian, 63,
                             (no. 351), 26-31

1968

1588. Kidwell, E. G.   : Disraeli in Shropshire in
                             Transactions of the Caradoc
                             and Severn Valley Field Club,
                             16 (1961-67), 1968, 109-119

1589. McCabe, Bernard   : Disraeli and the "baronial
                             principle": some versions of
                             romantic medievalism in VNL
                             34, 7-13 (Fall 1968)

Dissertations

1590. Hamilton, Herbert B.: On the portrayal of the life
                             and character of Lord Byron
                             in ... Venetia. Leipzig,
                             1884.

1591. Aronstein, Philipp : Benjamin Disraeli's Dichtun-
                             gen. Münster, 1891. See
                             826, 1470

1592. Hahn, Gustav   : Lord Beaconsfield's Roman
                             Venetia, ein Denkmal Byrons
                             und Shelleys. Dresden, 1898.

1593. Krug, Isidor   : Beiträge zur Weltanschauung
                             Disraelis. Vienna, 1912.

1594.	Kohlund, Johanna	:	Benjamin Disraelis Stellung zur englischen Romantik. Freiburg, 1913.
1595.	Otto, Friedrich K.	:	Autobiographisches aus Disraeli's Jugendromanen, "Vivian Grey," "Contarini Fleming," "The Young Duke." Leipzig, 1913.
1596.	Thoma, Otto	:	Das englische Verfassungs- und Gesellschaftsideal in den politischen Romanen Benjamin Disraelis. Heidelberg, 1913.
1597.	Herzog, Edgar	:	B. Disraeli als Imperialist. Leipzig, 1922.
1598.	Kammer, Paul	:	Disraeli als Romantiker. Bonn, 1923.
1599.	Schubert, Paul	:	Die Metapher bei Disraeli. Leipzig, 1923.
1600.	Wapler, Rudolf	:	Studien zu Disraelis "Coningsby." Leipzig, 1924.
1601.	Waelder, Hedi	:	Benjamin Disraelis Stellung zum Judenthum. Freiburg, 1925.
1602.	Heuer, Erich	:	Enstehungsgeschichte von Disraelis Erstlingsroman "Vivian Grey." Berlin, 1925.
1603.	Story, Irving C.	:	Disraeli the novelist. Cornell, 1926.
1604.	Caspar, Maria	:	Disraeli's "Vivian Grey" als politischer Schlüsselroman. Bonn, 1928. See 54
1605.	Segalowitsch, Boris	:	Benjamin Disraelis Orientalismus. Bonn, 1930. See 986
1606.	Dahle, A.	:	Disraelis Beziehungen zu Bolingbroke. Freiburg, 1931.

1607. Herrmann, Irmgard : Benjamin Disraelis Stellung
zur Katholischen Kirche.
Freiburg, 1932.

1608. Smith, Mrs. Virginia P.: The Parliamentary novels
of Benjamin Disraeli and An-
thony Trollope. Cornell,
1933.

1609. Sauer, Eugen : Die Politik Lord Beaconsfields
in der orientalischen Krisis
(1875-78). Tübingen, 1934.

1610. Cline, Clarence L. : Benjamin Disraeli, a study in
the development of a novelist.
Texas, 1938.

1611. Arnold, Carroll C. : The Parliamentary oratory of
Benjamin Disraeli, 1842-1852.
Iowa, 1942. See 1558-1559

1612. Frietzsche, Arthur H.: The early novels of Benjamin Disraeli. California,
1949.

1613. Kallsen, Anni Marta : Disraeli, Dickens und Thackeray in ihrer Stellung zur
englisch-aristokratischen Ge-
sellschaftschicht. Hamburg,
1949.

1614. Jerman, Bernard R. : Disraeli's relationship with
the Austens during his "mise-
rable youth, " 1825-1839, an
essay and an edition of letters.
Ohio State, 1952. See 1028

1615. Grate, William H. : The satiric content of Disraeli's fiction. Washington,
St. Louis, 1953.

1616. Müller, Ekkehard : Technik und Ideen der Romane
des Politikers Benjamin Dis-
raeli. Vienna, 1955.

1617. Parsons, Olive W. : The Ideas of Benjamin Disraeli, Lord Beaconsfield, Indiana,

214

1955.

1618. Lewis, Clyde Joseph: Disraeli's Conservatism. Kentucky, 1956.

1619. Bindmann, Werner : Wortschatz und Syntax bei Benjamin Disraeli. Jena, 1957.

1620. Maitre, Raymond : Disraeli, Lord Beaconsfield: la personnalité, la pensée, l'oeuvre littéraire. Paris, 1957. See 1047

1621. Painting, David E. : A study of Disraeli's contribution to the political novel, 1826-1844. Wales, 1959.

1622. Levine, Richard Allan: Disraeli and the Middle Ages: the influence of medievalism in the nineteenth century. Indiana, 1961.

1623. McCabe, Bernard : From "Vivian Grey" to "Tancred," a critical study of Disraeli's development as a novelist. Stanford, 1962.

1624. Merritt, J. D. : The novels of Benjamin Disraeli. Wisconsin, 1964.

1625. Painting, David E. : A Critical examination of Disraeli's novels from "Sybil" to "Falconet," with special reference to the Hughenden MSS. Wales, 1964.

1626. Liebermann, Marcia R.: Disraeli the novelist. Brandeis, 1966.

1627. Lawless, J. T. : Disraeli's concepts of English social classes. St. Louis, 1967.

"Notes and Queries"

The entries in "Notes and Queries" which relate to particular books are listed under the book. Other entries are listed here by subject. Some entries which refer only incidentally to Disraeli, or which repeat information to be found elsewhere in "Notes and Queries," are omitted. Each entry appears once only in this list.

1628. The name "Disraeli"
    1st ser.,   8, 441 (5.xi.1853)
    6th ser.,   3, 449 (4.vi.1881)
    7th ser., 11, 346 (2.v.1891); 436 (30.v.1891);
           12, 70 (25.vii.1891); 134 (15.viii.1891);
              258 (26.ix.1891); 310 (17.x.1891)
    8th ser., 11, 484 (19.vi.1897)

1629. Birthplace
    6th ser.,   3, 360 (30.iv.1881) (Date of birth);
           10, 309 (18.x.1884); 352 (1.xi.1884);
              457 (6.xii.1884);
           11, 16 (3.i.1885)
    7th ser.,   3, 441 (4.vi.1887)
    9th ser.,   4, 395 (11.xi.1899); 526 (23.xii.1899);
            8, 317 (19.x.1901); 426 (23.xi.1901);
              512 (21.xii.1901);
           9, 15 (4.i.1902), by W. L. Rutton;
              297 (12.iv.1902);
          10, 482 (20.xii.1902), by W. L. Rutton
    12th ser., 5, 204 (Aug. 1919); 328 (Dec. 1919);
           6, 50 (Feb. 1920)

1630. Baptism
    6th ser., 10, 473 (13.xii.1884)
    11th ser., 3, 268 (8.iv.1911); 314 (22.iv.1911)

1631. Schooldays
    10th ser., 9, 46 (18.i.1908);
          11, 362 (8.v.1909); 454 (5.vi.1909)
    12th ser., 5, 287 (Nov. 1919)

1632. Legal training
    6th ser.,   3, 384 (14.v.1881)

1633. Political career
    6th ser.,   3, 427 (28.v.1881) Maiden Speech;

		12,	466 (12. xii. 1885) "I intend to be Prime Minister")
7th ser.,	5,	146 (25. ii. 1888); 416 (26. v. 1888);
	6,	55 (21. vii. 1888); 116 (11. viii. 1888);
	7,	354 (4. v. 1889) The Primrose.
10th ser.,	9,	125 (15. ii. 1908) Abyssinian speech, by W. F. Prideaux
12th ser.,	2,	508 (23. xii. 1916);
	3,	56 (20. i. 1917) Speeches;
	7,	41 (17. vii. 1920), and Derby Ministry, 1858;
		106 (7. viii. 1920), Speech in 1878;
	8,	226 (19. iii. 1921), "Popkin's plan"

1634. Writings

Bibliography by G. Angus see 1.

10th ser.,	6,	149 (25. viii. 1906) Keys to novels
12th ser.,	4,	159 (June 1918) Keys to novels
15th ser.,	183,	110 (15. viii. 1942), 173 (12. ix. 1942), 263 (24. x. 1942) Characters in novels, keys.

1635. Quotations, words and sayings, letters

4th ser.,	1,	295 (28. iii. 1868) exchange with Sir G. C. Lewis
5th ser.,	2,	168 (29. viii. 1874); 234 (19. ix. 1874); 398 (14. xi. 1874); 525 (26. xii. 1874);
	3,	233 (20. iii. 1875);
	5,	277 (1. iv. 1876) ("Flouts, gibes and sneers")
6th ser.,	12,	88 (1. viii. 1885) "Do not ask who wrote 'Junius.' "
7th ser.,	7,	428 (1. vi. 1889), 518 (29. vi. 1889) "jockey, the western substitute for the eunuch";
	9,	287 (12. iv. 1890), 398 (17. v. 1890) Nickname for Horsman
8th ser.,	4,	49 (15. vii. 1893) Letter from, on writing for the press;
	11,	324 (24. iv. 1897) Letter from, on peasantry and trees
10th ser.,	6,	429 (1. xii. 1906);
	8,	510 (28. xii. 1907) "Protection, dead and damned";

           9,   70 (25. i. 1908) use of "revert";
          10, 486 (19. xii. 1908) eggs like prim-
                   roses;
          11,   37 (9. i. 1909) primroses, as salad;
          12, 490 (18. xii. 1909) on Radicals and
                   Conservatives
11th ser., 2, 267 (1. x. 1910) "plundering and blun-
                   dering";
           8, 170 (30. viii. 1913); 216 (13. ix. 1913);
               255 (27. ix. 1913);
          12, 359 (6. xi. 1915); 405 (20. xi. 1915)
                   on Thames Street;
               360 (6. xi. 1915); 406 (20. xi. 1915)
12th ser., 3,   29 (13. i. 1917), 74 (27. i. 1917) Sir
                   John Cutler's hose;
           4,   81 (March 1918) tax on hairpowder;
               233 (Sept. 1918) "Thank God there
                   is a House of Lords";
           7, 470 (11. xi. 1920) "at last we have
                   got something hot"
13th ser., 150, 127 (20. ii. 1926) Letter to Montagu;
          151, 154 (28. viii. 1926); 233 (25. ix. 1926);
          155, 11 (7. vii. 1928); 52 (21. vii. 1928)
15th ser., 170, 283 (18. iv. 1936); 323 (2. v. 1936);
               340 (9. v. 1936);
          183, 284 (7. ix. 1942) Borrowings;
          184, 223 (10. iv. 1943) quotations proposed
                   for inclusion in Oxford Diction-
                   ary of Quotations;
          205, 389 (Oct. 1960) J. C. Maxwell:
                   Two words from Disraeli; 456
                   (Dec. 1960) D. E. Painting:
                   "Juvenile delinquency" and
                   "Banausic": Young England
                   coinage?

        Disraeli and others: anecdotes and sayings

1636. Arnold, Matthew
       15th ser., 184, 106 (13. ii. 1943)

1637. Baum, his servant
       14th ser., 161, 190 (12. ix. 1931)
       15th ser., 183, 312 (21. xi. 1942)

1638. Blessington, Countess of
       15th ser., 192, 426-28 (4. x. 1947) (C. L. Cline)

1639. D'Arblay, Madame
11th ser., 3, 348 (6.v.1911)

1640. Dickens, Charles
209, 233 (June 1964) S. M. Smith: An unpublished letter from Dickens to Disraeli.

1641. Dillon
11th ser., 4, 449 (2.xii.1911);
498 (16.xii.1911) "a harp struck by lightning"

1642. Gladstone
7th ser., 11, 424 (30.v.1891)
10th ser., 2, 67 (23.vii.1904);
110 (6.viii.1904)
12th ser., 3, 229 (24.iii.1917);
5, 11 (Jan. 1919) "a good man, in the worst sense of the word"

1643. Goethe
7th ser., 11, 165 (28.ii.1891);
12, 508 (26.xii.1891)

1644. Greenwood, Frederick
194, 62 (5.ii.1949) J. W. Robertson-Scott: Beaconsfield and Frederick Greenwood

1645. Heine
7th ser., 12, 508 (26.xii.1891)

1646. Lamb, Lady Caroline
7th ser., 10, 167 (30.viii.1890) alleged to be a character in novels

1647. Lytton
11th ser., 4, 25 (8.vii.1911)

1648. Macready, William Charles
11th ser., 2, 506 (24.xii.1910) his Reminiscences

1649. Salisbury
15th ser., 180, 353 (17.v.1941)

219

1650. Shelley, Mary
        <u>195</u>, 475-76 (28.x.1950) C. L. Cline: Two Mary Shelley letters

1651. Tupper, Martin
    12th ser., <u>5</u>, 11 (Jan. 1919)

1652. Ude, the cook
    12th ser., <u>10</u>, 110 (11.ii.1922) worth £10,000 a year

1653. Willis, N. P.
    5th ser., <u>7</u>, 166 (3.iii.1877) erroneous prediction by

1654. <u>Death</u>
    6th ser., <u>3</u>, 363 (7.v.1881)
    14th ser., <u>161</u>, 333 (7.xi.1931), 431 (12.xii.1931) assertions that he died a Roman Catholic, or a Jew

1655. <u>Memorials</u>
    10th ser., <u>6</u>, 357 (3.xi.1906) In Theobald's Road
    11th ser., <u>8</u>, 119 (9.viii.1913) In Park Lane
    12th ser., <u>5</u>, 312 (Dec. 1919) In Bolton

1656. <u>Miscellaneous</u>
    3rd ser., <u>3</u>, 300 (11.iv.1863) Appointed Trustee of the British Museum
    5th ser., <u>6</u>, 399 (11.xi.1876) Coat of arms;
           <u>8</u>, 7 (7.vii.1877); 72 (28.vii.1877) arms, crest and motto
           8, 108 (11.viii.1877), 215 (15.ix.1877) Notices of Disraeli and Gladstone
          <u>10</u>, 206 (14.ix.1878) His "George and Garter"
    6th ser., <u>3</u>, 403 (21.v.1881) Recollections
    7th ser., <u>8</u>, 405 (23.ix.1889) "A man of great gumption"
          <u>11</u>, 145 (21.ii.1891) Scholarship
    9th ser., <u>4</u>, 498 (16.xii.1899) Jewish Jesuits
    10th ser., <u>3</u>, 367 (13.v.1905) Faith
          <u>11</u>, 186 (6.iii.1909), 276 (3.iv.1909) His habit of writing the names of his enemies on pieces of paper

```
              10th ser.,    12,   449 (4.xii.1909) Portrait
              13th ser.,   154,   156 (3.iii.1928) Portraits
              15th ser.,   179,    11 (6.vii.1940) Knowledge of Spanish
                           192,   150 (5.iv.1947) "Beaconsfield ward-
                                       robe" (a piece of furniture)
```

1657. Disraeli family
```
              11th ser.,     8,   154,   217 (23.viii, 13.ix.1913) Dis-
                                       raelis' burial place
              15th ser.,   177,   313-14 (28.x.1939) C. L. Cline:
                                       Movements of the Disraeli fam-
                                       ily
```

1658. Benjamin Disraeli of Dublin
```
              7th ser.,      3,    89,   152,   232,  295,  371;
                             4,   258   (1887)
              11th ser.,     3,    28,   134,   278 (Jan.-April 1911)
```

1659. Abraham Disraeli
```
              6th ser.,      8,   406   (24.xi.1883)
```

Novels and plays

1660. Disraeli a play by Louis N. Parker ... New York
       John Lane Company   MCMXI
          Pp. (iv)+114+(2), with photograph of Arliss as Dis-
       raeli.
          Based on the purchase of the Suez Canal shares.
       Produced in Montreal, 1911, with George Arliss as Dis-
       raeli, and at the Royalty Theatre, London, in 1916,
       with Dennis Eadie as Disraeli.   Later filmed.

1661. (Another edition).   London and New York, John Lane,
       1916.

1662. Disraeli by Louis N. Parker   The story of the play
       and of the film starring George Arliss as Disraeli   The
       Readers Library Publishing Company Ltd.   66-66A,
       Great Queen Street, Kingsway, London, W.C.2   n.d.
       (1930)
          Pp. 190

1663. T. L. S., 21 August 1930

1664.   "Dizzy" a domestic comedy in a prologue and three acts by T. Pellatt (W. T. Coleby) ... Macmillan & Co., Limited   St. Martin's Street, London   1932.
Pp. vi+ 122+ (2)
The main action is set in 1878.   Produced at the Westminster Theatre, London, 1932.

1665.   Victoria and Disraeli by Hector Bolitho   London Eyre & Spottiswoode
Pp. xxii+ (iv)+ 69+ (1)
150 copies printed, signed by the author and Dame Marie Tempest.   "Produced for the National Programme of the British Broadcasting Corporation by John Cheatle, on 25th September, 1938."   Marie Tempest as Victoria; Robert Farquharson as Disraeli.

1666.   Young Mr. Disraeli   A Play in Three Acts by Elswyth Thane ... Samuel French, London (&c.) 1935
Pp. 95+ (5)
"Produced at the Kingsway Theatre, London, on November 12th, 1934."

1667.   Elswyth Thane Young Mr. Disraeli   Constable & Company Ltd.   London   n. d. (1936)
Pp. (xii)+ 337+ (3)
A novel based on Disraeli's life up to his marriage.

1668.   Also published in New York by Harcourt Brace

1669.   Abbott, W. C. in Saturday Review of Literature, 13, no. 20, p. 6 (14 March 1936)

1670.   Kronenberger, L. in Nation, 142, 520 (22 April 1936)

1671.   Simpson, H. in New Republic, 89, 27 (4 November 1936)

1672.   Young, G. M. in Observer, 31 January 1937

Disraeli appears in the following works.   There are no doubt other fictional references.

1673.   Skelton, John: Thalatta.   Parker, 1862.
This is dedicated to Disraeli, who is supposed to be the model for the hero, "Mowbray."   (See 1261)

1674.   The Fall of Haman: a tragedy.   Appropriate for

222

school theatricals. Leeds: R. Jackson, 18, Commercial Street; and all respectable booksellers. 1874.
Pp. 16
A squib on the dismissal of Henry Hayman from the Headmastership of Rugby. The characters include "Disraeli, Vizier to the Queen."

1675. Trollope is said (Sadleir, M.: Trollope, a commentary, 1945, 418) to have admitted that "Mr. Daubeny" in the "political novels" was Disraeli. The question is discussed by A. O. J. Cockshut, who does not accept a simple identification, in the appendix "The political novels and history" to his, "Anthony Trollope," 1955.

1676. (Sir) Anthony Hope (Hawkins): Quisanté. Methuen, 1900. Grey (in 461) says that Hawkins denied that Quisanté was Disraeli, "yet readers, like critics, saw the similitude, and such things can be done unawares ... If his hero is not Disraeli, he is his near relation." Sir Charles Mallet, "Anthony Hope and his books ...," 1935, 152: "Quisanté had little in common with Disraeli, whose early life had dimly suggested the story, beyond political genius, strong determination, an exotic imagination, and occasional lapses from good taste ..."

1677. John Oliver Hobbes (Mrs. Craigie): Robert Orange. 1902. Disraeli is introduced under his own name.

1678. Brahms, Caryl and Simon, S. J.: Don't, Mr. Disraeli! Michael Joseph, 1940, has little to do with Disraeli, who makes occasional appearances.

1679. Bonnet, Theodore: The Mudlark. London, W. H. Allen, 1949. Filmed with Sir Alec Guinness as Disraeli.

1680. Sheppard, Elizabeth Sara: Charles Auchester. This precocious musical novel, published in 1853, is dedicated "To the author of "Contarini Fleming" whose perfect genius suggested this imperfect history." Disraeli had encouraged her to publish it. See the introduction by Jessie A. Middleton to the "Everyman's library" edition, 1911.

1681. Picciotto, James   : Sketches of Anglo-Jewish history, 1875 (new edition by I. Finestein, 1956)

The chapter "Isaac D'Israeli and his family" gives an account of the quarrel with the synagogue, and settled the date of Disraeli's birth, which had been variously given, by printing the relevant extract from the synagogue register.

1682. Foster, J.   : The Disraeli pedigree in Collectanea genealogica, 1881, I, 6-16, gives some facts relating to Isaac D'Israeli's immediate family, with documents.

1683. Wolf, Lucien   : The Disraeli family in The Times, 20 and 21 December 1904 and in Transactions of the Jewish Historical Society of England, 5, (1902-05), 202-18

See 1657

Isaac D'Israeli

1684. Ogden, James   : Isaac D'Israeli. Oxford, Clarendon Press, 1969; and see the works cited there. Disraeli's "Memoir" of his father (704), previously the chief source of information, is unreliable, particularly on the question of their ancestry.

Mary Anne Disraeli

1685. Her portrait, by A. E. Chalon, appeared in the "Book of Beauty for 1841," with verses by George Dawson, p. 236

1686. Sykes, James   : Mary Anne Disraeli. Benn, 1928

1687. T. L. S., 27 Sept. 1928, 681

1688. Baily, F. E.   : Lady Beaconsfield and her
                                  times. Hutchinson, 1935

1689. Elletson, D. H.   : Mrs. Disraeli in Maryannery,
                                  Mary Ann Lincoln and Mary
                                  Anne Disraeli, Murray, 1959,
                                  65-152

1690. Buckle, G. E.   : Lady Beaconsfield in T. L. S.,
                                  4 Oct. 1928, 710

1691. Leslie, Doris   : The Perfect Wife (a novel).
                                  Hodder & Stoughton, 1960

Benjamin Disraeli, Disraell, or Disrael, of Dublin

1692. Quane, Michael   : The D'Israeli School, Rathvilly
                                  in Journal of the Royal Society
                                  of Antiquaries of Ireland, 78,
                                  10-23 (1948)
       This Disraeli was thought by some to be an illegiti-
       mate half-brother of Isaac. See 1658

Election addresses and ephemera

        Many more placards and other election ephemera must
have appeared than have survived. Some, of which no copy
has been traced, are referred to in contemporary accounts.
The following list does not attempt to be complete, but gives
only those items which have been readily traceable.

Wycombe (June and December 1832)

1693. "To the free and independent electors of Wycombe,"
       dated June 27th, 1832. (H. P., B/I/A/16) Issued after
       his defeat in his first election.

1694. "The Wycombe Sentinel," a sheet issued free by Dis-
       raeli's supporters during his second election campaign
       in Wycombe in 1832. There were eight issues, weekly
       from 19 October to 7 December. No. 7, November, 30,

contains a report of Disraeli's speech at a dinner in
Wycombe, which is reprinted in 606 and 696.

Taunton (The poll was declared 29th April 1835)

1695. Taunton Election. EXTRACT FROM THE Morning
Chronicle, Saturday, April 25th, 1835. MR. D'ISRAELI,
"What is he?" s. s., ptd., Marriott, Taunton.
Contains extracts from 136, accusing Disraeli of
having been a Radical, and now pretending to be a Tory.

1696. TO THE Worthy and Independent ELECTORS OF THE
Borough of Taunton. s. s., ptd., Court, Taunton.
Signed, B. DISRAELI, Bradenham, May 12th, 1835.
In reply to the attack on him by Daniel O'Connell a
few days previously.

1697. A LETTER TO THE Electors of Taunton, IN REPLY
TO THE QUESTION "What is Mr. D'ISRAELI?"
Pp. 12. Ptd., Bragg, Taunton. Signed, AN ELEC-
TOR, Taunton, 29th, May 1835. A violent attack.

1698. A FULL TRUE AND PARTICULAR ACCOUNT OF
THE ROW IN TAUNTON, On the 1st. of JUNE, 1835,
By an EYE WITNESS. For nearly a month past the
Public have had their expectations excited by advertise-
ments in the Public Papers, and in every other possible
shape, with the Triumphant Entrance of, and the Dinner ,
to be given to the "IMPENITENT" POLITICAL APOSTATE
On the aniversary (sic) of the Glorious 1st. of June. s. s.
Signed "NO GO," Dated June 4th, 1835.
A scurrilous account of Disraeli's entry to Taunton
with his supporters.

1699. TO Mr. Edwards Beadon, Mr. W. P. Pinchard, AND
Mr. J. E. White.
s. s., signed 'The COMPILER of the Pamphlet "What
is Mr. D'Israeli?", Taunton, June 6th 1835.'
Recapitulates charges in 1697. The three named had
spoken at the dinner on 1st June.

1700. TO THE ELECTORS AND INHABITANTS OF THE
BOROUGH OF TAUNTON.
Pp. 7+ (1) Ptd., Court, Taunton.
Signed, BENJAMIN DISRAELI. London, June 13th
1835.
Refuting the allegations in 1699.

1701. TO Benjamin D'Israeli, Esq.
Pp. 12. Ptd., Bragg, Taunton. Signed, Edward W.
Cox, Taunton, June 29th 1835.
The charges of inconsistency served up again.

1702. TO THE INHABITANTS OF TAUNTON.
Pp. iv+ 18. Ptd., Barnicott's Albion Press, Taunton.
Contains: To the inhabitants of Taunton, signed Ed-
wards Beadon, Taunton, July 9th 1835. (Pp. (i)-iv), To
Edwards Beadon, Esq., signed B. Disraeli, London,
July 2nd 1835. (Pp. (1)-18.)
Disraeli's defence repeated. He here claims the
authorship of "The Gallomania" (85), and denies writing
for or being editor of Star Chamber and The Represen-
tative (see 723, 735)

1703. SECOND LETTER TO B. D'Israeli, Esq.
Pp. vi, (5)-22. Ptd., Bragg, Taunton.
Contains: Letter to the electors of Taunton, signed
Edward W. Cox, July 27th 1835, and To Benjamin Dis-
raeli, Esq., signed Edward W. Cox. (n.d.)

Nos. 1695-1703 are noted from copies in the Somerset Record Office.

Maidstone (July 1837. Disraeli's first successful contest)

1704. TO THE FREEMEN AND ELECTORS OF THE Borough
of Maidstone. s.s. Ptd., Smith, Maidstone. Signed,
B. DISRAELI. July 1st, 1837 (H.P., B/I/A/97.)

1705. "Who and What is Mr. D'Israeli?" Let his speech
reply! Speeches of Wyndham Lewis, Esq., M.P. and
B. D'Israeli, Esq., at the Corn Exchange, Maidstone,
July 3rd, 1837. s.s. Ptd., Hall, Maidstone. (H.P.,
B/I/A/96.)

1706. To the freemen and electors of the Borough of Maidstone. (Disraeli and Wyndham Lewis) s.s., Ptd., Hall,
Maidstone. July 8th, 1837. (H.P., B/I/A/99.)

1707. Speeches of the Conservative candidates Mr. Wynd-
ham Lewis, and Mr. Disraeli, at the Corn Exchange,
Maidstone, Last Evening, July 17, 1837. s.s., Ptd.,
Hall, Maidstone. (H.P., B/I/A/91.)

227

Shrewsbury (July 1841. Disraeli was M. P. for Shrewsbury, 1841-1847)

1708. TO THE FREE AND INDEPENDENT ELECTORS OF SHREWSBURY. (Disraeli and George Tomline, London, 8th June 1841) s. s., Ptd., Eddowes, Shrewsbury. (H. P., B/I/B/33.)

1709. TO THE FREE AND INDEPENDENT Electors OF THE BOROUGH OF SHREWSBURY. (Disraeli and Tomline) Dated, 18th June 1841. s. s., Ptd., Davies, Shrewsbury. (H. P., B/I/B/32.)

1710. JUDGEMENTS AGAINST B. D'ISRAELI, Esq. s. s. "John Doe and Richard Roe, Printers, Fleet." n. d. (June 1841) Alleging that Disraeli owed a total of £22, 036. (H. P., B/I/B/29.)

1711. TO THE FREE AND INDEPENDENT Electors OF THE BOROUGH OF SHREWSBURY. Shrewsbury, June 25th, 1841. s. s., Ptd., Davies, Shrewsbury. Disraeli's reply. (H. P., B/I/B/30.)

1712. TO THE ELECTORS OF Shrewsbury. (Signed, An elector.) n. d., no printer. (H. P., B/I/B/31.) Rebutting Disraeli's denial.

1713. TO THE ELECTORS OF SHREWSBURY. s. s., Ptd., Shrewsbury News Office. Signed W. Yardley, June 25th, 1841. (Salop C. R. O., 665/3/1722.) Reiterating charges regarding Disraeli's debts.

1714. Mr. B. D'Israeli. s. s., n. d., no printer. Paragraphs attributed to a "London Paper." (Salop C. R. O., 665/3/1718.) A violent attack.

1715. SHREWSBURY RACES, 1841. THE BOROUGH STAKES. HORSES ENTERED. THE Black horse, BENJAMIN, own brother to Conqueror, by Tory out of Confidence. He won at Maidstone in 1837, and has challenged the Irish horse Mendicant out of Derrynane by Popery, for the Whip. A fast winner, sound in wind and limb, and warranted "To win." (With similar remarks on the other candidates) s. s. "Printed at the Confidence Office, Shrewsbury." (Salop C. R. O., 665/3/1720.)

1716. ELECTORS OF SHREWSBURY. s. s. "Conservative
Office, Wyle Cop" (An attack on the policy of the Whigs.)
"WHO TRANSPORTED THE DORCHESTER LABORERS?
The Whigs!" &c., ending "Disraeli, and no Poor Law.
Tomline, and the happiness of the People!" (Salop C.
R. O., 665 /3 /1729.)

Buckinghamshire (Disraeli was M. P. for the County,
1847-1876)

Only a few items from this period have so far been
traced.

1717. TO THE ELECTORS OF THE COUNTY OF BUCKING-
HAM. Bradenham, May 22, 1847.
Pp. (1) and (2) of d. s. (H. P., B /I/C /192.)

1718. TO THE ELECTORS OF THE COUNTY OF BUCKING-
HAM. Downing Street, 18th June, 1852.
P. (1) of d. s. (Bucks. C. R. O., A. R. 30 /63 (L).)

1719. TO THE ELECTORS OF THE COUNTY OF BUCKING-
HAM. Hughenden Manor, March 17, 1857. s. s. (H. P.,
B /I /D /90.)

1720. TO THE ELECTORS OF THE COUNTY OF BUCKING-
HAM. Hughenden Manor, Jan. 24 (1874).
P. (1) of d. s. (H. P., B /I /D /97.)

Addenda

The numbers in parenthesis indicate the position which
the item would take if included in the main list, e. g., 111 /2
indicates "between 111 and 112," and does not necessarily
imply any relation to the previous number.

Disraeli's writings

1721. (111 /2)   (Contarini Fleming) Czech, 1932

1722. (174 /5)   (Henrietta Temple) With an introduction
by Anthony Hern, 1969

1723. (252/3) (Coningsby) With a foreword by Asa
                Briggs, New York, 1962

1724. (285/6) (Sybil) Third Edition (1845) Sadleir, XIX
                C. F., 726 b. Referred to in adver-
                tisements in Tancred.

1725. (497/8) (Letters of Runnymede. Review in) The
                Times, 1 Aug. (1836)

1726. (549/50) (Lord Beaconsfield's correspondence with
                his sister) Second edition

1727. (560/1) (Whigs and Whiggism) Political Science
                Quarterly, 30, 320-21 (1915) (Edward
                Porritt)

1728. (712/3) "An admirer of the blonde," Benjamin
                Disraeli, First Earl of Beaconsfield
                in Letters to mother, edited by
                Charles Van Doren, New York, 1959,
                271-75. (A letter from Disraeli to
                his mother, 1 August 1830, from
                Granada)

1729. (727/8) Letters by "Pittacus" in The Times, 2
                Aug., 20 Aug. 1841. Ascribed at the
                time to Disraeli, who denied the au-
                thorship. See 1053, 163-64

Writings on Disraeli

1730. (790/1) (Hitchman) Third edition, Sampson Low,
                1884

1731. (920/1) (Monypenny & Buckle) Political Science
                Quarterly, 36, 314-17 (1921) (Annie
                G. Porritt)

1732. (1054/5) (Blake) Briggs, A. in Political Science
                Quarterly, 83, 285-86 (1968)

1733. (1077/8) Gladstone, Disraeli and later Victorian
                politics   Paul Adelman ... Longman
                (1970)
                Pp. xii+119+(1) (Seminar studies in
                history)

1734. (1077/8)   Gladstone and Disraeli (Quotation) by
Patrick Rooke Wayland Publishers
London (1970)
Pp. 128 (The Wayland documentary
history series)

1735. (1087/8)   To your tents O Israel." "The country
betrayed." Gladstone, Bright, &
D'Israeli detected! or the late nego-
ciations! with the refreshing and hu-
morous dialogue between Pam, "The
Times," and Lord John Russell, with
Cobden's "soliloquy." By "The Witty
Wag," M. P. for the Boro' of Diddle'm.
London: Published by (There is a
blank after 'by' on the title-page)
Pp. 30. n. d. (1855?)

1736. (1172/3)   The battle of the genii. or, Gladiolus
and Beakitorus. A story of the Gene-
ral Election. Illustrated by J. P.
Stafford. (drawing) F. E. Longley,
39, Warwick Lane, London, E. C.
Pp. 28+ (4), including wrapper (1880)

1737. (1179/80) (Hyndman) Third edition, revised

1738. (1219/20) Hodge-podge Gladdy and Dizzy or the ri-
vals   A little comedy in two acts
(Quotation) William Blackwood and
Sons 1884
Pp. 23+ (1) (Verse)
An attack on the Reform Bill

1739. (1261/2)   Traill, Henry Duff: Lord Beaconsfield
and Sir Robert Peel in The New Lu-
cian, being a series of dialogues of
the dead, 1884, 85-106

1740. (1357/8)   Boyle, Sir Edward: Benjamin Disraeli in
Great Conservatives. Conservative
Political Centre, 1953, 16-29

1741. (1361/2)   Hollis, C.: Disraeli's political novels in
Tradition and change, by R. A. Butler
and others. (Conservative Party.
Political Centre. National Summer

School), 1954, 98-117. (A symposium
on the 150th anniversary of Disraeli's
birth.)

1742. (1364/5) Sacher, Harry: Disraeli in Zionist portraits and other essays, 1959, 41-45
(from New Judaea, March 1944) A
perceptive essay on Disraeli's relationship with Judaism.

1743. (1367/8) Pearson, Hesketh: Benjamin Disraeli in
Lives of the wits, 1962, 142-162

1744. (1370/1) Fisch, H.: Disraeli's Hebraic compul-
sions in Essays presented to Chief
Rabbi Israel Brodie on the occasion of
his seventieth birthday, edited by H.
J. Zimmels and others (Jews' College
publications, new ser., 3, 1967, 81-94.)

1745. (1372/3) Pike, Edgar Royston: Benjamin Disraeli
(Earl of Beaconsfield) in Britain's
Prime Ministers from Walpole to Wil-
son, 1968, 263-280

1746. (1587/8) Pilát, J.: Benjamin Disraeli a Suezský
průplav in Dějiny a současnost, 1967,
5

DISRAELI'S SPEECHES

Speeches published separately (611-646), in collections (596-610, 713-722) &c. are listed here chronologically.

1832
June	9	At Wycombe	606
Nov.	27	At Wycombe	606, 696, 1694

1834
Dec.	16	At Wycombe	558, 606, 611

1835
April	29	At Taunton	606, 696

1837
July	3	At Maidstone	1705
	17	At Maidstone	1707
Dec.	7	Maiden speech	601, 606

1839
July	12	Chartism	696, 713

1841
May	27	Melbourne's government	601

1842
May	10	Tariffs	606

1843
April	25	Tariffs	606
May	9	At Shrewsbury	606, 696, 713
Aug.	9	Ireland	606

1844
Feb.	16	Ireland	601, 670

1844 (cont.)
June   17   Sugar duties   606
Oct.   3   At Manchester   601, 606, 715, 716
         11   At Bingley   715

1845
Feb.   28   Mazzini's letters   606
March   17   Agriculture   606, 713
April   8   Printers' Pension Society 613
         11   Maynooth   606

1846
Jan.   22   Corn Laws   606
Feb.   20   Corn Laws   606
May   15   Corn Laws   601, 606, 614

1847
June   26   At Aylesbury   606
Dec.   16   Jewish question   713

1848
March   10   Income Tax   606
April   19   Denmark   615
June   20   Reform   599, 601, 618
Aug.   30   Labours of the Session   606, 619
Sept.   21   At Darlington   717

1849
Feb.   1   On the Address   606
March   8   Local taxation   606
May   2   Brompton Hospital   606, 621
July   2   State of the Nation   606

1850
Feb.   19   Agriculture   606
July   9   Locke King's motion   599

1851
Feb.   11   Agriculture   606
April   2   Locke King's Bill   599
June   30   Financial policy   622

1852
Feb.   9   Reform Bill   599
March   25   Hume's motion   599, 623
April   27   Locke King's motion   599
May   10   On St. Albans & Sudbury   599

234

235

1862 (cont.)

<u>Oct.</u>   30   At Wycombe   597, 606, 628

1863

<u>Feb.</u>   17   Italian Treaty   606
June   9   Act of Uniformity   597, 606

1864

<u>July</u>   4   Denmark   606
Nov.   25   Church Policy   597, 606, 629

1865

<u>April</u>   3   Cobden   601
May   8   Reform   598, 599, 606

1866

<u>Feb.</u>   1   Palmerston   601
April 27   Reform   599
May   14   Reform   599, 631
June   4   Reform   599
         7   Reform   599

1867

<u>Feb.</u>   25   Reform   601
March   5   Reform   601
       18   Reform   601, 606
       26   Reform   606
April 12   Reform   606
July   15   Reform   606, 713
Oct.   29   At Edinburgh
                 (Corn Exchange)   600, 606
       30   At Edinburgh
                 (Music Hall)   600, 632
Nov.   Lord Mayor's Banquet   714

1868

<u>April</u>   3   Irish Church   601
May   22   Irish Church   601
June 17   Church and State   633
July   2   Abyssinia   606
Nov.   Lord Mayor's Banquet   714

1869

<u>March</u> 18   Irish Church   601
May   31   Irish Church   606

```
1870
Feb.      8  Ireland                      606
March   11  Ireland                      606

1871
Feb.     24  Black Sea                    606
         27  Westmeath                    606

1872
April     3  At Manchester
                (Free Trade Hall)    606,  610,  634,  635,  713
          4  At Manchester
                (Deputation)              719
May       8  Literary Fund              602,  606
June     24  At the Crystal Palace    606,  610,  637,  638,  692

1873
March   11  Irish University Bill        606
         20  Refusal to take office       606
         26  Burials Bill                 639
Nov.     19  Glasgow Inaugural          603,  605,  640
             Glasgow Banquet           603,  605
         20  Freedom of Glasgow          603
         22  Glasgow Conservative
                Association              603,  605,  642
         23  Glasgow Short Time
                Committee                603,  605

1874
May      13  County Franchise            606
Nov.         Lord Mayor's Banquet        714

1875
Nov.         Lord Mayor's Banquet        714

1876
Feb.     21  Suez                         713
March     9  Royal Titles Bill           606
Aug.     11  Bulgaria                    606
Sept.    20  At Aylesbury               643,  644
Nov.         Lord Mayor's Banquet        714

1877
Nov.         Lord Mayor's Banquet        714

1878
April     8  Reserves                    606
```

INDEX

This index includes

Personal names: all authors of entries in the list, and persons mentioned as associated with Disraeli, including the publishers of first editions of Disraeli's works, editors, illustrators and translators of Disraeli's works, and translators of works about him; editors of collectaneous works, and persons written about.

Pseudonyms used by Disraeli and others.

The titles of Disraeli's works, including works ascribed to him, and of other works published anonymously; titles of periodicals ("transactions" of societies being entered under the name of the society); titles, where they are distinctive, of anonymous periodical articles; names of organizations.

Entries for events in Disraeli's life, general works on his life and writings, and places with which he was associated, are listed under DISRAELI.

Names of peers have been given only in the form in which they appear in the list.

The titles of periodicals and newspapers are underlined.

The titles of Disraeli's works have (D), the titles of anonymous works have (A) after the titles.

pseud is used to indicate pseudonyms

This index includes the items in the "Addenda."

Abbott, Wilbur Cortez 917, 1318, 1669
Abrahams, Israel 133
Academy 51-53, 370, 430, 544, 774, 787, 809, 814, 830, 842, 1479, 1496
Adams, W. Davenport 149
Address ... at the Manchester Athenaeum (D) 715, 716
Addresses on education, finances, and politics (D) 605
Adelman, Paul 1733
After the turtle 714
Age of lawn tennis, The (A) 285
Agricola pseud 1088, 1089
Agricultural Situation, The (D) 646
Ainsworth's Magazine 207, 267
Alaman, Don Lucas 12
Albert Prince Consort 673
Aldag, Peter 1544
Aldington, Richard 1354
Alguien pseud 1205
Allen, Walter 252
Allusions in Lothair, The 409
Alroy see Wondrous tale of Alroy
Althaus, Friedrich 1242
American Academy of Political and Social Science. Annals 1020
American Catholic Quarterly Review 431
American Hebrew 563
American Historical Review 582, 831, 862, 873, 884, 903, 918, 1011, 1021, 1033, 1060, 1554
American Literature 1545
American Monthly Magazine (New York) 115, 140, 159, 185
American Monthly Review (Boston) 116
Andzhaparidze, G. A. 301
Anglia, Zeitschrift für englische Philologie 1470
Angus, George 1
Annan, Noel 1054
Answer to some of the opinions and statements respecting the Jews ... 352
Anti-Coningsby 235
Apjohn, Lewis 796-798
Apparition of the late Lord Derby ... (A) 1165
Appleton's Journal 432, 1392, 1398
Apt, I. R. 1356

240

Baum, D's servant 1637
Baumann, Arthur A. 895, 910, 1324, 1335, 1507, 1517
Beaconsfield, a mock-heroic poem (A) 1203, 1204
Beaconsfield, a national poem (A) 1223
Beaconsfield acrostic, The (A) 1222
Beaconsfield ballads (A) 1209
Beaconsfield Birthday Book, The (D) 682
Beaconsfield brilliants ... (D) 681
Beaconsfield buried at Hughenden 1217
Beaconsfield maxims (D) 687, 688
Beaconsfield Quarterly 133, 717, 1498
Beaconsfield sermons, The 1138-1140
Beaconsfield the immaculate 1171, 1172
"Beaconsfield Wreath, The" 1163, 1164, 1171
Beadon, Edwards 1699, 1702
Beckford, William 94, 135
"Bede, Cuthbert" 324
Beebe, Elswyth Thane see "Elswyth Thane"
Beeley, Harold 994-996
Beeton, Samuel O. 759ff.
Beiblatt zur Anglia 991
Belaney, Archibald 1090
Ben changes the motto 1120
Ben D'Ymion. By the Author of "Loafair" &c. 451, 452
Ben's dream about the "Schemers of Philistia" (A) 1146
Ben-Dizzy the bold (A) 1211
Bendizzy's vision (A) 1145
Benjameni de Israeli. Who is this uncircumcised Philistine?
    (A) 803
Benjamin D-------, his little dinner (A) 1122, 1123
Benjamin Disraeli and R. Shelton Mackenzie (D) 595
Benjamin Disraeli, Earl of Beaconsfield (1881) (A) 795
Benjamin Disraeli Earl of Beaconsfield, being forty years
    and upward of political life 757
Benjamin Disraeli, Esquire, M. P. (1841) (A) 1079
Benjamin Disraeli on the grotesque in literature (D) 587
Benjamin Disraeli, the past and the future 1106
Benjamin Disraeli's letters to Robert Carter (D) 593
"Benjamins, Mr." see Bret Harte
Benson, E. F. 585
Bentinck, Lord George 336-368
Bentinck, Lord Henry 336
Bentley, Horatio 1177
Bentley's Miscellany 306
Berlin Congress 720, 721
Berman, Harold 1538
Best of all good company, The 673

Bibliographical Society of America, Papers 1579
Bibliographies 1-6
Bickley, Francis 499
Bicknell, Percy F. 835
Biggs-Davison, John 1357
Bigham, Clive 1312
Bindmann, Werner 1619
Birrell, Augustine 553, 936, 939, 1283
Bismarck, Prince Otto von 1152, 1256, 1367
Bits of Beaconsfield (A) 1173
Bjerre, Birger 259
Blackwood's Magazine 17, 339, 373, 378, 396, 747, 816, 833,
    854, 868, 881, 890, 905, 932, 1384, 1433, 1473, 1475,
    1476, 1486, 1487
Blake, Robert 462, 1029, 1053-1067, 1074-1076, 1368, 1583,
    1584, 1585, 1732
Blessington, Countess of 537, 1638
Blind, K. 1453
Bloomfield, Paul 1045
Blot on the Queen's Head, The 1119
Bodelsen, C. A. 992
Bolingbroke, Henry Lord 1040, 1606
Bolitho, Hector 1341, 1665
Bonghi, Ruggero 799
Bonnet, Theodore 1679
Book of Beauty 486, 489, 506, 508, 516, 520, 522, 529, 530,
    532, 533, 1685
Book of Benjamin, The 1157, 1158
Bookman (London) 666, 834, 855, 891, 906, 1467, 1485, 1492
Bookman (New York) 964, 981, 1481, 1519
Booth, B. A. 1019
Borring, L. E. 617
Bosphorus, The (D) 467
Bosworth, G. F. 975
Bousfield, John 717
Boyle, Sir Edward 610, 1740
"Bradenham" edition (D) 663-667
Bradford, Selina Countess of 564
Brahms, Caryl and Simon, S. J. 1678
Brandes, Georg 771-783
Brandl, A. 134
Brasher, Norman Henry 1372
Breakers ahead! 1142
Brewster, F. Carroll 811, 812
Briggs, Asa 1361, 1723, 1732
Bright, John 148, 855, 1203, 1735
Brinton, Crane 1337

243

British Home Rule Association 685
British Prime Ministers of the Nineteenth Century 713
British Quarterly Review 257, 270, 630, 1394, 1407
Brittain, Henry 675
Britten, James 1518
Broadsheets 1228-1234
Brodie, Sir Israel 1744
Brompton Hospital for Consumption 621
Brougham, Henry 1081
Brown, Alfred Barratt 1343
Brown, Cornelius 800, 801
Bruce, J. D. 1493
Brunner, Karl 990
Bryan, Daniel 1218, 1219
Bryant, W. C. 27, 35
Bryce, James Viscount 918, 1281, 1431, 1432, 1445, 1454
Bryden, Ronald 1030
Buccleuch, Duke of 721
Bucher, L. 732
Buckinghamshire County Record Office 1718
Buckinghamshire elections 825, 1717-1720
Buckinghamshire Infirmary 138
Buckle, George Earle 1531, 1690 and see Monypenny, W. F.
    and Buckle, G. E.
Bulley, John F. 598, 601, 602
Bundy, J. M. 1393
Burney, Fanny see D'Arblay
Burton, Sir Richard F. 1190
Butler, Sir (George) Geoffrey G. 1294
Butler, Richard Austen 1741
Byron, Lord 184, 1590, 1592

C., J. 1148
Calantha (D) 508
Callendar 709
Cambridge Historical Journal 1552 see also Historical Jour-
    nal
Canadian Historical Review 1511
Canadian Journal of Economics and Political Science 1577
Canadian Magazine 1474
Canadian Monthly 1411
Canning, George 11, 12
Capel, Thomas John Monsignor 413
Caradoc and Severn Valley Field Club. Transactions 1588
Carlyle, Thomas 463, 517, 1396
Caro, Joseph 1534
Carré, Jean Marie 1304
Carrier-Pigeon, The (D) 486

Colquhoun, A. H. U. 1474
Colson, Percy 1355
Commentary 1567
Comyn-Platt, T. 692
Congregationalist 1432
Coningsby (D) 206-265, 671, 699, 1267, 1362, 1600, 1723
"Coningsby" pseud 731
Conservative Party. Political Centre 1740, 1741
Conservative Watchman, A pseud 1147
Constantinople, and who is to have it? (A) 1147
Constitutional Reform (D) 598
Consul's daughter, The (D) 489-491
Contarini Fleming (D) 94-113, 669, 1595, 1721
"Contarini Fleming," a Psychological Satire 1208
Contemporary Review 112, 565, 863, 874, 885, 892, 907,
    1418, 1419, 1430, 1436, 1441, 1500, 1504, 1529
Cook, E. Thomas 708
Cook, Mrs. Elsie Thornton 1340
Cooper, Alfred Duff 1360
Copley, Sarah, Susan, and Sophia 519
Cornhill Magazine 461, 1471, 1495, 1525, 1536, 1585
Corry, Montagu Lord Rowton 2, 599
Costigan, Giovanni 1033
Coulton, D. T. 739
Count Alarcos (D) see Tragedy of Count Alarcos
Country betrayed, The (A) 1735
Courcelle, Maurice 828
Court Journal 71, 97, 119, 143, 162, 188, 201, 211, 271,
    308
Court Magazine 478, 480
Court of Egypt, The (D) 465
Cowan, Samuel K. 1215
Cowell, Herbert 816, 1433
Cowling, Maurice 1068, 1581
Cox, Edward W. 1701, 1703
Cracroft, Bernard 1383
Craemer, Rudolf 997-1000, 1549
Craigie, Mrs. P. M. T. 1677
Crisis examined, The (D) 611, 612
Criterion, The 566, 1520
Critic (New York) 435, 677, 1443
Critic, London Literary Journal 212, 272, 309, 340
Croker, John Wilson 625
Cromer, Evelyn Baring earl of 561, 871, 894, 931, 932,
    1290, 1295, 1297
Crosbie, William 1131

246

Cucheval-Clarigny, Athanase 444, 794, 1421
Cuckson, John 1148
Cullum, of Exeter, printer 495
Curiosities of Literature, by I. D'Israeli 703, 704
Curtis, L. P. 1056
Cutler, Sir John (proverbial) 1635

Dahl, Curtis 5, 333
Dahle, A. 1606
Daiches, David 638
Daily News 1245, 1289
Dalhousie Review 1555
Daniels, Emil 921
D'Arblay, Mme. (Fanny Burney) 94, 1639
Dartmouth, Earl of 1110
Dasent, G. W. 392
D'Aumale, Henri Duc 369
D'Avigdor-Goldsmid, Sir Henry 262, 1572
Dawson, George 1685
Day with ... Disraeli, A (D) 673
Day-book of Benjamin Disraeli, A (D) 693, 694
Daydreams of a Prime Minister (A) 1025
De Morgan, John 1132-1134
"De Tankard" 323
De Vere 24
Debrett's Illustrated House of Commons 737
Dějiny a Součansost 1746
Democratic Tory, A pseud of J. Skelton
Derby, 14th earl of 1165, 1581
Derby, 15th earl of 148, 536, 739, 1165
"The Derby" (race) 302
Despot, Lord B., The (A) 1232
Dial (Chicago) 436, 835, 864, 875, 886, 1437
Dickens, Charles 1397, 1587, 1613, 1640
Dickensian, The 1587
Dilke, Charles Wentworth 1102
Dillon 1641
Diplomatic Review 1149
Disraeli (name) 1628
Disraeli family 1657, 1681-1692
Disraeli, Abraham 1659
Disraeli, Benjamin of Dublin 1658, 1692
Disraeli, Benjamin earl of Beaconsfield
    (References, chiefly to pamphlets, articles in books and
    periodicals, and dissertations, to particular aspects of
    D's life. References to persons and books are in the
    main sequence of this index. Numbers referring to D's

247

D's known pseudonyms
　　"Atticus" 531
　　"Coeur-de-Lion" 517
　　"Laelius" 523-525
　　"Marco Polo Junior" 467, 468, 477
　　"Mesr" 465
　　"Runnymede" 493, 494, 509, 513
　　"Skelton, Jun." 510-512
D also used the following descriptions
　　"The Author of 'Vivian Grey' " 61, 69, 138, 158, 199,
　　　480, 486, 489, 506, 508, 516
　　"The Author of 'Vivian Grey,' 'Contarini Fleming' &c. "
　　　114, 478
　　"The Author of 'Vivian Grey' and 'Henrietta Temple' "
　　　184
　　"The Author of 'Lothair' " 429
　　"The Author of 'Contarini Fleming' and 'Vivian Grey' "
　　　470
The following were anonymous 7, 11, 12, 14, 15, 85, 94,
　　136, 466 and newspaper articles, 488, 503-505, 514,
　　515, 536
The following books had D's name on the title-page 139,
　　151, 206, 266, 303, 336, 369
Particular places connected with D
　　Austria 1081
　　Aylesbury 643, 644, 646
　　Berlin 645
　　Bingley 715
　　Bradenham 139n.
　　Buckinghamshire 825, 1378, 1717-1720
　　Crystal Palace 637, 638, 692
　　Cyprus 1533
　　Darlington 717
　　Deepdene 206n.
　　Denmark 615-617
　　Edinburgh 600, 632
　　Eton 258
　　Flanders 588
　　Germany 112, 588
　　Glasgow 603, 605, 640-642
　　High Wycombe see Wycombe below
　　Hughenden 1251, 1356, 1448
　　India 1091, 1563
　　Ireland 670-672, 685, 1109, 1116, 1154, 1194, 1452,
　　　1460 and see Religion above
　　Italy 1081, 1529
　　London 1509

Maidstone 518, 1078, 1184, 1704-1707
Malacca 1575
Manchester 634, 713, 715, 716, 719
Marylebone 136n.
Mexico 12
Oxford 629
Rhineland 588
Scotland 1535
Shrewsbury/Shropshire 713, 1588, 1708-1716
Southend 139n.
Taunton 1695-1703
Thebes (Egypt) 468, 529
Troy 139n.
Walthamstow 975
West Pacific 1573
Willenhall 300
Wycombe 469, 611-612, 628, 1693-1694 and see Events
     above
Foreign views of D 1415, 1426, 1557 and see the list of
     publications in languages other than English, below
D'Israeli, Isaac 33, 587, 703, 704, 742, 1681, 1684
D'Israeli, Maria 1728
Disraeli, Mary Anne 266, 709, 742, 1048, 1685-1691
Disraeli, Ralph 151, 538, 543, 551
Disraeli, Sarah 42, 69, 114, 538ff., 563, 594, 704, 723,
     1570
Disraeli, a key to the characters with notes and portraits
     852
Disraeli and Conservatism (D) 700
Disraeli as journalist (A) 562
Disraeli in love (A) 576
D'Israeli School, Rathvilly 1692
Disraeli to an agent (D) 712
Dissolution of Parliament (A) 1210
Dizzey & the Wycombe lion (A) 1228
Dizzi-ben-Dizzi (A) 1153
Dizzy heights, a prospect of Beaconsfield (A) 1066
Dizzy's lament (A) 1229
D'Orsay, Alfred 158, 1374
Douglas Jerrold's Shilling Magazine 273, 310
Dover Standard 1209
Dowden, Edward 430, 774
Drew, Edwin 1216
Drew, F. Bickerstaffe 1170
Du Vivier, J. H. 1155
Dublin Review 376, 437, 567, 865, 876, 887, 893, 908, 1499
Dublin University Magazine 311, 341, 1400

Duerksen, Roland A. 1578
Dunciad of Today, The (D?) 723ff.
Dunlop, Charles 681

E., G. R. 1191
E., W. 406
Eadie, Dennis 1660
Earl Beaconsfield, a political sketch (A) 1148
Eastern Question, The (D) 644
Eclectic Magazine 447, 1420
Eclectic Review 213, 312, 342, 748
Economist 1379, 1380, 1382, 1406
Edda 259
Edelman, Maurice 262
Eden and Lebanon (D) 532
Edinburgh Review 163, 214, 313, 343, 377, 438, 546, 604,
   607, 866, 894, 909
Edler, P. J. 1336
Edmonds, Edward 1510
Edwards, H. W. J. 696
Egerton, Lord Francis 199
Egyptian Thebes (D) 468
Elector of Bucks., An pseud 351
Elletson, Daniel Hope 1689
Elliot, Walter 610
Ellis, Stewart Marsh 912, 1321
Embryo M. P., An pseud 235
Eminent Persons, Biographies reprinted from "The Times"
   1270
"Empire" edition (D) 659
Empire Review 568, 939
Endymion (D) 426, 429-464, 799, 1258, 1266
Endymion (title of burlesque of "Ixion in Heaven") 474
England and Denmark (D) 615-617
England and France (D) 85-93, 1702
"England under seven administrations, " by A. Fonblanque
   514
English Historical Review 569, 1035, 1059, 1533
English Illustrated Magazine 150
English Review 570, 923, 966
English Studies (Amsterdam) 992
Escott, T. H. S. 818, 1500, 1501, 1504, 1516
Esher, Reginald Brett 2nd Viscount 913, 1274
"Essays and Reviews" 630
Essays and Studies 1562
Essays by Divers Hands 1583
Essays in Criticism 1565

Espinasse, Francis 1269, 1467
Essex Weekly News 1192
Etudes Anglaises 55, 1012, 1023
Evans, T. M., D's letters to 707
Ewald, Alexander Charles 707, 802
Examiner 72, 87, 120, 164, 215, 274, 314, 344, 378, 439, 760

Faber, Richard 1040-1043
Fairlie, Louisa 519, 528, 537
Falconet (D) 555-557
Fall of Haman, The (A) 1674
Famous speeches, selected and edited by Herbert Paul 718,
   720
Fantasia (D) 534
Farquharson, Robert 1665
Farrer, J. A. 1465
Fawcett, Henry 1127
Feiling, Sir Keith 924, 1329, 1368
Feuchtwanger, E. J. 1071
Fido, Martin 58, 1057
Figaro, Le 135
Financial Policy (D) 622
Fine, H. A. 1567
Finestein, I. 1681
Finkelhaus, J. J. 785
Finsk Tidskrift 922
Fiscal Oppression (A) 1096
Fisch, Harold 1744
Fisher, H. A. L. 1525
Five letters from Benjamin Disraeli to his sister Sarah (D)
   594
Flaccus-cum-Whimsicalus 1090
Foggo, Algernon 763
Fonblanque, Albany 514
Forbes-Boyd, Eric 698, 1562
Forcade, Eugène 226, 347
Foreign Affairs Committees 1149
Forschungen zur englischen Philologie 988
Forschungen zur Judenfrage 1549
Fortnightly Review 379, 440, 560, 856, 877, 895, 910, 1383,
   1405, 1413, 1447, 1472, 1484, 1491, 1501, 1507, 1516,
   1517, 1526
Forum (New York) 963, 1468
Foster, Joseph 1682
Francis, George Henry 743, 744, 1375, 1376
Fraser, Peter 1058
Fraser, Sir William 822-824, 1283

Fraser's Magazine 144, 189, 216, 236, 275, 366, 380, 441, 501, 727, 743, 1246, 1373, 1375-1377, 1414
Freed, Clarence I. 563
Freeman, Philip 1098
Freeman-Ishill, Rose 699
Frietzsche, Arthur H. 263, 1027, 1044, 1612
Friswell, J. Hain 1243
Friswell, Laura A. 1488
Froude, James Anthony 813-821
Fulford, R. 1010, 1034
Fuller, M. W. 436

G., A. W. 1210
G., E 407
Galaxy 1397, 1409
"Gallomania" (D) see England and France
Garnett, Richard 807, 1279, 1457
Garrod, Herbert B. 544
Gash, Norman 1035, 1059
Gaster, T. H. 1007
Geffcken, Friedrich Heinrich 1265
Gegenwärtige Krisis, Die 732
Gelber, Natan Michael 1006, 1007
"General Preface" (D) 389, 398, 419, 673
Gentleman's Magazine 8, 98, 217, 381, 1402, 1408, 1465, 1469
Geographical and historical account of the great world ... (A) 733
George, R. E. Gordon 1521
Gerard, Morice 1458, 1459
German Life and Letters 1546
Geyl, Pieter 911
Gids, De 382, 911
Gilbert, Felix 112
Gilfillan, George 1235
Ginx's blot removed 1201, 1202
Gladdy and Dizzy (A) 1738
Gladiolus and Beakitorus 1736
Gladstone, William Ewart 15, 596, 799, 938, 993, 1068, 1076, 1099, 1111, 1117, 1155, 1160, 1171, 1389, 1642, 1656, 1733, 1734, 1735
Gladstone Papers 1228-1233
Gleanings from Beaconsfield (D) 683, 684
Gleig, G. R. 1384
Globe, The 492
Goethe, J. W. von 1304, 1330, 1643
Good Company 1428

Hardcastle, J. A. 604
Harries, Frederick J. 1498
Harris, Christopher 1118
Harris, Harold M. 427
Harris, Leon A. 1370
Harrison, Frederic 379, 1262, 1272, 1468
Harte, Bret 403, 404
Hawkins, Sir Anthony Hope 1676
Haworth, Sir Lionel 1543
Haye, Alexandre de 550, 1197, 1464
Hayes, T. T. 1135-1137
Hayman, Henry 1674
Hayward, Abraham 214, 343, 386, 392
Hayward, John 1341
Hayward, Walter S. 956
Head, Mrs. Henry 693
Hearnshaw, Fossey John C. 1323
Hebrew, the Saracen, and the Christian, The (A) 306
Hebrew Race, The (D) 699
Heine, Heinrich 94, 1645
Hellman, George S. 1481
Henderson, Gavin Burns 1552
Henley, William Ernest 1268
Hennessy, Sir John Pope 1194, 1452
Henrietta Temple (D) 158-183, 1315, 1316, 1722
Hentschel, Cedric 1546
Hern, Anthony 1722
Heroic epistle, An (D) 512
Herrick, Francis H. 582
Herrmann, Irmgard 1607
Hertford, Marquis of 259
Herzog, Edgar 1597
Heuer, Erich 1602
Hewit, A. F. 374
Hi-Bealdarc-Benali pseud of A. Belaney
Higginson, Thomas Wentworth 1249
Hill, Frank Harrison 1245, 1413
Hirsch, Leo 1539
Historical Journal 1581 see also Cambridge Historical Jour-
nal
Historical Studies, Australia and New Zealand 1573
Historische Zeitschrift 998
History 1058
History Today 1029, 1564, 1584
Hitchman, Francis 155, 246, 426, 498, 786-790, 1730
"Hobbes, John Oliver" (pseud of Mrs. Craigie) 1677
Hobhouse, Sir John Cam 727

Hochschule und Ausland 1544
Hodge-Podge (A) 1738
Hoeltje, Hubert J. 593
Hoey, Cashel 376
Holbeach, Henry 1401
Holland, Bernard 887
Hollis, Christopher 1741
Holloway, John 638, 1359, 1565
Home Letters (D) 538-542, 553
Hood, Edwin Paxton 1138-1141
Hood's Magazine 218
"Hope, Anthony" pseud of A. H. Hawkins 1676
Hope, Henry 206
Hopkins, John Baker 1402
Horrabin, J. Frank 53
Horsman 1635
Hoste, James W. 1472
Houghton, Lord see R. M. Milnes
Hours at Home (New York) 383, 1386
House of Commons, D's speeches in 596, 599, 614-631 passim, 639
Howe, Julia Ward 435
Howe, Susanne 1330
Howes, R. W. 852
Hoyt, Charles Alva 1371
Hubbard, John Gellibrand 1086
Hudson, Derek 729
Hudson, Ruth Leigh 1545
"Hughenden" edition (D) 654
Hughenden Papers 742; cited passim
Hugins, Roland 1505
Hume, Joseph 492, 618, 623, 1166
Hurst, Gerald 569
Hutcheon, William 558, 591, 727, 728
Hyatt, Alfred H. 689
Hyndman, Frederick Arthur 156, 1179, 1737

Ibrahim Pacha (D) 477
Iddesleigh, 2nd earl of 47, 83, 109, 127, 172, 195, 249, 290, 327, 662, 1483
Illustrated London News 1378, 1404, 1434
Impeachment of Lord Beaconsfield (A) 1149
Imperium et Libertas (A) 1230
Importance of literature to men of business 716
In Memoriam 19th April 1883 (A) 1233
Inaugural address delivered to the University of Glasgow (D) 603, 604, 640, 641

Jones, Granville (fictitious author of "The Young Venetian") 105
Jones, John Paul 701
Journal of British Studies 1582
Journal of Comparative Legislation and International Law 1532
Journal of Modern History 1032, 1547
"Juden, Die" (translation of chapter 24 of "Lord George Bentinck") 365
"Judgements against B. D'Israeli" (election placard) 1710
Judy 1227

Kallsen, Anni Marta 1613
Kammer, Paul 1598
Kapur, Anup Chand 1563
Kebbel, Thomas Edward 606-609, 808-810, 817, 1240, 1241, 1263, 1286, 1381, 1422, 1455
Keepsake, The 534, 535
Key to "Almack's" (A) 733
Key to the Characters in Coningsby (A) 232
Key to Vivian Grey (A) 36, 37 see also 851, 852
Keys to D's novels 36, 37, 232-233, 464, 851, 852
Keys to the famous characters ... 851
Kidd, Joseph 1462
Kidwell, E. G. 1588
King, E., of Wycombe, publisher 138
Kirk, Russell 1566
Kluke, Paul 638
Kohlund, Johanna 1594
Kolischer see Külischer
Komroff, Manuel 1046
Kronenberger, Louis 1670
Krug, Isidor 1593
Külischer, Alexander 937

Laelius pseud of D 523-525
Lake, Henry 825
Lakeside Monthly (Western Monthly) 1390
Lamartine, Alphonse de 1197, 1464
Lamb, Lady Caroline 1646
Landon, Letitia E. 99
Langdon-Davies, Bernard N. 44, 248, 250, 289, 326, 661
Laparra, Mme. William 579
Larson, Laurence M. 864, 875
Las Almenas, Count de 1260
Laski, Harold J. 898
Lassalle, Ferdinand 1539, 1546

Late Earl of Beaconsfield's first constituency, The (A) 1184
Late Lord Beaconsfield, The (A) 1189
Laugel, A. 1415, 1426
Lawless, Joseph Timothy 1627
Lawrenny, H. 370
Lawyers and Legislators (D) 11   •
Layard, Sir Austen Henry 552
Lazaron, Morris S. 1331
Lazarus, Emma 1446
Le Clerc, Percy 1111
(Leading articles in the Morning Post) (D) 488
(Leading articles in The Times) (D) 503, 504
Leask, William Keith 247
Lee, Rose 964
Legacy of Disraeli, Toryism and democracy, The (A) 697
Leinad pseud 1218
Leisure Hour 733, 734, 1395, 1448
Leith Burghs Pilot 1099
Leopold, Duke of Albany 84n.
Leslie, Doris 1691
Lester, Horace Francis 451, 452
Lethbridge, Roper 1497
(Letter on a speech at Wycombe) (D) 469
Letter on the present wine duty (A) 1108
Letter to Benjamin D'Israeli, A (1846) (A) 1080
(Letter to Joseph Hume) (D) 492
Letter to Lord Beaconsfield, A (1878) (A) 1150
Letter to the Right Hon. Benjamin Disraeli, A (1869) (A)
      1200
Letter to the Right Hon. Benjamin Disraeli, on the culture
      of the field, A (A) 1088, 1089
Letters (D) see also Home letters; Lord Beaconsfield's cor-
      respondence; Lord Beaconsfield's letters; A new sheaf of
      Disraeli letters; Benjamin Disraeli's letters to Robert
      Carter; Five letters from Benjamin Disraeli; Benjamin
      Disraeli and R. Shelton Mackenzie; Some early letters ...
(Letters between Disraeli, and Daniel and Morgan O'Connell
      ...) 487
Letters from Benjamin Disraeli to Frances Anne Marchioness
      of Londonderry 581-586
(Letters in reply to the allegations in The Globe) (D) 492
Letters of Disraeli to Lady Bradford and Lady Chesterfield
      564-580
Letters of Laelius (D) 523-525
Letters of Runnymede (D) 493-502, 1725
(Letters to the editor of The Times) (D) 492
Letters to the Whigs (Lytton) 728

260

MacKnight, Thomas 745-752
Maclise, Daniel 66
Maclise Portrait-Gallery 1259
Macmillan's Magazine 386, 1440, 1489
MacMunn, Sir George Fletcher 1344
Macready, William Charles 1648
Macrone, John publisher 496
McTimon, Isaac 1208
Madden, R. R. 537
Maddyn, Daniel Owen 1238
Magazine of Art 1456, 1480
Maginn, William 1246, 1373
Magnus, Sir Philip 1360, 1564
Mahon, Lady 520
Maidstone and Kent County Standard 1184
Mair, R. H. 738
Mairet, Jeanne 445
Maitre, Raymond 55, 1012, 1023, 1047, 1620
Malleson, G. B. 1097, 1121
Mallet, Sir Charles 1676
Manchester Guardian 1275
Manilius pseud of Lytton 728
Manners, Janetta duchess of Rutland 1181-1183
Manners, John 7th duke of Rutland 279, 715
Marchant, Sir James 1270
Marco Polo, junior pseud of D 467, 468, 477
Marlborough, Duke of 706
Marriott, Sir John Arthur R. 1338
Marsh, William publisher 36, 723
Marshall, Edward 491
Marshall, Julian 285
Martin, Kingsley 571
Martin, Sir Theodore note after 113
Martineau, Harriet 515
Masefield, Muriel 1022-1025
Massingham, H. J. and H. 1335
Maurois, André 251, 255, 579, 960-979
Maury, Lucien 972
Maxwell, J. C. 57, 68, 84, 1635
Mayfair 761
Medlicott, W. Norton 1367
Meester, Marie E. de 1298
Melbourne, William Lamb, 3rd viscount 512, 513, 525
Melville, Lewis (L. S. Benjamin) 834, 856, 1285, 1484
"Memoir" of Isaac D'Israeli (D) 554, 704
Memoir of the Earl of Beaconsfield, A (1881) (A) 1186
Memoirs of D (A) 455, 655

Memorials of Lord Beaconsfield (1881) 1187
Mendes, Henry Pereira 851
Meredith, William George 590, 723n.
Merewether, Francis 1084
Merritt, James D. 463, 1624
Merrypebble, Mr. 1117
Mesr pseud of D 465
Meynell, Wilfrid 150, 829-840, 1485
Micklewright, F. H. A. 411
Middleton, Jessie A. 1680
Midland Ocean, The (D) 533
Miles, Hamish 962
Mill, John 753-755
Millbank, Edith note after 335
Milman, Henry Hart 94
Milnes, Richard Monckton Lord Houghton 218, 313, 377, 440
Miriam Alroy (title given to "The Wondrous Tale of Alroy")
    126
Mirror 221
Modder, Montagu Frank 1349, 1535, 1541
Modern Aesop, The (D?) 723
Modern Language Notes 1548
Modern Language Review 1038, 1049
Moers, Ellen 1365
Monatsschrift für Geschichte und Wissenschaft des Judenthums
    1534
Moncrieff, J. 224
Montagu, A. F. W. 710, 1635
Monteagle, Lord see T. S. Rice
Month 387, 1518, 1537
Monthly Review 22, 32, 90, 122, 146, 497
Monthly Review (1900-1907) 1483
Monypenny, William Flavelle and Buckle, G. E. 555, 853-
    930, 1731, and cited passim
Mordell, Albert 1364
More, Paul Elmer 1299, 1503
Morgan, Osborne 639
Morgen, Der 1539
Morison, J. L. 1511
Morley, John 861
Morning Chronicle 91, 222, 277, 1362, 1695
Morning Post 488, 518, 591
Mornings of the recess 729
Mortimer, Raymond 583
Moscow. University. Vestnik. Filologiya 301
Motley, J. L. 1416
Moxon, Edward publisher 139

New Parliamentary Reform (D) 618
New Republic 299, 573, 898, 949, 969, 1671
New sheaf of Disraeli letters (D) 563
New Statesman 583, 1014, 1037, 1064, 1556, 1569
New Voyage of Sindbad the Sailor, A (D) 505
New World 1510
New York Review of Books 1054
New York Times 556
Newman, John Henry 1485
Newmarket pseud 1512
Nickerson, Charles C. 59
Nihilism in Russia (A) 284
"Nine Hours' Movement for Factory Workers" 719
Nineteenth Century 817, 858, 878, 889, 899, 1422, 1452, 1462,
    1482, 1497, 1506, 1521
Nineteenth Century Fiction 264, 334, 463, 1019, 1031, 1051,
    1055, 1568
No Popery Premier and the Irish People (A) 1109
Norgate, G. Le Grys 570, 940
Norma, G. W. 1195, 1196
North, William 235
North American Review 34, 317, 867, 879, 1460
North British Review 224, 390
Notes and Queries 1, 46, 57, 58, 60, 68, 82, 84, 113, 183,
    198, 260, 261, 265, 302, 333, 335, 368, 411, 428, 464,
    479, 485, 491, 507, 521, 526, 527, 548, 589, 592, 711,
    758, 859, 1050, 1413, 1628-1659
Notestein, Wallace 584, 925, 973
Nottingham University Miscellany 1048
Nouvelle Revue Française 970
Nouvelle Revue Internationale 1464
Noyes, George C. 1437
Nulty, Roman Catholic Bishop of Meath 1116

Obituary of Lord Lyndhurst 729
Observer 1672
O'Connell, Daniel 487, 1166, 1696
O'Connell, Morgan 487
O'Connor, Thomas Power 757-770
Oedipus, David pseud 803
Ogden, James 704, 1684
Ogden, Rollo 857, 869, 888, 897
Old and New (Boston) 391
Old England (D) 517
On the Life and Writings of Mr. Disraeli. By his Son (D)
    704
On the portrait of the Lady Mahon (D) 520, 521

On the portrait of the Viscountess Powerscourt (D) 522
Once a Week 1247
Open Court (Chicago) 1538
Open Questions (D) 511
Otto, Friedrich K. 1595
Outlook 694
Oxford and Cambridge Review 279
Oxford Book of Victorian Verse 526
Oxford Diocesan Society for the Augmentation of Small Benefices 628, 629
Oxford Review 1057

P., G. G. 1233
P., U. 1221
Padley, Alfred 352
Paget, Edwin H. 971
Painting, David E. 1580, 1586, 1621, 1625, 1635
Palaestra 989
Palmer, William 1103, 1104
Palmerston, Lord 1081, 1092, 1552
Panjab. University. Research Bulletin 1563
Park, Joseph Hendershot 713
Parker, Louis Napoleon 1660-1663
Parliament and the Government, The (D) 619, 620
Parliamentary Reform (D) 599, 623, 626
Parsons, Olive W. 1617
Partisan Review 1062
Partridge, Eric 474, 482
Paston, George (Emily Morse Symonds) 1536
Patmore, Peter George 97
Patton, Lewis 951
Paul, Herbert 718, 720
Paul Jones (D) see Life of Paul Jones
Pearson, Hesketh 1008-1017, 1743
Peel, Sir Robert 151, 350, 496, 713, 744, 1080, 1166, 1547, 1571, 1739
(Peers and People) (D) 488
Pegram, F. 288, 292
Pelham (Lytton) 51
Pellatt, Thomas 1664
People's Magazine 1381
Perry-Robinson, H. 942
Pfeffer, Karl Heinz 998
Philipson, David 1267
Phillips, Olga Somech 1073
Philological Quarterly 593
Picciotto, James 1681

Princeton Studies in English 1334
Printers' Pension Society 613
Pritchett, V. S. 1353, 1556
Private history of the rise and fall of a morning newspaper,
  The (A) 736
Proserpine aux Infers (D) 484
Prowett, C. G. 1105
Psychological romance, The (D) Alternative title of "Conta-
  rini Fleming"
Public expenditure (D) 627
Pularinos, Oth 1144
Punch 318, 451, 1224-1226
Puppet-Showman's Album 323
Purcell, Sir Gilbert K. T. 258
Putnam's Monthly Magazine 1393

Quane, Michael 1692
Quarrel between Mr. Merrypebble and Mr. Bull ..., The
  (A) 1117
Quarterly Journal of Speech 971, 1009, 1559
Quarterly Review 56, 298, 392, 443, 552, 625, 818, 880,
  900, 913, 1002, 1081, 1494, 1560, 1580, 1586
Queen's Quarterly (Kingston, Ont.) 1566
Question du Slesvig, La (D) 617
Quiller-Couch, Sir Arthur 1322
Quincy, Edmund 388

R., J. 1230
Radical Tory, The (D) 696, 697
Raikes, H. St. J. 683, 684
Ramsay, A. A. W. 729
Rathborne, Anthony Blake 705, 1092-1095
Rathvilly School 1692
Ray, Gordon Norton 1362
Raymond, E. T. 948-953
Reede, Frank 1399
Reeve, Henry 438
Reform Bill, 1859 598
Reid, Sir Thomas Wemyss 1244, 1253
Religious creed and opinions of the Caucasian champion of
  the Church, The (A) 366
Renaissance and Modern Studies 1575
Rendall, Magnus C. 1099
Representative, The 14, 735ff., 1702
Review of English Studies 300, 462, 587, 1553
Revolutionary Epick, The (D) 139-150
Revue Anglo-Américaine 987

Saintsbury, George 1352, 1456
Salisbury, 3rd Marquis of 721, 722, 1517, 1649
Salisbury, 4th Marquis of 692
Salmon, Edward 1466
Salop County Record Office 1713-1716
Saltus, Edgar 1490
Sampson, George 690
Sampson, R. V. 1042
Samuel, Horace B. 51, 52, 1293, 1491
Sarkissian, A. O. 1367
Sarolea, Charles 966
Saturday Review 395, 446, 574, 665, 708, 755, 788, 950,
    955, 982, 1439, 1449, 1523, 1540, 1542, 1543
Saturday Review of Literature 584, 925, 956, 973, 983, 1669
Saturnalia (A) 1221
Sauer, Eugen 1609
Saunders and Otley publisher 114, 151, 611
Scattered Nation 396
Schapiro, J. Salwyn 968
Scherer, Edmond 1258
Schlumberger, Jean 970
Schmitz, Oscar A. H. 933-935
Schramm, Rudolph 645
Schubert, Paul 1599
Schuyler, Robert Livingstone 1013
Schwartz, C. 396
Scotch Distiller, A pseud 1096
Scott, Ernest 1306
Scribner's Monthly 1412, 1438 see also Century Magazine
Seager, Rob 1231
Seccombe, Thomas 1492
Second Book of Benjamin, The 1159
Sedgwick, Arthur George 442, 777, 836, 844
Segalowitsch, Boris 986, 987, 1605
Seikat, Hildegard 988
Selected speeches of the late Right Honourable the Earl of
    Beaconsfield (D) 606-609
Selections from the novels (D) 698
Seton, Matthew 1126, 1410
Seton-Watson, Robert William 993
Sewanee Review 1493
Seyd, Richard 714
Shahani, Ranjee G. 1557
Shand, A. I. 399, 546
Shanks, Edward 665, 950
Sharpe's London Magazine 397
Shaw, A. Capel 1157-1159

Shaw, Byam 44, 248, 289, 326, 661
Shelburne Essays 1299
Shelley, Mary 1650
Shelley, Percy Bysshe 184, 807, 1279, 1457, 1578, 1592
Shelley Society 1457
Sheppard, Elizabeth Sara 1680
Sheppard, Nathan 1390
Shepperson, Claude A. 247
Sherburne, John Henry 701
Sherman, Stuart Pratt 1319, 1519
Shilling Book of Beauty 324
Shoubra (D) 535
"Shrewsbury Races, 1841" (Election placard) 1715
Sichel, Walter 291, 560, 841-850, 855, 858, 878, 889, 891,
    899, 906, 909, 1440, 1461, 1476, 1482
Simon, S. J. 1678
Simpson, H. 1671
Simpson, Richard 390
Skelton, Jun. pseud of D 510-512
Skelton, Sir John 380, 1106, 1261, 1273, 1441, 1673
Sketchley, Arthur pseud of G. Rose
Smith, G. Barnett 1264
Smith, George 1160
Smith, Sir George Adam 1160
Smith, Goldwin 401, 409-411, 1413
Smith, Lloyd E. 695
Smith, Paul 1070
Smith, Sheila M. 300, 1038, 1048-1052, 1640
Smith, Virginia P. 1608
Smith, W. Roy 831
Smythe, George Sydney Lord Strangford 715, 749
Snape, Joseph 1161
Socialist Review 1528
Society in America, by H. Martineau 515
Some early letters of Lord Beaconsfield (D) 708
Somerset County Record Office 1695-1703
Somervell, David Churchill 938-947, 1343
Somerville, H. 1537
Song of King Benjamin 1231
South Atlantic Quarterly 951, 1505, 1570
Southern Literary Messenger (Richmond, Va.) 167, 227
Southern Quarterly Review 1417
Speaking Harlequin, The (D) 466
Speare, Morris Edmund 1320
Spectator 75, 92, 102, 147, 153, 168, 191, 228, 281, 348,
    398, 447, 448, 473, 540, 561, 575, 585, 609, 688, 750,
    778, 789, 819, 837, 845, 860, 870, 871, 882, 901, 914,

942, 957, 974, 1030, 1061, 1442, 1450, 1513, 1522
Speech Monographs 1558
Speech on the death of the Duke of Wellington (D) 741
Speeches on the Conservative policy of the last thirty years
(D) 601, 602
Spirit of Whiggism, The (D) 494, 496
Spofforth, W. 712
Spring-Rice, Thomas see T. S. Rice
Squire, Sir John Collings 694, 1313
Squire Bull and his bailiff Benjamin (A) 1169
Stafford, J. P. 1171, 1172, 1736
Stammers, Joseph 1078
Standard, The 1187, 1286
Stanley, Arthur Penrhyn 1175
Stanley, Lord see 15th earl of Derby
Stansfeld, Sir James 627
Stapledon, Sir Reginald George 1001-1005
Star Chamber 25, 26, 36, 723, 733, 734, 1702
State of the Case, The (D) 531
Statesman's adventures in search of a majority, A (A) 1210
Stembridge, Stanley R. 1582
Stephen, Sir Leslie 1250, 1405
Stevenson, G. H. 567
Stevenson, Lionel 5, 1530
Stewart, Robert Wilson 6, 56, 742
Stoddard, R. H. 1443
Story, Irving C. 1603
Strachey, Giles Lytton 916, 1339
Strachey, J. St. Loe 473, 957, 974
Strictures on "Coningsby" (A) 234
Stronach, George 1171, 1496
Strong, L. A. G. 1356
Stuart, Robert Montgomery 424
Sturge, Mrs. George 773
Sullivan, Margaret 1423
Summary of the Session, The (D) 504
Sunday Times 995, 1309
Swinnerton, Frank 666, 1524
Sybil (D) 266-302, 686, 1048, 1266, 1362, 1587, 1724
Sykes, James 1686
Symonds, Arthur G. 674
Syrian Sketch, A (D) 516

T. L. S. (Annual volume) 1066
Tait's Edinburgh Magazine 229, 319
Tales and Sketches (D) 554
Tancred (D) 303-335, 675, 699, 1235, 1267, 1292, 1298

Tancredi 324
Taylor, Alan John P. 1014, 1064, 1363, 1569
Taylor, G. R. Stirling 1307, 1328
Taylor, James 1162
Taylor, Sedley 1127-1129
Telford, J. 919
Temperley, Harold 1533, 1552
Tempest, Dame Marie 1665
Temple Bar 1451, 1454, 1458, 1459, 1463, 1488
Terry, Sir H. M. Imbert 568
Texas. University. Library Chronicle 594
Texas. University. Studies in English 205, 588, 1551
Thackeray, William Makepeace 222, 225, 259, 264, 277, 318,
    463, 1236, 1362, 1553, 1580, 1613
"Thane, Elswyth" (E. T. Beebe) 1666-1672
Thiers, Adolphe 1377
This is the tree that Ben raised (A) 1192
Thoma, Otto 1596
Thomas, Henry pseud of H. T. Schnittkind 1351
Thomas, W. 475
Thompson, Edward Raymond see E. T. Raymond
Thompson, George Carslake 806
Thornton-Cook, Mrs. Elsie see Mrs. Elsie Thornton Cook
Timbs, John 733
Time 1424, 1427, 1453, 1461
Times, The 93, 154, 169, 182, 230, 282, 320, 321, 349,
    399, 449, 469, 487, 492, 493, 494, 503, 504, 505, 509-
    515, 517, 518, 523-526, 531, 555, 611, 710, 712, 729,
    738, 751, 779, 1164, 1181, 1185, 1186, 1270, 1311, 1315,
    1444, 1531, 1683, 1725, 1729
Times Literary Supplement 59, 174, 258, 262, 367, 476, 483,
    502, 557, 562, 576, 586, 667, 697, 709, 726, 846, 861,
    872, 883, 902, 915, 924, 943, 952, 958, 975, 984, 996,
    1003, 1015, 1025, 1039, 1043, 1052, 1065, 1066, 1075,
    1514, 1515, 1663, 1687, 1690
Tinsley's Magazine 400
To a maiden sleeping after her first ball (D) 506, 507
To Lord John Russell (D) 523
To Lord Melbourne (D) 525
To Lord Viscount Melbourne (D) 513
To the Duke of Wellington (D) 526
To the electors and inhabitants of the Borough of Taunton
    (D) 1700
To the electors of the County of Buckingham (D) 1717-1720
To the free and independent electors of the Borough of
    Shrewsbury (D) 1711
To the free and independent electors of Wycombe (D) 1693

Velvet Lawn (D) 138
Venetia (D) 184-198, 1457, 1590, 1592
Victoria, Queen note after 113, 524, 1181, 1213, 1214, 1274, 1665
Victorian Newsletter 595, 1578, 1589
Victorian Studies 1036, 1042, 1056, 1574
Viebrock, Helmut 638
Villari, L. 929
Villiers, Sarah, Clementina, and Adela 528
Vincent, Leon 1296
Vindication of the English Constitution (D) 151-157
Virginia Quarterly Review 1530
Vissering, S. 382
Vivian Grey (D) 14-60, 665, 723, 1296, 1304, 1595, 1602, 1604
Vogüé, Vicomte Eugène de 1477
Voice from the grave, A (D) 635
Voice of Jacob 321
Voyage of Captain Popanilla, The (D) 61-68

W., J. F. T. 1192
Waddy, Frederick 1247
Waelder, Hedi 1601
Walford, Edward 804, 805
Walkley, Arthur Bingham 182, 1311, 1316
Walpole, Sir Spencer 607, 1287
Walstein (D) 478
Wapler, Rudolf 1600
Ward, Robert Plumer 24, 61
Ward, Wilfrid 876, 1297, 1499
Ward and Lock's Penny Books 1191
Warning Voice, A (D) 706
Warren, Samuel 139
Watson, J. G. 293
Watts, Charles A. 636
Watts' political series 1174
Weldon's Christmas Annual (A) 1153
Wellington, Duke of 526, 531, 741
Wenz, Heinrich 991
Western Humanities Review 1571
Western Monthly (Lakeside Monthly) 1390
Westminster Review 76, 152, 231, 283, 322, 350, 1204
What is duty? and What is faith? (D) 675
What is he? (D) 136, 137
Whibley, Charles 362, 905, 1278, 1301, 1317, 1475
Whigs and Whiggism (D) 558-562, 1727
White, J. E. 1699

REFERENCES IN LANGUAGES OTHER THAN ENGLISH

Translations of Disraeli's own works are underlined